The
Annotated
C++
Reference
Manual

Margaret A. Ellis

Bjarne Stroustrup

AT&T Bell Laboratories
Murray Hill, New Jersey

▲▼ **ADDISON-WESLEY PUBLISHING COMPANY**

Reading, Massachusetts · Menlo Park, California · New York
Don Mills, Ontario · Wokingham, England · Amsterdam · Bonn
Sydney · Singapore · Tokyo · Madrid · San Juan

Library of Congress Catalog Card No. 90-33932.

This book was typeset in Times and Courier by the authors, using a Linotronic 200P phototypesetter and a DEC VAX 8550 running the 10th edition of the UNIX® operating system.

DEC and VAX are trademarks of Digital Equipment Corporation. UNIX is a registered trademark of AT&T Bell Laboratories.

Reprinted with corrections May, 1991

ISBN 0-201-51459-1

4 5 6 7 8 9 10 HA 9594939291

The
Annotated
C++
Reference
Manual

Margaret A. Ellis

Bjarne Stroustrup

AT&T Bell Laboratories
Murray Hill, New Jersey

▲▼ ADDISON-WESLEY PUBLISHING COMPANY

Reading, Massachusetts · Menlo Park, California · New York
Don Mills, Ontario · Wokingham, England · Amsterdam · Bonn
Sydney · Singapore · Tokyo · Madrid · San Juan

AT&T

Library of Congress Catalog Card No. 90-33932.

This book was typeset in Times and Courier by the authors, using a Linotronic 200P photo-typesetter and a DEC VAX 8550 running the 10th edition of the UNIX® operating system.

DEC and VAX are trademarks of Digital Equipment Corporation. UNIX is a registered trademark of AT&T Bell Laboratories.

Reprinted with corrections May, 1991

ISBN 0-201-51459-1

4 5 6 7 8 9 10 HA 9594939291

Preface

This book provides a complete language reference for the expert C++ user. It consists of the C++ reference manual plus annotations and commentary sections.

The C++ reference manual alone provides a complete definition of C++, but the terse reference manual style leaves many reasonable questions unanswered. Discussions of what is *not* in the language, *why* certain features are defined as they are, and *how* one might implement some particular feature have no place in a reference manual but are nevertheless of interest to most users. Such discussions are presented as annotations and in the commentary sections.

The commentary also helps the reader appreciate the relationships among different parts of the language and emphasizes points and implications that might have been overlooked in the reference manual itself. Examples and comparisons with C also make this book more approachable than the bare reference manual.

This book does not provide information about standard libraries beyond discussion of the library functions providing the most basic run-time support nor docs it discuss C++ programming styles or techniques. Furthermore, this book does not attempt to teach C++ programming; it explains what the language is – not how to use it.

The index and the cross references embedded in the commentary and in the reference manual itself are important and integral parts of the book.

We hope that this reference manual will provide a firm base for the further evolution of C++. It has been chosen by ANSI to serve as a starting point for the formal standardization of C++.

Murray Hill, New Jersey

Margaret A. Ellis
Bjarne Stroustrup

Organization

The C++ reference manual consists of 16 major sections and two appendices each of which is used as the nucleus of a chapter of this book. The C++ reference manual proper is presented in 10 point Times Roman font.

■ Embedded annotations are presented in 9 point Times Roman font indented and bracketed, as this sentence is. □

Examples in the manual proper are presented using a constant width font:

```
int a;   // manual example
```

■ An italicized constant width font is used for examples in the commentary:

```
int b;   // commentary example
```

□

Major discussions are placed after the manual sections. Thus, each chapter consists of an abstract followed by an annotated manual section optionally followed by a commentary section. The heading

Commentary

separates the manual and the commentary parts of a chapter.

Commentary subsections contain the suffix 'c' to distinguish them from reference manual sections. Except for the chapter prefix, the numbering of commentary sections is unrelated to the section numbering of the manual proper.

Acknowledgments

C++ could never have matured without the constant use, suggestions, and constructive criticism of many friends and colleagues. In particular, we would like to thank Andrew Koenig and Doug McIlroy.

Brian Kernighan provided constant support and encouragement to us while we wrote this book; he read and commented on more drafts than anyone else.

Ravi Sethi showed us how to write the cross referencing software and Brian Kernighan helped us through the mysteries of *troff*, *pic*, *tbl*, *eqn*, *pj*, and his indexing software. Doris Ellis provided valuable editorial input.

Special thanks to Dennis Ritchie for C and for the original C manual that became the starting point for the C++ manual.

Further acknowledgements of people who specifically helped with the review of this manual can be found in §1.2c.

Contents

Overloading   307

Templates   341

Exception Handling   353

Preprocessing   383

1

Introduction

This chapter contains the introductory section of the C++ reference manual and demonstrates the mechanisms for presenting commentary to the reference manual proper. The commentary section summarizes the evolution of the C++ programming language and lists the people who took part in the 1989 reviews of the C++ reference manual.

1 Introduction

This manual describes the C++ programming language as of May 1991. C++ is a general purpose programming language based on the C programming language*. In addition to the facilities provided by C, C++ provides classes, inline functions, operator overloading, function name overloading, constant types, references, free store management operators, and function argument checking and type conversion. These extensions to C are summarized in §18.1. The differences between C++ and ANSI C† are summarized in §18.2. The extensions to C++ since the 1985 edition of this manual are summarized in §18.1.2. The sections related to templates (§14) and exception handling (§15) are placeholders for planned language extensions.

> ■ The pre-ANSI C dialects based on K&R plus structure assignment and enumerations will be collectively referred to as "Classic C." The adjectives "Classic" and "ANSI" will be used only where differences exist between Classic C and ANSI C. Most often, the name C will be used without an adjective. □

---

* "The C Programming Language" by Brian W. Kernighan and Dennis M. Ritchie, Prentice Hall, 1978 and 1988.
† American National Standard X3.159-1989.

1.1 Overview

This manual is organized like this:

1.2 Syntax Notation

In the syntax notation used in this manual, syntactic categories are indicated by *italic* type, and literal words and characters in `constant width` type. Alternatives are listed on separate lines except in a few cases where a long set of alternatives is presented on one line, marked by the phrase "one of." An optional terminal or nonterminal symbol is indicated by the subscript "*opt*," so

> { *expression*$_{opt}$ }

indicates an optional expression enclosed in braces.

Commentary

1.1c Evolution of C++

In 1980, classes, function argument type checking and conversion, and a few other features were added to C; the resulting language was called "C with Classes." This language was described in Bjarne Stroustrup: "*Classes: An Abstract Data Type Facility for the C Language,*" ACM SIGPLAN Notices Vol 17, no 1, January 1982 and in Bjarne Stroustrup: "*Adding Classes to C: An Exercise in Language Evolution,*" Software − Practice & Experience, Vol 13 (1983).

In 1983/84, C with Classes was redesigned, extended, and reimplemented; the resulting language was called C++. The major extensions were virtual functions and operator overloading. C++ was first described in Bjarne Stroustrup: "*Data Abstraction in C,*" AT&T Bell Laboratories Technical Journal Vol 63, No 8, October 1984. After a few further refinements, C++ became generally available in 1985 and was documented by Bjarne Stroustrup's book "*The C++ Programming Language*," Addison Wesley 1986.

This manual documents C++ as it now exists after the addition of support for multiple inheritance, type-safe linkage, abstract classes, refined mechanisms for overloading resolution, and other enhancements; see Chapter 18 for details. Templates (Chapter 14) and exception handling (Chapter 15) have only recently been added to the language and may not have made it into your implementation.

Since its conception, C++ has been evolving to meet the needs of its users. The experience of users of diverse backgrounds working in a wide range of applications has guided this evolution.

Because C++ has been in use for large software projects, stability and compatibility have been important considerations in the development of the language; so has run-time and space efficiency. Time and space overheads above those for C are considered unacceptable for C++.

The primary aim in extending C++ has been to enhance it as a language for data abstraction and object-oriented programming in general and as a tool for writing high quality libraries in particular.

Portability of at least some C++ implementations has been a key design goal, so extensions that would add significantly to the time required to port a C++ implementation or to the demands on system resources by a C++ compiler have been avoided.

1.2c Acknowledgements

The February 1990 C++ reference manual was written by Bjarne Stroustrup helped by an extensive review of several drafts. Many dozens of people were involved in this review and their contributions were invaluable. We do not know the names of everyone involved. In particular, several reviews are clearly the work of a group of people but contain only the name of a single individual and the name of an organization. The following, however, is the most complete list we have been able to compile. The list is sorted by affiliation and affiliations apply to the immediately preceding sublist of people. The affiliation of an individual is the affiliation at the time the review was written.

James Waldo (Apollo Computer Inc.), Ken Friedenbach (Apple), Mark Behm, Dave Brand, Phil Brown, Steve Buroff, Jim Coplien, Edna Edelman, Moshe Eliovson, Margaret Ellis, Roselle Fernandez, Doug Gibbons, Georges Gonthier, Tony Hansen, Bill Hopkins, Stacey Keenan, Andrew Koenig, Doug McIllroy, Brian Kernighan, Stan Lippman, Bill Mershon, Dave Prosser, Margaret Quinn, Johnathan Shopiro, Kathy Stark, Peter Weinberger (AT&T), Craig Bordelon, Joe Carfagno, Steve Carter, Bill Donahue, Stu Feldman, Wen-Yau Hsieh, Eric Krohn, Paul Matthews, Linda Schumacher (Bellcore), Michael B. Jones (Carnegie-Mellon University), Roger Scott (Data General), Donald Courtney, George Hetrick, Gary Pollice, Craig Hansen-Sturm, Laura Yaker (DEC), Steve Dewhurst (Glockenspiel), Timothy C. O'Konski, Mark Mathieu, Kathy Harris, Rob Seliger, Dmitry Lenkov,

Parag Patel, Nancy Sechrist, Paul Faust (Hewlett Packard), John J. Barton, Derek Lieber, Lee Nackman (IBM), Marc Shapiro (INRIA), Jesper Boelsmand (Jensen & Partners Inc.), Ron Guilmette (MCC), Jim Howard, Archie Lachner (Mentor Graphics), Tom Davies, Mitch Harter, Ross Garmoe, Jan Gray, David Jones, Jonathan Kimmich, Martin O'Riordan, Scott Randell, Tony Williams, Craig Wittenberg (Microsoft), Sam Haradhvala (Object Design Inc.), Mike Mowbray (Overseas Telecommunications Commission, Australia), Philippe Gautron (Rank Xerox France & LITP University of Paris VI), William Bulley (Schlumberger), Prescott K. Turner, Jr., William M. Miller, Michael J. Young (Software Development Technologies Inc.), Mark Linton, Michael Tiemann, Craig Chambers (Stanford University), Lily Chang (Sun Microsystems), Michael S. Ball, Stephen D. Clamage (TauMetric Corporation), Mark Rafter, Steve Rumsby (University of Warwick), Walter Bright (Zortech, Inc.), John M. Dlugosz, James Roskind.

C++ owes much to their efforts. Naturally, these people are in no way responsible for mistakes in the manual and naturally they made many suggestions for improvements that could not be accommodated for lack of time, because of compatibility issues, or for other reasons.

2

Lexical Conventions

This chapter presents the lexical conventions of C++. It defines tokens in a C++ program and describes comments, identifiers, keywords, and literals – integer, character, and floating point constants and string literals. Operators are discussed in §5. The C++ grammar based on these tokens is summarized in §17.

2   Lexical Conventions

A C++ program consists of one or more *files* (§3.3). A file is conceptually translated in several phases.

■ A file is a piece of text containing C++ source code and preprocessor commands. In other words, it is a source file on a traditional system. Dedicated C++ environments may have more elaborate ways of storing a file in a program data base. □

The first phase is preprocessing (§16), which performs file inclusion and macro substitution. Preprocessing is controlled by directives introduced by lines having # as the first character other than white space (§2.1). The result of preprocessing is a sequence of tokens. Such a sequence a tokens, that is, a file after preprocessing is called a *translation unit*.

■ Except for the treatment of C++ // comments and C++ tokens that are not also C tokens (. *, ->*, and : :), C++ preprocessing is ANSI C preprocessing. Originally, Classic C style preprocessors were used for C++, but the current definition of C++ preprocessing (§16) conforms to ANSI C preprocessing. □

2.1   Tokens

There are five kinds of tokens: identifiers, keywords, literals, operators, and other separators. Blanks, horizontal and vertical tabs, newlines, formfeeds, and comments (collectively, ''white space''), as described below, are ignored except as they serve to separate tokens. Some white space is required to separate otherwise adjacent identifiers, keywords, and constants.

If the input stream has been parsed into tokens up to a given character, the next token is taken to be the longest string of characters that could possibly constitute a token.

2.2 Comments

The characters `/*` start a comment, which terminates with the characters `*/`. These comments do not nest. The characters `//` start a comment, which terminates at the end of the line on which they occur. The comment characters `//`, `/*`, and `*/` have no special meaning within a `//` comment and are treated just like other characters. Similarly, the comment characters `//` and `/*` have no special meaning within a `/*` comment.

> ■ There are rare code sequences for which the C++ `//` commenting convention will cause C++'s interpretation of a program fragment to differ from C's interpretation of the same fragment. Consider
>
> ```
> int b = a//* divide by 4 */4;
> -a;
> ```
>
> With comments deleted, C++ parses this as
>
> ```
> int b = a -a;
> ```
>
> while C sees the same construct as
>
> ```
> int b = a/4;  -a;
> ```
>
> □

2.3 Identifiers

An identifier is an arbitrarily long sequence of letters and digits. The first character must be a letter; the underscore _ counts as a letter. Upper- and lower-case letters are different. All characters are significant.

> ■ C++ sets no maximum length for an identifier. Some implementations impose constraints on the length of identifiers. This is unfortunate and makes it harder for users of such systems to import software and to adhere to common naming conventions. It is, however, sometimes infeasible to upgrade basic system software and given the choice between accepting a limitation and not using C++ the limitation is often accepted. Similarly, experience shows that if (and only if) no alternative exists users will accept an implementation that is unable to distinguish upper-case from lower-case letters in external names. □

2.4 Keywords

The following identifiers are reserved for use as keywords, and may not be used otherwise:

```
asm      continue   float    new         signed     try
auto     default    for      operator    sizeof     typedef
break    delete     friend   private     static     union
case     do         goto     protected   struct     unsigned
catch    double     if       public      switch     virtual
char     else       inline   register    template   void
class    enum       int      return      this       volatile
const    extern     long     short       throw      while
```

In addition, identifiers containing a double underscore (_ _) are reserved for use by C++ implementations and standard libraries and should be avoided by users.

■ Identifiers starting with a single underscore (_) should also be avoided by ordinary users since C implementations reserve those for their own use. □

The ASCII representation of C++ programs uses the following characters as operators or for punctuation:

```
!   %   ^   &   *   (   )   -   +   =   {   }   |   ~
[   ]   \   ;   '   :   "   <   >   ?   ,   .   /
```

and the following character combinations are used as operators:

```
->    ++    --    .*    ->*   <<    >>    <=    >=    ==    !=    &&
||    *=    /=    %=    +=    -=    <<=   >>=   &=    ^=    |=    ::
```

Each is a single token.

In addition, the following tokens are used by the preprocessor:

```
                              #    ##
```

Certain implementation-dependent properties, such as the type of a sizeof (§5.3.2) and the ranges of fundamental types (§3.6.1), are defined in the standard header files (§16.4)

```
        <float.h>     <limits.h>     <stddef.h>
```

These headers are part of the ANSI C standard. In addition the headers

```
        <new.h>     <stdarg.h>     <stdlib.h>
```

define the types of the most basic library functions. The last two headers are part of the ANSI C standard; <new.h> is C++ specific.

■ Naturally, many other libraries and their associated header files will be available to the C++ programmer. For example,

```
<stdio.h>   <iostream.h>   <string.h>
```

These, however, do not affect the semantics of the language and are therefore not specified here. □

2.5 Literals

There are several kinds of literals (often referred to as "constants").

> *literal:*
> > *integer-constant*
> > *character-constant*
> > *floating-constant*
> > *string-literal*

2.5.1 Integer Constants

An integer constant consisting of a sequence of digits is taken to be decimal (base ten) unless it begins with 0 (digit zero). A sequence of digits starting with 0 is taken to be an octal integer (base eight). The digits 8 and 9 are not octal digits. A sequence of digits preceded by 0x or 0X is taken to be a hexadecimal integer (base sixteen). The hexadecimal digits include a or A through f or F with decimal values ten through fifteen. For example, the number twelve can be written 12, 014, or 0XC.

The type of an integer constant depends on its form, value, and suffix. If it is decimal and has no suffix, it has the first of these types in which its value can be represented: int, long int, unsigned long int. If it is octal or hexadecimal and has no suffix, it has the first of these types in which its value can be represented: int, unsigned int, long int, unsigned long int. If it is suffixed by u or U, its type is the first of these types in which its value can be represented: unsigned int, unsigned long int. If it is suffixed by l or L, its type is the first of these types in which its value can be represented: long int, unsigned long int. If it is suffixed by ul, lu, uL, Lu, Ul, lU, UL, or LU, its type is unsigned long int.

■ For example, *100000* is of type *int* on a machine with 32 bit *int*s, but of type *long int* on a machine with 16 bit *int*s and 32 bit *long*s. Similarly, *0XA000* is of type *int* on a machine with 32 bit *int*s, but of type *unsigned int* on a machine with 16 bit *int*s. These implementation dependencies can usually be avoided by using suffixes: *100000L* is *long int* on all machines and *0XA000U* is of type *unsigned int* on machines with at least 16 bits for an *unsigned int*. □

2.5.2 Character Constants

A character constant is one or more characters enclosed in single quotes, as in `'x'`. Single character constants have type `char`. The value of a single character constant is the numerical value of the character in the machine's character set.

> ■ In C, all character constants are of type `int`. Interestingly enough, having single character constants as type `char` in C++ does not cause compatibility problems. In C, the `int` value of the character constant is obtained by taking a `char` value and promoting it to an `int`. This is exactly what C++ will do in all contexts where integral promotion (§4.1) occurs. There is only one place in C where a character constant does not suffer integral promotion and consequently only one place where the difference in the type of a character constant can be detected in a program that is both legal C and C++: `sizeof('a')` has the value `1` in C++ and a value `sizeof(int)` in C.
>
> In C++, however, having character constants of type `char` is important because of overloading; it allows functions to distinguish between small integers and characters; see §13.2. □

Multicharacter constants have type `int`. The value of a multicharacter constant is implementation dependent.

> ■ For example, the value of
>
>   `'AB'`
>
> could reasonably expected to be `'A'` `'B'` and `('A'<<8)+'B'` on three different implementations. Multicharacter constants are usually best avoided. □

Certain nongraphic characters, the single quote `'`, the double quote `"`, the question mark `?`, and the backslash `\`, may be represented according to the following table of escape sequences:

new-line	NL (LF)	`\n`
horizontal tab	HT	`\t`
vertical tab	VT	`\v`
backspace	BS	`\b`
carriage return	CR	`\r`
form feed	FF	`\f`
alert	BEL	`\a`
backslash	`\`	`\\`
question mark	`?`	`\?`
single quote	`'`	`\'`
double quote	`"`	`\"`
octal number	*ooo*	`\ooo`
hex number	*hhh*	`\xhhh`

If the character following a backslash is not one of those specified, the behavior is undefined.

■ This differs from the interpretation by Classic C and early versions of C++, where the value of a sequence of a backslash followed by a character in the source character set, if not defined as an escape sequence, was equal to the numeric value of the character. For example, '\q' would equal 'q'. □

An escape sequence specifies a single character.

The escape \ooo consists of the backslash followed by one, two, or three octal digits that are taken to specify the value of the desired character. The escape \xhhh consists of the backslash followed by x followed by a sequence of hexadecimal digits that are taken to specify the value of the desired character. There is no limit to the number of hexadecimal digits in the sequence. A sequence of octal or hexadecimal digits is terminated by the first character that is not an octal digit or a hexadecimal digit, respectively. The value of a character constant is implementation dependent if it exceeds that of the largest char.

A character constant immediately preceded by the letter L, for example, L'ab', is a wide-character constant. A wide-character constant is of type wchar_t, an integral type (§3.6.1) defined in the standard header <stddef.h>. Wide-characters are intended for character sets where a character does not fit into a single byte.

2.5.3 Floating Constants

A floating constant consists of an integer part, a decimal point, a fraction part, an e or E, an optionally signed integer exponent, and an optional type suffix. The integer and fraction parts both consist of a sequence of decimal (base ten) digits. Either the integer part or the fraction part (not both) may be missing; either the decimal point or the letter e (or E) and the exponent (not both) may be missing. The type of a floating constant is double unless explicitly specified by a suffix. The suffixes f and F specify float, the suffixes l and L specify long double.

■ For example, *2.0, 2., 0.2e1*, and *.2E1* are *doubles*, *2.0F* and *20e-1F* are *floats*, and *2.0L* is a *long double*. □

2.5.4 String Literals

A string literal is a sequence of characters (as defined in §2.5.2) surrounded by double quotes, as in "...". A string has type "array of char" and storage class *static* (§3.5), and is initialized with the given characters. Whether all string literals are distinct (that is, are stored in nonoverlapping objects) is implementation dependent. The effect of attempting to modify a string literal is undefined.

Adjacent string literals are concatenated. Characters in concatenated strings are kept distinct. For example,

```
"\xA" "B"
```

contains the two characters '\xA' and 'B' after concatenation (and not the single hexadecimal character '\xAB').

After any necessary concatenation ' \0' is appended so that programs that scan a string can find its end. The size of a string is the number of its characters including this terminator. Within a string, the double quote character " must be preceded by a \.

A string literal immediately preceded by the letter L, for example, L"asdf", is a wide-character string. A wide-character string is of type "array of wchar_t," where wchar_t is an integral type defined in the standard header <stddef.h>. Concatenation of ordinary and wide-character string literals is undefined.

■ Given the two declarations

```
char* str1 = "Please enter name and address";
char* str2 = "name and address";
```

some implementations will create two nonoverlapping memory locations containing the string literals, while others will optimize the use of memory by initializing *str2* to point to the substring *"name and address"* within the string pointed to by *str1.*

This implies that string literals are best treated as constants by the programmer since modifying one string may modify another string that may not even be known to the programmer. For example, the second − unintentionally modified − string might be part of a standard library linked to the program.

String literals are of type *char[]* (see §2.5.4) and not *const char[]* for compatibility with Classic C where early software took advantage of string literals being distinct and modifiable. □

Commentary

2.1c Implementation Dependencies

Like C, C++ leaves many details "implementation-dependent." This is done partly to allow an implementation to take maximum advantage of the hardware (for example, the sign of the result of a % operation with a negative argument, §5.6), and partly to allow the programmer to manipulate the hardware directly rather than an implementation independent abstract machine. There are about thirty implementation-dependent features in the C++ language (the exact number depends on exactly what one considers separate features); they can be found by looking up "*implementation dependency*" in the index.

Clearly, use of implementation-dependent features can lead to portability problems. Consequently, the documentation for an implementation should provide a detailed explanation of the choices made for each implementation-dependent feature. In addition, tools that detect reliance on implementation-dependent features can be very useful.

Why couldn't C++ have resolved these implementation dependencies by defining a right answer for each? The reason is partly that some implementation dependencies are necessary to retain the closeness to the machine that allows C and C++ to serve for low-level systems programming and allows an implementation to use the full speed of a machine's arithmetic unit and memory access hardware. Another reason is that resolving such things in C++ but not in C would make it highly unlikely that compatible C and C++ implementations would be provided for a given system, thereby creating a whole new class of subtle compatibility and portability bugs.

3

Basic Concepts

This chapter presents the basic concepts of the C++ language. It explains the difference between an *object* and a *name* and how they relate to the notion of an *lvalue*. It introduces the concepts of a *declaration* and a *definition* and presents C++'s notion of *type*, *scope*, *linkage*, and *storage class*. The mechanisms for starting and terminating a program are discussed. Finally, this chapter presents the fundamental types of the language and lists the ways of constructing derived types from these.

This chapter does not cover concepts that affect only a single part of the language. Such concepts are discussed in the relevant chapters.

3   Basic Concepts

A name denotes an object, a function, a set of functions, an enumerator, a type, a class member, a template, a value, or a label. A name is introduced into a program by a declaration. A name can be used only within a region of program text called its *scope*. A name has a type, which determines its use. A name used in more than one translation unit may (or may not) refer to the same object, function, type, template, or value in these translation units depending on the linkage (§3.3) specified in the translation units.

An object is a region of storage (§3.7). A named object has a storage class (§3.5) that determines its lifetime. The meaning of the values found in an object is determined by the type of the expression used to access it.

3.1 Declarations and Definitions

A declaration (§7) introduces one or more names into a program. A declaration is a definition unless it declares a function without specifying the body (§8.3), it contains the extern specifier (§7.1.1) and no initializer or function body, it is the declaration of a static data member in a class declaration (§9.4), it is a class name declaration (§9.1), or it is a typedef declaration (§7.1.3). The following, for example, are definitions:

```
int a;
extern const c = 1;
int f(int x) { return x+a; }
struct S { int a; int b; };
enum { up, down };
```

whereas these are just declarations:

```
extern int a;
extern const c;
int f(int);
struct S;
typedef int Int;
```

There must be exactly one definition of each object, function, class, and enumerator used in a program (§3.3). If a function is never called and its address is never taken, it need not be defined. Similarly, if the name of a class is used only in a way that does not require its definition to be known, it need not be defined.

■ Note that declarations can be repeated whereas definitions cannot. For example,

```
struct S;
struct S;            // OK: redeclaration
typedef int Int;
typedef int Int;     // OK: redeclaration

int a;
int a;               // error: redefinition
extern const c = 1;
extern const c = 1;  // error: redefinition
```

The general model is that there must be exactly one definition of each object, function, class, and so on in a program, whereas there can be as many declarations as is desired.

Note that C++ differs from ANSI C by considering "*int a;*" (with no *extern* specifier) a definition. The reason for this is partly to ensure that there is no difference between saying "*int a;*" twice in a single translation unit and "*int a;*" twice in two separate translation units; partly to avoid having different rules for built-in and user-defined (§9) types . Consider

```
class Int { /* ... */ public: Int(); };
Int a;
Int a;               // error: two definitions of 'a'
```

Here, both occurrences of

```
Int a;
```

are clearly definitions because a call of the constructor *Int::Int()* is required for each. The global declaration

```
int a;
```

is considered equivalent to

```
Int a;
```

except for the difference in type and is considered *exactly* equivalent to

```
int a = 0;
```

☐

3.2 Scopes

There are four kinds of scope: local, function, file, and class.

> *Local*: A name declared in a block (§6.3) is local to that block and can be
> used only in it and in blocks enclosed by it after the point of declaration.
> Names of formal arguments for a function are treated as if they were
> declared in the outermost block of that function.

> *Function*: Labels (§6.1) can be used anywhere in the function in which they
> are declared. Only labels have function scope.

> *File*: A name declared outside all blocks (§6.3) and classes (§9) has file
> scope and can be used in the translation unit in which it is declared after the
> point of declaration. Names declared with *file* scope are said to be *global*.

> *Class*: The name of a class member is local to its class and can be used
> only in a member function of that class (§9.3), after the . operator applied
> to an object of its class (§5.2.4) or a class derived from (§10) its class, after
> the -> operator applied to a pointer to an object of its class (§5.2.4) or a
> class derived from its class, or after the : : scope resolution operator (§5.1)
> applied to the name of its class or a class derived from its class. A name
> first declared by a friend declaration (§11.4) belongs to the same scope as
> the class containing the friend declaration. A class first declared in a
> return or argument type belongs to the global scope.

Special rules apply to names declared in function argument declarations (§8.2.5),
and friend declarations (§11.4).

> ■ Note that class and typedef names nest properly within classes. They do not in C
> nor did they previously in C++; see §9.7, §18.3.5. ☐

   A name may be hidden by an explicit declaration of that same name in an
enclosed block or in a class. A hidden class member name can still be used when
it is qualified by its class name using the : : operator (§5.1, §9.4, §10). A hidden

name of an object, function, type, or enumerator with file scope can still be used
when it is qualified by the unary : : operator (§5.1). In addition, a class name
(§9.1) may be hidden by the name of an object, function, or enumerator declared in
the same scope.

■ The operator : : followed by an identifier refers to the object of file scope named
by that identifier. This allows an object to be visible even if its identifier has been
hidden. For example,

```
int g = 99;

int f(int g)
{
     return g ? g : ::g; // return argument if it
                         // is nonzero otherwise
                         // return global g
}
```

Similarly, a class name that has been hidden by a nontype name can still be used
with the : : operator, as follows:

```
class X {
     // ...
public:
     static int xval();
};

int f(X* p)
{
     int X = 44 ;        // hiding the class name
     // ...
     return X::xval(); // X before :: is a class name
}
```

□

If a class and an object, function, or enumerator are declared in the same scope (in
any order) with the same name the class name is hidden. A class name hidden by
a name of an object, function, or enumerator in local or class scope can still be
used when appropriately (§7.1.6) prefixed with class, struct, or union.
Similarly, a hidden enumeration name can be used when appropriately (§7.1.6) prefixed with enum.

■ See the commentary (§3.1c) for examples of hiding of class names. □

The scope rules are summarized in §10.4.

The *point of declaration* for a name is immediately after its complete declarator
(§8) and before its initializer (if any). For example,

```
int x = 12;
{ int x = x; }
```

Here the second x is initialized with its own (unspecified) value.

■ Consider

```
struct s { /*...*/ }; // declare struct s in file scope

f()
{
    extern int s(s*); // declare s() in local scope
    s(0);             // call s()
}
```

Here, a *struct* s is declared at file scope. Then a function s() taking a pointer to a *struct* s as its argument is declared at local scope in f(). Because the point of declaration of s() in

```
extern int s(s*);
```

is *after* the full declarator has been parsed (and the argument type is part of the declarator), *struct* s is still in scope and can be used to specify the type of the argument for the function s().

Consider also

```
int x = 7;
int f(int x, int y = x);        // error
```

Here, the point of declaration for the argument x is at the comma, so y's default value is the argument x and not the global x; see §8.2.6. Using one argument as the default value for another happens to be illegal (§8.2.6). □

The point of declaration for an enumerator is immediately after the identifier that names it. For example,

```
enum { x = x };
```

Here, again, the enumerator x is initialized to its own (uninitialized) value.

3.3 Program and Linkage

A program consists of one or more files (§2) linked together. A file consists of a sequence of declarations.

■ This may seem peculiar to those accustomed to thinking of a program as consisting of a series of executable statements, along with the appropriate declarations of variables. Consider though, that executable statements are contained within functions and that a function definition is itself a declaration. Conversely, because declarations can contain initializers, declarations can also be considered executable. □

A name of file scope that is explicitly declared static is local to its translation unit and can be used as a name for other objects, functions, and so on, in other translation units. Such names are said to have internal linkage. A name of file scope that is explicitly declared inline is local to its translation unit. A name of file scope that is explicitly declared const and not explicitly declared extern is local to its translation unit. So is the name of a class that has not been used in the

declaration of an object, function, or class that is not local to its translation unit and
has no static members (§9.4) and no noninline member functions (§9.3.2). Every
declaration of a particular name of file scope that is not declared to have internal
linkage in one of these ways in a multifile program refers to the same object (§3.7),
function (§8.2.5), or class (§9). Such names are said to be external or to have
external linkage. In particular, since it is not possible to declare a class name
`static`, every use of a particular file scope class name that has been used in the
declaration of an object or function with external linkage or has a static member or
a noninline member function refers to the same class.

> ■ Note that two classes that in any way have been used to specify a form of external
> linkage may not have the same name. C++ relies on name equivalence (§9.1). □

Typedef names (§7.1.3), enumerators (§7.2), and template names (§14) do not
have external linkage.

Static class members (§9.4) have external linkage.

Noninline class member functions have external linkage. Inline class member
functions must have exactly one definition in a program.

> ■ This last constraint is almost impossible to enforce in an environment with
> genuinely independent compilation of the parts of a program, but easy to check
> where a compiler uses information stored between compilations. It is essential
> where virtual functions are used. Had definitions of different versions of a member
> function in different parts of a program been allowed the definition of a class would
> have been incoherent and it would have been undefined which version of a virtual
> function should be called (§10.2). The only safe use of class member inline func-
> tions is to define each once and include it with its class declaration. □

Local names (§3.2) explicitly declared `extern` have external linkage unless
already declared `static` (§7.1.1).

The types specified in all declarations of a particular external name must be
identical except for the use of typedef names (§7.1.3) and unspecified array bounds
(§8.2.4). There must be exactly one definition for each function, object, class and
enumerator used in a program. If, however, a function is never called and its
address is never taken, it need not be defined. Similarly, if the name of a class is
used only in a way that does not require its definition to be known, it need not be
defined.

> ■ If a name is just declared and never used, it need not be defined. For example,
>
> ```
> extern f();
> main() { }
> ```
>
> Is a complete and correct program. □

A function may be defined only in file or class scope.

Linkage to non-C++ declarations can be achieved using a *linkage-specification*
(§7.4).

3.4 Start and Termination

A program must contain a function called `main()`. This function is the designated start of the program. This function is not predefined by the compiler, it cannot be overloaded, and its type is implementation dependent. It is recommended that the two examples below be allowed on any implementation and that any further arguments required be added after `argv`. The function `main()` may be defined as

```
int main() { /* ... */ }
```

or

```
int main(int argc, char* argv[]) { /* ... */ }
```

In the latter form `argc` shall be the number of parameters passed to the program from an environment in which the program is run. If `argc` is nonzero these parameters shall be supplied as zero-terminated strings in `argv[0]` through `argv[argc-1]` and `argv[0]` shall be the name used to invoke the program or `""`. It is guaranteed that `argv[argc]==0`.

The function `main()` may not be called from within a program. The linkage (§3.3) of `main()` is implementation dependent. The address of `main()` cannot be taken and `main()` may not be declared `inline` or `static`.

■ This is to ensure full freedom of the implementer of the interface between a C++ program and its environment. One could even imagine an implementation where *main ()* was not implemented as a function. □

Calling the function

```
void exit(int);
```

declared in `<stdlib.h>` terminates the program. The argument value is returned to the program's environment as the value of the program.

A return statement in `main()` has the effect of calling `exit()` with the return value as the argument.

The initialization of nonlocal static objects (§3.5) in a translation unit is done before the first use of any function or object defined in that translation unit. Such initializations (§8.4, §9.4, §12.1, §12.6.1) may be done before the first statement of `main()` or deferred to any point in time before the first use of a function or object defined in that translation unit. The default initialization of all static objects to zero (§8.4) is performed before any dynamic (that is, run-time) initialization. No further order is imposed on the initialization of objects from different translation units. The initialization of local static objects is described in §8.4.

■ Note that it is not in general possible to complete dynamic initialization of every nonlocal static object before its use.
Consider

```
//file1:
    extern y;
    int x = y+1;


// file2:
    extern x;
    int y = x+1;
```

Here, a mutual dependency exists that makes it impossible to define the values of x
and y at the start of *main ()*, that is after the dynamic initialization has taken place.
Either the dynamic initialization for *file1* takes place before the dynamic initialization of *file2* and *x==1* and *y==2* or the order is reversed and we get *x==2*
and *y==1*. Because the static initialization to *0* takes place before dynamic initialization there are no further possibilities for the values of x and y.

For a given implementation it is possible to control the order of dynamic initialization, but it is usually wise to avoid dependencies on dynamic initialization order.
Where such order is essential, placing the definitions of the global objects involved
in a single translation unit is the only portable way of assuring a specific order.

A useful technique for ensuring that a global object is initialized only once and
before its first use is to maintain a count of the number of translation units using it.
For example, consider writing a library that provides some statically allocated objects
that must be initialized before the first use of the facilities of the libraries.

```
// file nifty_library.h:

// ...
extern X1 obj1;
// ...
extern Xn objn;
```

If these objects require dynamic initialization, we have a problem: the dynamic
initialization of the translation unit or translation units holding the definitions cannot
(except by special system-dependent and extra-linguistic magic) be assumed to be
performed before the dynamic initialization of all users. To solve this problem we
add to *nifty_library.h*

```
class nifty_counter {
    static count;
public:


    nifty_counter()
    {
        if (count++ == 0) {
            // initialize obj1 ... objn
        }
    }
```

```
~nifty_counter()
{
    if (--count == 0) {
        // clean up obj1 ... objn
    }
}
};
```

```
static nifty_counter nifty;
```

Now every file that includes the library header also creates a *nifty_counter* object and initializes it with the effect of increasing *nifty_counter::count*. The first time this happens the library objects will be initialized. Since the library header appears before any use of the library facilities this ensures proper initialization. Since destruction is done in reverse order of construction, this technique also ensures that cleanup is done after the last use of the library.

We believe this technique has been independently discovered many times. Jerry Schwarz pioneered its use in C++ by using it for construction and destruction of *cout*, *cin*, and others, in the iostream library. These objects are constructed before the first I/O operation, and destroyed (with the effect of flushing their buffers) after the last. □

Destructors (§12.4) for initialized static objects are called when returning from `main()` and when calling `exit()`. Destruction is done in reverse order of initialization. The function `atexit()` from `<stdlib.h>` can be used to specify that a function must be called at exit. If `atexit()` is to be called, objects initialized before an `atexit()` call may not be destroyed until after the function specified in the `atexit()` call has been called. Where a C++ implementation coexists with a C implementation, any actions specified by the C implementation to take place after the `atexit()` functions have been called take place after all destructors have been called.

Calling the function

```
void abort();
```

declared in `<stdlib.h>` terminates the program without executing destructors for static objects and without calling the functions passed to `atexit()`.

■ Typically, *abort()* has additional, system-dependent, effects. For example, *abort()* often saves information that allows a post-mortem on the program. □

3.5 Storage Classes

There are two declarable storage classes: automatic and static.

Automatic objects are local to each invocation of a block.

Static objects exist and retain their values throughout the execution of the entire program.

Automatic objects are initialized (§12.1) each time the control flow reaches their definition and destroyed (§12.4) on exit from their block (§6.7).

A named automatic object may not be destroyed before the end of its block nor may an automatic named object of a class with a constructor or a destructor with side effects be eliminated even if it appears to be unused.

■ There are programming techniques relying exclusively on side effects of the initialization and cleanup of such objects. For example,

```
class Tracer {
    char* p;
public:
    Tracer(char* s)
        { p = s; cerr << s << " entered\n"; }
    ~Tracer()
        { cerr << "exit from " << p << '\n'; }
};

void f()
{
    Tracer tr("f"); // Tracer variable
    // ...
}
```

□

Similarly, a global object of a class with a constructor or a destructor with side effects may not be eliminated even if it appears to be unused.

■ Such objects are sometimes used for library initialization as described in §3.4. □

Static objects are initialized and destroyed as described in §3.4 and §6.7. Some objects are not associated with names; see §5.3.3 and §12.2. All global objects have storage class *static*. Local objects and class members can be given static storage class by explicit use of the `static` storage class specifier (§7.1.1).

3.6 Types

There are two kinds of types: fundamental types and derived types.

3.6.1 Fundamental Types

There are several fundamental types. The standard header <limits.h> specifies the largest and smallest values of each for an implementation.

■ The minimum values that will satisfy the ANSI C Standard are given in §3.2c. □

Objects declared as characters (`char`) are large enough to store any member of the implementation's basic character set. If a character from this set is stored in a character variable, its value is equivalent to the integer code of that character. Characters may be explicitly declared `unsigned` or `signed`. Plain `char`, `signed char`, and `unsigned char` are three distinct types. A char, a `signed char`, and an `unsigned char` consume the same amount of space.

■ An implementation must specify whether the high-order bit of a *char* object that is neither explicitly *signed* nor *unsigned* is treated as a sign bit. Generally, the treatment chosen will take advantage of the instructions the target hardware executes most efficiently. Leaving this aspect of the language implementation-dependent is a common source of portability problems. Resolving these problems by simply defining *chars* to be *unsigned* (or *signed*) would lead to incompatibilities with C, however, and programmers rightfully expect C compatibility in such basic matters. □

Up to three sizes of integer, declared `short int`, `int`, and `long int`, are available. Longer integers provide no less storage than shorter ones, but the implementation may make either short integers or long integers, or both, equivalent to plain integers. Plain integers have the natural size suggested by the machine architecture; the other sizes are provided to meet special needs.

■ This implies that the *signed char*, *short*, *int*, and *long* types may all be of the same size. A *signed char* will usually be smaller than a *short*, but it is not uncommon for an *int* to be the same size as either a *short* or a *long*. □

For each of the types `signed char`, `short`, `int`, and `long`, there exists a corresponding `unsigned` type, which occupies the same amount of storage and has the same alignment requirements. An *alignment requirement* is an implementation-dependent restriction on the value of a pointer to an object of a given type (§5.4).

■ Typically implementations impose restrictions on where objects of given types may be allocated to ensure better use of memory access hardware. For example, it is often required that *int*s are allocated so that they do not straddle hardware word boundaries. □

Unsigned integers, declared `unsigned`, obey the laws of arithmetic modulo 2^n where n is the number of bits in the representation. This implies that unsigned arithmetic does not overflow.

■ Typical integer type sizes and alignments:

type	size (in bytes)	byte alignment
char	1	1
short	2	2
int	2 or 4	2 or 4
long	4 or 8	4 or 8

□

There are three *floating* types: `float`, `double`, and `long double`. The type `double` provides no less precision than `float`, and the type `long double` provides no less precision than `double`. An implementation will define the

characteristics of the fundamental floating point types in the standard header
`<float.h>`.

■ The minimum values that will satisfy the ANSI C Standard are given in §3.2.2c.
  Typical floating point type sizes and alignments:

type	size (in bytes)	byte alignment
float	4	4
double	8	4 or 8
long double	12 or 16	4 or 8 or 16

□

Types `char`, `int` of all sizes, and enumerations (§7.2) are collectively called
integral types. *Integral* and *floating* types are collectively called *arithmetic* types.

The `void` type specifies an empty set of values. It is used as the return type
for functions that do not return a value. No object of type `void` may be declared.
Any expression may be explicitly converted to type `void` (§5.4); the resulting
expression may be used only as an expression statement (§6.2), as the left operand
of a comma expression (§5.18), or as a second or third operand of `?:` (§5.16).

3.6.2 Derived Types

There is a conceptually infinite number of derived types constructed from the fundamental types in the following ways:

arrays of objects of a given type, §8.2.4;

functions, which take arguments of given types and return objects of a given
type, §8.2.5;

pointers to objects or functions of a given type, §8.2.1;

references to objects or functions of a given type, §8.2.2;

constants, which are values of a given type, §7.1.6;

classes containing a sequence of objects of various types (§9), a set of functions for manipulating these objects (§9.3), and a set of restrictions on the
access to these objects and functions, §11;

structures, which are classes without default access restrictions, §11;

unions, which are structures capable of containing objects of different types
at different times, §9.5;

pointers to class members, which identify members of a given type within objects of a given class, §8.2.3.

In general, these methods of constructing objects can be applied recursively; restrictions are mentioned in §8.2.1, §8.2.4, §8.2.5, and §8.2.2.

■ We refer to classes (including structures and unions) as *user-defined* types and other types as *built-in* types. □

A pointer to objects of a type T is referred to as a "pointer to T." For example, a pointer to an object of type int is referred to as "pointer to int" and a pointer to an object of class X is called a "pointer to X."

Objects of type void* (pointer to void), const void*, and volatile void* can be used to point to objects of unknown type. A void* must have enough bits to hold any object pointer.

■ A pointer to a nonstatic member is not considered an object pointer. Thus, the requirement that type *void** be large enough to hold any object pointer does not mean that *void** must be large enough to hold a pointer to function or a pointer to member.

A pointer to a static member, however, is treated as an ordinary pointer. Thus, given

```
class X {
public:
    static int Xcount;
};
```

applying the & operator to *X::Xcount* yields type *int**, not type *int X::**. Therefore the following is correct:

```
int* p = &X::Xcount;
```

□

Except for pointers to static members, text referring to "pointers" does not apply to pointers to members.

3.6.3 Type Names

Fundamental and derived types can be given names by the typedef mechanism (§7.1.3), and families of types and functions can be specified and named by the template mechanism (§14).

3.7 Lvalues

An *object* is a region of storage; an *lvalue* is an expression referring to an object or function. An obvious example of an lvalue expression is the name of an object. Some operators yield lvalues. For example, if E is an expression of pointer type, then *E is an lvalue expression referring to the object to which E points. The name "lvalue" comes from the assignment expression E1 = E2 in which the left operand `E1` must be an lvalue expression. The discussion of each operator in §5 indicates whether it expects lvalue operands and whether it yields an lvalue. An lvalue is *modifiable* if it is not a function name, an array name, or `const`.

Commentary

3.1c Name Spaces

C++ puts type names in the same name space as other names, unlike C, which provides a separate name space for structure tags. For example,

```
struct stat {
     // ...
};

extern struct stat stat(int, struct stat *);
```

was originally not legal C++, although even early implementations accepted it for compatibility.

On the other hand, providing a single name space gives important notational conveniences to C++ programmers. Consider a class *complex*

```
class complex {
     // ...
};
```

for which an object can be declared as follows:

```
complex c1;
```

Without the single name space, every declaration of a *complex* object or argument type would have to include the *class* keyword.

```
class complex c1;
```

All casts to class types would be similarly burdened.

Requiring that such prefixing always appear would compromise the effort to make use of user-defined types, such as *complex*, as similar as possible to use of built-in types, such as *int*.

Experience has shown, however, that simply imposing a single name space causes too much confusion and too much inconvenience for too many users. Consequently, a refined version of the C/C++ compatibility compromise is now incorporated into C++; see §9.1.

This name space compromise enables all accepted uses of multiple name spaces in C while preserving the notational convenience of C++ when compatibility with C isn't an issue. In particular, every formerly legal C++ program remains legal.

A typedef can declare a name to refer to the same type more than once. For example,

```
typedef struct s { /* ... */ } s;
typedef s s;
```

A name s can be declared as a type (struct, class, union, enum, typedef) *and* as a nontype (function, object, value, and so on) in a single scope. In this example, after both declarations of s have been seen, the name s refers to the nontype and `struct s` can be used to refer to the type. The order of declaration does not matter. For example,

```
struct stat { /* ... */ };
stat a;              // same as ''struct stat a;''
void stat(stat* p);
struct stat b;    // struct keyword is needed
stat(0);             // function call

int f(int);
f(1);
union f { /* ... */ };
union f g;      // union keyword is needed
```

A name cannot simultaneously refer to two types.

```
class c { /* ... */ };
typedef int c;    // error
```

If a nontype name s hides a type name s, `struct s` (or `class s`, `union s`, or `enum s`, as the case may be) can be used to refer to the type name. For example,

```
struct s { /* ... */ };
void f(int s) { struct s a; s++; }
```

If a type name hides a nontype name the usual scoping rules apply (§3.2).

```
int s = 0;

void f()
{
    struct s { /* ... */ }; // global int s is hidden
    s a;
    ::s = 3;                          // refers to global int s
}
                                          // struct s is out of scope
                                          // int s is visible
int q = s;
```

3.2c Numerical Limits

This section defines the minimum numerical limits that a C++ implementation consistent with the ANSI C Standard will provide in the header files `<limits.h>` and `<float.h>`.

3.2.1c Integral Limits

An implementation that provides functionality consistent with ANSI C will define the sizes of integral types in the `<limits.h>` header file. Where a maximum value is given below, it is the minimum value that will satisfy ANSI; an implementation may provide larger values. Where a minimum value is given below, it is the maximum value that will satisfy ANSI; an implementation may provide smaller values.

CHAR_BIT	8	maximum bits in a byte
SCHAR_MIN	−127	minimum value of `signed char`
SCHAR_MAX	+127	maximum value of `signed char`
UCHAR_MAX	255	maximum value of `unsigned char`
CHAR_MIN	0	
	or SCHAR_MIN	minimum value of `char`
CHAR_MAX	UCHAR_MAX	
	or SCHAR_MAX	maximum value of `char`
MB_LEN_MAX	1	maximum bytes in a multibyte character
SHRT_MIN	−32767	minimum value of `short`
SHRT_MAX	+32767	maximum value of `short`
USHRT_MAX	65535	maximum value of `unsigned short`
INT_MIN	−32767	minimum value of `int`
INT_MAX	+32767	maximum value of `int`
UINT_MAX	65535	maximum value of `unsigned int`
LONG_MIN	−2147483647	minimum value of `long`
LONG_MAX	+2147483647	maximum value of `long`
ULONG_MAX	4294967295	maximum value of `unsigned long`

The value of *CHAR_MIN* will be *SCHAR_MIN* if the value of a *char* is sign-extended when used in an expression, and *0* otherwise. The value of *CHAR_MAX* will be *SCHAR_MAX* if a *char* is sign-extended in an expression, and *UCHAR_MAX* otherwise.

3.2.2c Floating Limits

An implementation that provides functionality consistent with ANSI C will define the characteristics of floating types in the `<float.h>` header file. Where a maximum value is given below, it is the minimum value that will satisfy ANSI; an implementation may provide larger values. Where a minimum value is given below, it is the maximum value that will satisfy ANSI; an implementation may provide smaller values.

FLT_RADIX	2	radix of exponent representation
FLT_MANT_DIG		number of base FLT_RADIX digits in mantissa
FLT_DIG	6	decimal digits of precision
FLT_MIN_EXP		minimum negative integer n such that FLT_RADIX raised to the nth minus 1 is a normalized floating point number
FLT_MIN_10_EXP	−37	minimum negative integer n such that 10 raised to the nth is within the range of normalized floating point numbers
FLT_MAX_EXP		maximum integer n such that FLT_RADIX raised to the nth minus 1 is representable
FLT_MAX_10_EXP	+37	maximum integer n such that 10 raised to the nth is representable
FLT_MAX	1E+37	maximum representable floating point number
FLT_EPSILON	1E−5	minimum positive number x such that $1.0 + x$ does not equal 1.0
FLT_MIN	1E−37	minimum normalized positive floating point number
DBL_MANT_DIG		number of base FLT_RADIX digits in mantissa
DBL_DIG	10	decimal digits of precision
DBL_MIN_EXP		minimum negative integer n such that FLT_RADIX raised to the nth minus 1 is a normalized floating point number
DBL_MIN_10_EXP	−37	minimum negative integer n such that 10 raised to the nth is within the range of normalized floating point numbers
DBL_MAX_EXP		maximum integer n such that FLT_RADIX raised to the nth minus 1 is representable
DBL_MAX_10_EXP	+37	maximum integer n such that 10 raised to the nth is representable
DBL_MAX	1E+37	maximum representable floating point number
DBL_EPSILON	1E−9	minimum positive number x such that $1.0 + x$ does not equal 1.0
DBL_MIN	1E−37	minimum normalized positive floating point number
LDBL_MANT_DIG		number of base FLT_RADIX digits in mantissa
LDBL_DIG	10	decimal digits of precision

`LDBL_MIN_EXP`		minimum negative integer n such that `FLT_RADIX` raised to the nth minus 1 is a normalized floating point number
`LDBL_MIN_10_EXP`	-37	minimum negative integer n such that 10 raised to the nth is within the range of normalized floating point numbers
`LDBL_MAX_EXP`		maximum integer n such that `FLT_RADIX` raised to the nth minus 1 is representable
`LDBL_MAX_10_EXP`	$+37$	maximum integer n such that 10 raised to the nth is representable
`LDBL_MAX`	`1E+37`	maximum representable floating point number
`LDBL_EPSILON`	`1E-9`	minimum positive number x such that $1.0 + x$ does not equal 1.0
`LDBL_MIN`	`1E-37`	minimum normalized positive floating point number

Many implementations will also provide the definitions required to satisfy the *IEEE Standard for Binary Floating-Point Arithmetic*.

4

Standard Conversions

This chapter presents standard type conversions, including integral promotions, integral conversions, floating point conversions, conversions between floating and integral types, and arithmetic conversions, as well as pointer, reference, and pointer to member conversions.

4   Standard Conversions

Some operators may, depending on their operands, cause conversion of the value of an operand from one type to another. This section summarizes the conversions demanded by most ordinary operators and explains the result to be expected from such conversions; it will be supplemented as required by the discussion of each operator. These conversions are also used in initialization (§8.4, §8.4.3, §12.8, §12.1). §12.3 and §13.2 describe user-defined conversions and their interaction with standard conversions. The result of a conversion is an lvalue only if the result is a reference (§8.2.2).

> ■ Conversions for the fundamental types (§3.6.1) are defined in C++ as they are in ANSI C. The conversion rules for arithmetic types and the way implementation dependencies affect them are summarized in the commentary section at the end of this chapter. □

4.1 Integral Promotions

A char, a short int, enumerator, object of enumeration type (§7.2), or an int bit-field (§9.6) (in both their signed and unsigned varieties) may be used wherever an integer may be used. If an int can represent all the values of the original type, the value is converted to int; otherwise it is converted to unsigned int. This process is called *integral promotion*.

■ C++ follows ANSI C in defining integral promotions as "value-preserving." That is, a *char*, a *short*, or an *int* bit field, or their signed or unsigned varieties, will be widened to *int* if *int* can represent all the values of the original type or to *unsigned int* otherwise.

In this respect, however, ANSI C introduces an incompatibility with Classic C, from which most older C++ implementations are derived. Many Classic C compilers use "unsigned-preserving" integral promotions. When an *unsigned char* or an *unsigned short* is widened, it becomes an *unsigned int*.

Although the two schemes will usually yield the same result, value-preserving promotion will give different results from an unsigned-preserving promotion when the following two conditions are both true (yielding a "questionably signed" result):

[1] An integral constant with a value greater than the largest signed *int* value on the target machine appears in an expression, or an expression involving an *unsigned char*, an *unsigned short*, or a bit field with any *unsigned* type except *unsigned long* and size smaller than *int* produces a result in which the high-order bit is set.

[2] The result of that expression
   − is an operand of a predefined operator /, %, /=, %=, <, <=, >, or >=, or
   − on a machine for which >> is a signed right shift, is the left operand of the predefined >> or >>= operator, or
   − is an operand of a user-defined operator (§13) for which the result depends on the sign of its operand.

The following code, for example, yields a questionably signed result if *sizeof(short)<sizeof(int)*:

```
void f(int i,unsigned short us)
{
    // ...
    int k = (i + us) < 42;
    // ...
}
```

Suppose *f()* is passed the values −1 for *i* and 2 for *us*. Under the ANSI C rule *us* will be promoted to *int*, yielding the expression *(−1 + 2)* < *42* and *k* will be assigned 1. Under the Classic C rule, *us* will be promoted to *unsigned int* and *i*'s value *must also* be promoted to *unsigned int* before the addition. The result of this promotion of −1 is some large value, which when added to 2 is not less than 42, so *k* is assigned 0.

The appropriate use of casts will ensure consistent evaluation using both Classic C and ANSI C rules. For example,

```
k = (i + (unsigned int)us) < 42; // force Classic C style
k = (i + (int)us) < 42;          // force ANSI C style
```

It will take some time before all C++ implementations follow the ANSI C rule by default. □

4.2 Integral Conversions

When an integer is converted to an *unsigned* type, the value is the least unsigned integer congruent to the signed integer (modulo 2^n where n is the number of bits used to represent the unsigned type). In a two's complement representation, this conversion is conceptual and there is no change in the bit pattern.

When an integer is converted to a signed type, the value is unchanged if it can be represented in the new type; otherwise the value is implementation dependent.

> ■ An unsigned type must be of the same size as its corresponding plain type, which must be of the same size as the corresponding explicitly signed type (§3.6.1). It follows that an unsigned type can hold a larger value than its corresponding signed type. Thus it is not safe to convert from an unsigned type to its corresponding signed type. It is safe to convert from an unsigned type to a larger signed type. Thus, for example, converting from `unsigned short` to `int` on an implementation for which an `int` is larger than a `short` will be safe. Note, however, that an implementation may define the types `char`, `short`, `int`, and `long` all to be of the same size. On such an implementation no conversion from an unsigned integral type to a signed integral type is safe, not even `unsigned char` to `long`.
>
> The result of demoting an integer to a shorter signed integer is implementation dependent. Typically the low-order bits from the longer integer will be copied to the shorter signed integer; a negative value may result.
>
> Similarly, the result of converting an unsigned integer to a signed integer of equal length is implementation dependent. If the bits from the unsigned integer are copied to the signed integer, as will usually be done, a negative value may result. □

4.3 Float and Double

Single-precision floating point arithmetic may be used for `float` expressions. When a less precise floating value is converted to an equally or more precise floating type, the value is unchanged. When a more precise floating value is converted to a less precise floating type and the value is within representable range, the result may be either the next higher or the next lower representable value. If the result is out of range, the behavior is undefined.

> ■ The set of values that can be represented as a `float` is a subset of the set of values that can be represented as a `double`; the set of values that can be represented as a `double` is a subset of the set of values that can be represented as a `long double` (see §3.2.2). Thus it is always safe to convert from `float` to `double` or from `double` to `long double`. □

4.4 Floating and Integral

Conversion of a floating value to an integral type truncates; that is, the fractional part is discarded. Such conversions are machine dependent; for example, the direction of truncation of negative numbers varies from machine to machine. The result is undefined if the value cannot be represented in the integral type.

Conversions of integral values to floating type are as mathematically correct as the hardware allows. Loss of precision occurs if an integral value cannot be represented exactly as a value of the floating type.

> ■ C++ defines integral and floating point types consistently with ANSI C, in terms of minimum magnitude values (see §3.2.1 and §3.2.2). Other than these minimum magnitudes, there is no defined relationship between the floating point and integral types. In particular, there is no upper limit on the maximum value an implementation can support in any of the integral types. It follows, contrary to popular misconception, that the safety of any conversion from an integral type to a floating type is implementation dependent.
>
>   The result of the conversion of a value of an integral type to a floating type when the value is in the range of values that can be represented but cannot be represented exactly will be implementation dependent. It can be either the nearest higher or nearest lower value. In many implementations the result will depend on the setting of a rounding mode provided in a library. □

4.5 Arithmetic Conversions

Many operators cause conversions and yield result types in a similar way. This pattern will be called the "usual arithmetic conversions."

If either operand is of type `long double`, the other is converted to `long double`.

Otherwise, if either operand is `double`, the other is converted to `double`.

Otherwise, if either operand is `float`, the other is converted to `float`.

Otherwise, the integral promotions (§4.1) are performed on both operands.

Then, if either operand is `unsigned long` the other is converted to `unsigned long`.

Otherwise, if one operand is a `long int` and the other `unsigned int`, then if a `long int` can represent all the values of an `unsigned int`, the `unsigned int` is converted to a `long int`; otherwise both operands are converted to `unsigned long int`.

Otherwise, if either operand is `long`, the other is converted to `long`.

Otherwise, if either operand is `unsigned`, the other is converted to `unsigned`.

Otherwise, both operands are `int`.

■ The rules for arithmetic conversion specify an order of conversions to be applied to bring the values of operands of differing types to a common type before their operator is applied; they do not, however, imply a mechanism for disambiguating calls to overloaded functions (§13, §13.2).

Consider

```
int a = 8;
a *= .5;          // 'a' becomes 4.0
```

According to the arithmetic conversion rules, the generated code for the multiplication will first promote the value of *a* to *double*, then do a floating point multiplication, convert the resulting value to *int*, and finally assign the result to the *a*. Some implementations will issue a warning about the assignment of a *double* to an *int*.

Now consider

```
float b = 8.0;
b *= 1/2;         // 'b' becomes 0.0
```

Because both operands of the division operator are of type *int*, an integer division is done and the result is the *int* value *0*. This value is converted to *float* and then the multiplication is done, yielding *0.0*. Even though the result of the division will be used in an expression with a *float* operand, it is an integer operation with integer operands. Any of the following would involve floating point division:

```
float c = 8.0;
c *= 1.0/2;       // 'c' becomes 4.0
c *= 1/2.0;       // 'c' becomes 2.0
c *= 1.0/2.0;     // 'c' becomes 1.0
```

Like ANSI C, C++ generates code for operations involving only *float* (and not *double* or *long double*) operands without widening to *double*. Classic C, however, promotes *float* operands in expressions to *double* before evaluation. Code generated for computations without widening *float* operands may produce a difference in the least significant bits for each floating point operation compared with code that promotes *float* operands. Declaring objects to be of type *double* or using casts will yield evaluation of floating point expressions as done by Classic C.

Some conversions lose information and others cause the bit pattern representing the value to be interpreted differently; see §4.1. □

4.6 Pointer Conversions

The following conversions may be performed wherever pointers (§8.2.1) are assigned, initialized, compared, or otherwise used:

A constant expression (§5.19) that evaluates to zero is converted to a pointer, commonly called the null pointer. It is guaranteed that this value will produce a pointer distinguishable from a pointer to any object or function.

■ Note that the null pointer need not be represented by the same bit pattern as the integer *0*. □

A pointer to any non-`const` and non-`volatile` object type may be converted to a `void*`.

A pointer to function may be converted to a `void*` provided a `void*` has sufficient bits to hold it.

A pointer to a class may be converted to a pointer to an accessible base class of that class (§10) provided the conversion is unambiguous (§10.1); a base class is accessible if its public members are accessible (§11.1). The result of the conversion is a pointer to the base class sub-object of the derived class object. The null pointer (0) is converted into itself.

An expression with type ''array of `T`'' may be converted to a pointer to the initial element of the array.

An expression with type ''function returning `T`'' is converted to ''pointer to function returning `T`'' except when used as the operand of the address-of operator `&` or the function call operator `()`.

■ The standard conversion of a derived class pointer to a pointer to one of its bases can be done only by a function that can access that class. That is, if the base is a public base then every function can do the conversion. If the base is private, the function needs to be a friend, member, or a member of a class that has the base as its immediate base class. In those cases the conversion is performed implicitly. □

■ C++ differs from ANSI C in the treatment of *void**. ANSI C allows an implicit conversion from a pointer to *void* to a pointer to another object type (but not to a pointer to function type – see §5.4); in C++ a *void** cannot be assigned to an object of any type other than *void** without an explicit cast. Thus, the following is legal ANSI C, but is not accepted in C++:

```
void f(char* cptr, void* vptr)
{
    cptr = vptr;  // error: cannot assign void* to char*
}
```

By accepting this, ANSI C opens a hole in the type system that was not present in Classic C. We surmise that the hole was opened to save programmers tedious casting of the result of *malloc()*. For example,

```
int* p1 = (int*)malloc(sizeof(int)*sz);  // tedious

int* p2 = malloc(sizeof(int)*sz);  // error, but
                                   // allowed in ANSI C
```

In C++, operator *new* is a safer and more convenient alternative.

```
int* p3 = new int[sz];
```

Consequently, C++ need not open that hole in the type system. □

■ The restriction against implicit conversions that remove ''constness'' is an example of the more general rule that constraints may not simply disappear without the use of an explicit cast. For example,

```
const char v[] = "Nicholas";
void* p = v;            // error: v points to const
void* q = (char*)v;     // ok (on your head be it!)
```

It is implementation dependent whether an attempt to write elements of *v* through *q* will succeed; see §2.5.4. □

■ A pointer to any non-*const* and non-*volatile* type can be converted, by a standard conversion, to a pointer to *void*, provided *void** is big enough to hold the result of the conversion (§4.6).
    For example,

```
char* cptr;
int* iptr;
void* vptr;

void f(int i)
{
    vptr = i ? iptr : vptr;
    vptr = i ? vptr : cptr;
}
```

Here, each of the pointers *iptr* and *cptr*, when used in an expression with the pointer to *void*, *vptr*, will be implicitly converted to *void**. Use of pointers to different types in the same expression, as in

```
vptr = cptr ? iptr : cptr;     // error: type mismatch
```

is not legal − there is no standard conversion from a pointer to one type to a pointer to another type (other than *void**). If a pointer to one type absolutely must be converted to a pointer to another type (other than *void**), an explicit conversion can be used (§5.4). □

■ The rule that says that the null pointer is converted into itself is relevant for conversions of the null pointer between different derived types in a multiple inheritance lattice (§10.1). □

■ Except for pointers to static members, pointers to members are not implemented or handled as ordinary pointers. The discussions of conversions and uses of pointers do not apply to pointers to members; conversions of pointers to nonstatic members are discussed in §4.8. □

4.7 Reference Conversions

The following conversion may be performed wherever references (§8.2.2) are initialized (including argument passing (§5.2.2) and function value return (§6.6.3)) or otherwise used:

A reference to a class may be converted to a reference to an accessible base class (§10, §11.1) of that class (§8.4.3) provided this conversion can be done unambiguously (§10.1.1). The result of the conversion is a reference to the base class sub-object of the derived class object.

■ Reference conversions behave much like pointer conversions. Note, however, that reference conversions occur only where references are initialized.
    Given the declarations

```
class B {
    // ...
};
class D : public B {
    // ...
};
void f(B&);
D d;
D& dr=d;
```

the following call is legal:

```
f(dr);     // equivalent to f((B&)d);
```

□

■ Note that since copying is defined in terms of reference arguments, the implicit conversions of a reference to a derived class to references to its base classes implies implicit conversion of an object of a derived class to objects of its base classes; see §5.17, §12.8. □

4.8 Pointers to Members

The following conversion may be performed wherever pointers to members (§8.2.3) are initialized, assigned, compared, or otherwise used:

A constant expression (§5.19) that evaluates to zero is converted to a pointer to member. It is guaranteed that this value will produce a pointer to member distinguishable from any other pointer to member.

A pointer to a member of a class may be converted to a pointer to member of a class derived from that class provided the (inverse) conversion from the derived class to the base class pointer is accessible (§11.1) and provided this conversion can be done unambiguously (§10.1.1).

The rule for conversion of pointers to members (from pointer to member of base to pointer to member of derived) appears inverted compared to the rule for pointers to objects (from pointer to derived to pointer to base) (§4.6, §10). This inversion is necessary to ensure type safety.

■ This may seem backwards at first. Consider

```
class B {
public:
      int bi;
};

class D : public B {
public:
      int di;
};

B b;
B* bp = &b;
int B::*bpm;

D d;
D* dp = &d;
int D::*dpm;
```

Now suppose *bpm* is implicitly converted to pointer to member of *D*, as follows:

```
bpm = &B::bi;
d.*bpm = 1;       // OK - sets d.bi
dp->*bpm = 2;     // OK - sets d.bi
```

Because a *D* object always contains an object of its base class, *B*, converting *bpm* (which points to a member of a *B* object) to a pointer to member of *D* makes it point to *D*'s *bi*.

On the other hand, an implicit conversion of *dpm* to pointer to member of *D*'s base class cannot be allowed. The following is illegal:

```
dpm = &D::di;
b.*dpm = 3;       // error: b has no member di
bp->*dpm = 4;     // error: b has no member di
```

An object of class *B* has no member *di*. Thus implicit conversion from a pointer to a derived class to a pointer to member of its base class cannot be allowed.

There are no other standard conversions involving pointers to members, not even between a pointer to a member and *void** or between a pointer to member and an integer. □

Note that a pointer to member is not a pointer to object or a pointer to function and the rules for conversions of such pointers do not apply to pointers to members. In particular, a pointer to member cannot be converted to a void*.

■ Pointers to static members are ordinary pointers (§3.6.2). □

Commentary

4.1c Arithmetic Conversions

The original idea behind the variety of integral and floating point types in C was to have computation done at the natural precision of a machine and also to provide ways to store values of lesser precision compactly. For example, all integer computation was done in *int*s and small integers could be stored in *short*s and *char*s.

Some conversions lose information about the value converted and some cause the bit pattern representing the value to be interpreted differently. For example, converting a floating point value to an integer loses precision; the floating point value *4.261745* converted to an *int* is *4*. Converting the value *−1* stored as an *int* to an unsigned type yields a large positive value.

The C++ rules for arithmetic conversions are summarized below. Arrows show conversions that are guaranteed safe. A conversion is said to be *safe* if all values of the operand type can be represented as values of target type without loss of precision or change of numerical value.

Conversions for the types *char* and *w_char* are not shown because *w_char* is a synonym for some integer type, usually *short* or *unsigned short*, and it is also implementation dependent whether *char* is signed or unsigned.

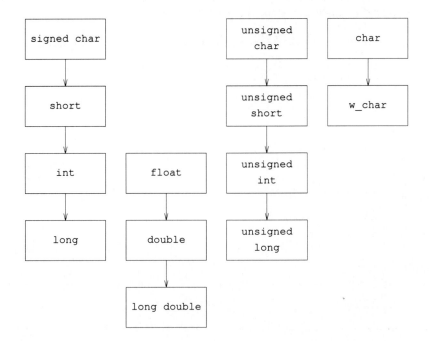

One might expect many more conversions to be safe. For example, it is hard to imagine an implementation where an *unsigned char* cannot be converted to a *long*, but since only

```
sizeof(char) <= sizeof(long)
```

is guaranteed, an implementation might (perversely) define the types such that

```
sizeof(char) == sizeof(long)
```

This would make it impossible to convert the highest *unsigned char* value to a *long* with the same integer value.

An implementation, however, must not only be correct; it must also be useful. A typical implementation chooses the sizes of its basic types to provide a variety of object sizes, thus making many more conversions safe. To illustrate this we provide examples of safe conversions for a couple of plausible implementations.

A machine, such as a VAX, where

$$1 < sizeof(short) < sizeof(int) == sizeof(long)$$

$$sizeof(int) == sizeof(float)$$

$$sizeof(float) < sizeof(double) == sizeof(long\ double)$$

gives these safe coercions:

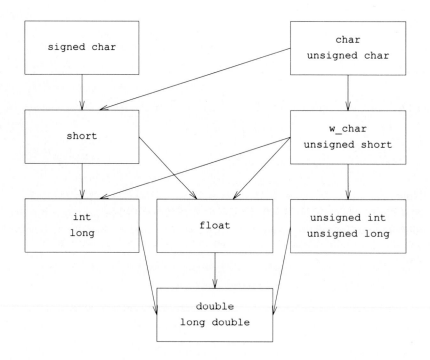

Note that different implementations for the same hardware may make different choices for sizes.

Some machines, such as Crays, designed for very high performance, lack the hardware to extract part of a word or store into a part of a word efficiently. Thus

$$sizeof(short) == sizeof(int) == sizeof(long)$$

becomes a reasonable implementation choice. Speed is bought at the expense of space. This gives these safe conversions:

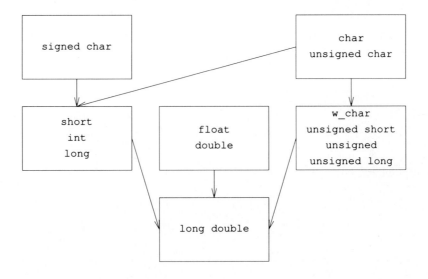

Note that a conversion from an integer type to a floating type depends on the range of numbers that can be represented exactly in the floating point type (the size of the mantissa) and not just the size of the floating point type.

The only truly safe advice is: be careful. Machine architectures differ more than we like to imagine.

Expressions

This chapter discusses C++ expressions, the primary building blocks for computation. C++ provides the usual arithmetic operators (+, −, *, and so on), bit manipulation operators (&, |, ^, and so on), operators for pointer manipulation (*, &, [], −>), storage management (new and delete), conditional evaluation (?:, ||, &&), and the pointer to member operators (.* and −>*).

This chapter also describes explicit type conversions ("casting").

5   Expressions

This section defines the syntax, order of evaluation, and meaning of expressions. An expression is a sequence of operators and operands that specifies a computation. An expression may result in a value and may cause side effects.

Operators can be overloaded, that is, given meaning when applied to expressions of class type (§9). Uses of overloaded operators are transformed into function calls as described in §13.4. Overloaded operators obey the rules for syntax specified in this section, but the requirements of operand type, lvalue, and evaluation order are replaced by the rules for function call. Relations between operators, such as ++a meaning a+=1, are not guaranteed for overloaded operators (§13.4).

This section defines the operators when applied to types for which they have not been overloaded. Operator overloading cannot modify the rules for operators applied to types for which they are defined by the language itself.

■ We repeat: the rules in this chapter do not cover expressions involving overloaded operators or user-defined conversion operations. See §13 for an explanation of those mechanisms.

Note that C++ is extensible in the sense that meanings of operators can be defined for user-defined types (that is, classes §9) but not mutable because the operations described in this chapter cannot be redefined for the types for which they are defined here. The exception to this rule is assignment of class objects, the address-of operator applied to class objects, and the comma operator when applied to a class object; these can be redefined. □

The order of evaluation of subexpressions is determined by the precedence and grouping of the operators. The usual mathematical rules for associativity and commutativity of operators may be applied only where the operators really are associative and commutative. Except where noted, the order of evaluation of operands of individual operators is undefined. In particular, if a value is modified twice in an expression, the result of the expression is undefined except where an ordering is guaranteed by the operators involved. For example,

```
i = v[i++];       // the value of 'i' is undefined
i=7,i++,i++;      // 'i' becomes 9
```

■ Compilers can detect and warn against the use of expressions with undefined order of evaluation. □

■ C++ differs from Classic C in that a floating point operation may be performed in single precision provided both its arguments are *floats* (after standard conversions have been performed; §4). In this, C++ agrees with ANSI C. Classic C required all floating point computation to be performed in double precision. □

The handling of overflow and divide check in expression evaluation is implementation dependent. Most existing implementations of C++ ignore integer overflows. Treatment of division by zero and all floating point exceptions vary among machines, and is usually adjustable by a library function.

■ If an exception handling scheme, such as the one described in §14, is adopted, one would map such events into standard exceptions so that they could be handled by user-provided code in a standard manner. □

Except where noted, operands of types const T, volatile T, T&, const T&, and volatile T& can be used as if they were of the plain type T. Similarly, except where noted, operands of type T*const and T*volatile can be used as if they were of the plain type T*. Similarly, a plain T can be used where a volatile T or a const T is required. These rules apply in combination so that, except where noted, a const T*volatile can be used where a T* is required. Such uses do not count as standard conversions when considering overloading resolution (§13.2).

If an expression has the type "reference to T" (§8.2.2, §8.4.3), the value of the expression is the object of type "T" denoted by the reference. The expression is an lvalue. A reference can be thought of as a name of an object.

■ Despite appearances, no operator operates on a reference. For example,

```
int ivar = 0;
int& int_ref = ivar;
int_ref++;
```

Here *int_ref++* does not increment the reference *int_ref*; rather, *++* is applied to the *int* referred to by *int_ref*, in this case, *ivar*. □

User-defined conversions of class objects to and from fundamental types, pointers, and so on, can be defined (§12.3). If unambiguous (§13.2), such conversions may be applied by the compiler wherever a class object appears as an operand of an operator, as an initializer (§8.4), as the controlling expression in a selection (§6.4) or iteration (§6.5) statement, as a function return value (§6.6.3), or as a function argument (§5.2.2).

5.1 Primary Expressions

Primary expressions are literals, names, and names qualified by the scope resolution operator : :.

> *primary-expression:*
>> *literal*
>> this
>> : : *identifier*
>> : : *operator-function-name*
>> : : *qualified-name*
>> (*expression*)
>> *name*

A *literal* is a primary expression. Its type depends on its form (§2.5).

In the body of a nonstatic member function (§9.3), the keyword this names a pointer to the object for which the function was invoked. The keyword this cannot be used outside a class member function body.

The operator : : followed by an *identifier*, a *qualified-name*, or an *operator-function-name* is a primary expression. Its type is specified by the declaration of the identifier, name, or *operator-function-name*. The result is the identifier, name, or *operator-function-name*. The result is an lvalue if the identifier is. The identifier or *operator-function-name* must be of file scope. Use of : : allows a type, an object, a function, or an enumerator to be referred to even if its identifier has been hidden (§3.2).

■ Examples of use of the scope resolution operator, *: :*, can be found in §3.2. □

A parenthesized expression is a primary expression whose type and value are identical to those of the unadorned expression. The presence of parentheses does not affect whether the expression is an lvalue.

A *name* is a restricted form of a *primary-expression* that can appear after . and -> (§5.2.4):

name:
> *identifier*
> *operator-function-name*
> *conversion-function-name*
> ~ *class-name*
> *qualified-name*

An *identifier* is a *name* provided it has been suitably declared (§7). For *operator-function-name*s, see §13.4. For *conversion-function-name*s, see §12.3.2. A *class-name* prefixed by ~ denotes a destructor; see §12.4.

> *qualified-name:*
> > *qualified-class-name* : : *name*

A *qualified-class-name* (§7.1.6) followed by : : and the name of a member of that class (§9.2), or a member of a base of that class (§10), is a *qualified-name*; its type is the type of the member. The result is the member. The result is an lvalue if the member is. The *class-name* may be hidden by a nontype name, in which case the *class-name* is still found and used. Where *class-name* : : *class-name* or *class-name* : : ~ *class-name* is used, the two *class-name*s must refer to the same class; this notation names constructors (§12.1) and destructors (§12.4), respectively. Multiply qualified names, such as N1::N2::N3::n, can be used to refer to nested types (§9.7).

■ For *N1::N2::N3::n* to be meaningful, *N1* must be a class in which a class *N2* is declared, and a class *N3* with a member *n* must be declared within *N2*. □

5.2 Postfix Expressions

Postfix expressions group left-to-right.

> *postfix-expression:*
> > *primary-expression*
> > *postfix-expression* [*expression*]
> > *postfix-expression* (*expression-list$_{opt}$*)
> > *simple-type-name* (*expression-list$_{opt}$*)
> > *postfix-expression* . *name*
> > *postfix-expression* -> *name*
> > *postfix-expression* ++
> > *postfix-expression* --

> *expression-list:*
> > *assignment-expression*
> > *expression-list* , *assignment-expression*

5.2.1 Subscripting

A postfix expression followed by an expression in square brackets is a postfix expression. The intuitive meaning is that of a subscript. One of the expressions must have the type "pointer to T" and the other must be of integral type. The type of the result is "T." The expression E1[E2] is identical (by definition) to *((E1)+(E2)). See §5.3 and §5.7 for details of * and + and §8.2.4 for details of arrays.

■ For example, given

```
int i, a[10];
```

the array can be indexed by the integer like this *a[i]*. The value of *i* must be between *0* and *9* for the result to be well-defined (§5.7). By definition, the expression *a[i]* means **(a+i)*; since addition is commutative (§5.7 discusses addition of pointers), this is equivalent to **(i+a)*. It follows therefore, that *i[a]* means the same thing as *a[i]*.

Note again that this chapter does not discuss overloaded operators; there is no guarantee that *i[a]==a[i]* for user-defined types. □

■ The use of negative indices is legal, provided the index points into an array. For example,

```
char v[] = "Marian";
char* p = &v[2];
char ch = p[-2];
```

is a complicated way of assigning *'M'* to *ch*. □

5.2.2 Function Call

A function call is a postfix expression followed by parentheses containing a possibly empty, comma-separated list of expressions which constitute the actual arguments to the function. The postfix expression must be of type "function returning T," "pointer to function returning T," or "reference to function returning T," and the result of the function call is of type "T."

■ See also: function declarations (§7.1.2), function definitions (§8.3), linkage (§7.4), pointers to functions (§8.2.5), use of temporaries (§12.2, §12.1c), overloading resolution (§13). □

When a function is called, each formal argument is initialized (§8.4.3, §12.8, §12.1) with its actual argument. Standard (§4) and user-defined (§12.3) conversions are performed. A function may change the values of its nonconstant formal arguments, but these changes cannot affect the values of the actual arguments except where a formal argument is of a non-const reference type (§8.2.2). Where a formal argument is of reference type a temporary variable is introduced if needed (§7.1.6, §2.5, §2.5.4, §8.2.4, §12.2). In addition, it is possible to modify the values of nonconstant objects through pointer arguments.

A function may be declared to accept fewer arguments (by declaring default arguments §8.2.6) or more arguments (by using the ellipsis, . . .   §8.2.5) than are specified in the function definition (§8.3).

A function can be called only if a declaration of it is accessible from the scope of the call. This implies that, except where the ellipsis (. . .) is used, a formal argument is available for each actual argument.

■ This differs from C in that C allows calling an undeclared function and treats it as returning type *int* and having unchecked arguments. This is a well known major source of errors in C programs. □

Any actual argument of type float for which there is no formal argument is converted to double before the call; any of char, short, enumeration, or a bit-field type for which there is no formal argument are converted to int or unsigned by integral promotion (§4.1). An object of a class for which no formal argument is declared is passed as a data structure.

■ That is, the object is passed without the use of a copy constructor, as described in §12.8. □

An object of a class for which a formal argument is declared is passed by initializing the formal argument with the actual argument by a constructor call before the function is entered (§12.2, §12.8).

The order of evaluation of arguments is undefined; take note that compilers differ. All side effects of argument expressions take effect before the function is entered. The order of evaluation of the postfix expression and the argument expression list is undefined.

■ For example,

```
int i = 1;
extern f(int, int);

void g()
{
    f(i++,i++);
}
```

Here, *f()* is called with the arguments *(1,2)* or *(2,1)* or even *(1,1)* depending on the order of evaluation of the arguments. Should *f()* examine the value of the global variable *i* during the call it would find it to have the value *3* since the side effects on the arguments take place before *f()* is entered.

It is also possible to have an order dependence between the expression denoting the function to be called and the argument list.

```
int i = 1;
extern int (*p[10])(int);   // array of 10 pointers
                            // to functions

void h()
{
    (*p[i++])(i++);
}
```

Here, *p[1]* will be called with the argument *2*, or *p[2]* will be called with the argument *1*, or *p[1]* will be called with the argument *1*.

Naturally, such order dependencies should be avoided since they lead to very obscure errors. Compilers can detect them and warn about them. □

Recursive calls are permitted.

■ For example,

```
int fac(int i) { return 1<i ? i*fac(i-1) : 1; }
```

□

A function call is an lvalue only if the result type is a reference.

■ Given, for example,

```
class X {
public:
    int i;
};
X f();
X* g();
```

the assignment

```
f().i = 1;    // error: function returns rvalue
```

is invalid. One can, of course, write

```
j = f().i;
```

Further, if a function returns a pointer to a class object, assignment to a member of that object is legal, as in the following:

```
g()->i = 1;
```

If an lvalue is needed as the result of a function call, a reference should be returned.

```
extern int v[];

int& elem(int i) { return v[i]; }

void f()
{
    int x = elem(7);
    elem(7) = 27;
}
```

Note that calls such as $f().g()$ are legal when $f()$ returns an object for which $g()$ may be called. See §12.2 for an explanation of the lifetime of temporaries generated to hold the results of such calls.

Such constructs are not uncommon. In addition to being written explicitly, they often occur where conversion functions (§12.3.1, §12.3.2) are used and also for certain styles of overloading (§13). For example,

```
class X {
    // ...
public:
    X operator+(X);
    X operator*(X);
};


void f()
{
    X a, b, c, d;
    // ...
    a = b*c+d;
    // ...
}
```

Here, $b*c+d$ is resolved as $b.operator*(c).operator+(d)$. □

5.2.3 Explicit Type Conversion

A *simple-type-name* (§7.1.6) followed by a parenthesized *expression-list* constructs a value of the specified type given the expression list. If the expression list specifies more than a single value, the type must be a class with a suitably declared constructor (§8.4, §12.1).

A *simple-type-name* (§7.1.6) followed by a (empty) pair of parentheses constructs a value of the specified type. If the type is a class with a suitably declared constructor that constructor will be called; otherwise the result is an undefined value of the specified type. See also (§5.4).

■ For example,

```
class complex {
    // ...
public:
    complex(double,double);
    complex();
};


f()
{
    complex z = complex(1,2);
    z = complex();
```

```
                    int i = int (1.2);
                    i = int ();
        }
```

The last statement assigns an undefined *int* value to *i*. □

5.2.4 Class Member Access

A postfix expression followed by a dot (.) followed by a *name* is a postfix expression. The first expression must be a class object, and the *name* must name a member of that class. The result is the named member of the object, and it is an lvalue if the member is an lvalue.

A postfix expression followed by an arrow (->) followed by a *name* is a postfix expression. The first expression must be a pointer to a class object and the *name* must name a member of that class. The result is the named member of the object to which the pointer points and it is an lvalue if the member is an lvalue. Thus the expression E1->MOS is the same as (*E1).MOS.

Note that ''class objects'' can be structures (§9.2) and unions (§9.5). Classes are discussed in §9.

■ When a member of a union is accessed after a value has been stored in a different member of the object, the result will be implementation dependent. No conversion will be done between the type of the member by which the value was stored and the type of the member by which the value is retrieved. Thus storing a value through a member of one type and retrieving it through a member of a different type implies a reinterpretation of the bit pattern stored. For example,

```
        union u_tag {
            int ival;
            float fval;
        } u_obj;
        int i;

        u_obj.fval = 4.0;
        i = u_obj.ival;
```

The bit pattern that represents *4.0* as a floating point value on the target machine will be stored in *u_obj.fval*. This bit pattern will be accessed and assigned to the integer variable *i* with no conversion. Naturally, the result is highly implementation dependent. □

5.2.5 Increment and Decrement

The value obtained by applying a postfix ++ is the value of the operand. The operand must be a modifiable lvalue. The type of the operand must be an arithmetic type or a pointer type. After the result is noted, the object is incremented by 1. The type of the result is the same as the type of the operand, but it is not an lvalue. See also §5.7 and §5.17.

The operand of postfix `--` is decremented analogously to the postfix `++` operator.

■ A typical use of the increment and decrement operators is to step through an array. The example below copies a null-terminated string pointed to by *p* to a location pointed to by *q*.

```
while (*q++ = *p++) ;
```

This code is simpler, but less readable to those unfamiliar with C++ and C, than the equivalent code not using the increment operator, which would be

```
while (*p != '\0') {
    *q = *p;
    p = p + 1;
    q = q + 1;
}
*q = '\0';
```

□

■ The increment and decrement operators are *not* defined for enumerations; they are defined only for other arithmetic types. When applied to an enumeration the value of the enumeration is converted to an integer and incremented or decremented. The resulting type is an integer, *not* an enumeration, and cannot be assigned to the enumeration. Thus, applying an increment or decrement operation to a variable of an enumeration type is an error. For example,

```
enum E { a, b=2, c=4, d=8 };

void f(E e)
{
    e++;     // error: integer assigned to enumeration 'e'
}
```

□

5.3 Unary Operators

Expressions with unary operators group right-to-left.

> *unary-expression:*
> > *postfix-expression*
> > `++` *unary-expression*
> > `--` *unary-expression*
> > *unary-operator cast-expression*
> > `sizeof` *unary-expression*
> > `sizeof` (*type-name*)
> > *allocation-expression*
> > *deallocation-expression*

unary-operator: one of
      *   &   +   -   !   ~

The unary * operator means *indirection*: the expression must be a pointer, and the result is an lvalue referring to the object to which the expression points. If the type of the expression is "pointer to T," the type of the result is "T."

The result of the unary & operator is a pointer to its operand. The operand must be a function, an lvalue, or a *qualified-name*. In the first two cases, if the type of the expression is "T," the type of the result is "pointer to T." In particular, the address of an object of type const T has type const T*; volatile is handled similarly. For a *qualified-name*, if the member is not static and of type "T" in class "C," the type of the result is "pointer to member of C of type T."

■ Note that the type of a member includes the class in which it was defined (and *not* any class derived (§10) from that class). For example,

```
struct B { void f(); int i; };
struct D : B { };
```

Here, the types of &B::f and &D::f are the same: *void (B::*)()*. □

■ Note that the address-of operator must be explicitly used to get a pointer to member; there is no implicit conversion of a member name to a pointer to member the way there is an implicit conversion of a function name to a pointer to function (§4.6, §4.8). Had there been, we would have had an ambiguity in the context of a member function. The reason is that within a member function the name of a member of that class refers to that member of the specific object for which the member function was invoked (§9.3); that is, except when prefixed by the address-of operator, a mention of B::i within B::f() is interpreted as this->i. For example,

```
void B::f()
{
    int B::* p = &B::i;    // ok
    p = B::i;              // error: 'B::i' is an int
    p = &i;                // error: '&i' means '&this->i'
                           // which is an int*

    int* q = &i;           // ok
    q = B::i;              // error 'B::i' is an int
    q = &B::i;             // error '&B::i' is an int B::*
}
```

□

For a static member of type T, the type is plain "pointer to T." The address of an overloaded function (§13) can be taken only in an initialization or an assignment where the left side uniquely determines which version of the overloaded function is referred to (§13.3).

■ When the address of a reference is taken the result is the address of the object
referred to.

```
int  i = 1;
int&  r = i;
int*  p = &r;    // 'p' points to 'i'
```

□

■ Note also that the address-of operator may be overloaded so the programmer can
control the meaning of taking the address of an object of a class. □

The operand of the unary + operator must have arithmetic or pointer type and
the result is the value of the argument. Integral promotion is performed on integral
operands. The type of the result is the type of the promoted operand.

■ Unary plus is a historical accident and generally useless. □

The operand of the unary − operator must have arithmetic type and the result is
the negation of its operand. Integral promotion is performed on integral operands.
The negative of an unsigned quantity is computed by subtracting its value from 2^n,
where n is the number of bits in the promoted operand. The type of the result is
the type of the promoted operand.

The operand of the logical negation operator ! must have arithmetic type or be
a pointer; its value is 1 if the value of its operand is 0 and 0 if the value of its
operand is nonzero. The type of the result is int.

The operand of ~ must have integral type; the result is the one's complement of
its operand. Integral promotions are performed. The type of the result is the type
of the promoted operand.

5.3.1 Increment and Decrement

The operand of prefix ++ is incremented by 1. The operand must be a modifiable
lvalue. The type of the operand must be an arithmetic type or a pointer type. The
value is the new value of the operand; it is an lvalue. The expression ++x is
equivalent to x+=1. See the discussions of addition (§5.7) and assignment operators (§5.17) for information on conversions.

The operand of prefix −− is decremented analogously to the prefix ++ operator.

5.3.2 Sizeof

The sizeof operator yields the size, in bytes, of its operand. The operand is
either an expression, which is not evaluated, or a parenthesized type name. The
sizeof operator may not be applied to a function, a bit-field, an undefined class,
the type void, or an array with an unspecified dimension. A *byte* is undefined by
the language except in terms of the value of sizeof; sizeof(char) is 1.

When applied to a reference, the result is the size of the referenced object.

■ For example,

```
struct s {
    double d1;
    double d2;
};

s dd;
s& r = dd;
int i = sizeof(r);       // sizeof(r) >= 2*sizeof(double)
```

Note that this implies that the sum of the sizes of the members of a class may be larger than the size of the class itself.

```
struct r {
    s& r1;
    s& r2;
    // constructor required; see §12.6.2
};
```

Here *sizeof(r)* is probably *2*sizeof(s*)*, which is most likely less than *2*sizeof(s&)*.

See §12.6.2 for an explanation of how class members that are references can be initialized. □

When applied to a class, the result is the number of bytes in an object of that class including any padding required for placing such objects in an array.

■ A typical example of padding follows:

```
struct odd {
    int a;
    char c;
};
```

An *odd* can theoretically be allocated in *sizeof(int)+1* bytes, but most machines have an internal architecture that makes memory references faster when integers are placed starting at word boundaries, typically at addresses that are multiples of two or four. Thus, to avoid (significant) overheads an *odd* must be allocated on such a boundary. To ensure this for all elements in an array of *odds* the size of an *odd* is typically rounded up to *2*sizeof(int)*.

Another form of padding is the "housekeeping" information stored in objects of classes with virtual functions (§10.2, §10.7c, §10.8c) or virtual base classes (§10.5c). For example,

```
class non_trivial : virtual base {
    virtual f();
};

int i = sizeof(non_trivial);     // i > 1
```

The size of a *non_trivial* will most likely be at least *2*sizeof(int*)*. □

The size of any class or class object is larger than zero.

■ For example,

```
struct empty {};
int i = sizeof(empty);   // i >= 1
```

□

When applied to an array, the result is the total number of bytes in the array. This implies that the size of an array of *n* elements is *n* times the size of an element.

■ Note that the usual conversion of an array to a pointer to its first element does not take place when the array is the argument of `sizeof`. For example,

```
int a[10];
const int i = sizeof(a);           // i = 10*sizeof(int)
```

□

The `sizeof` operator may be applied to a pointer to a function, but not to a function.

■ Note that the usual conversion of a function to a pointer to the function (§4.6) does not take place when the array is the argument of `sizeof`. For example,

```
void f() { /* ... */ }

const int i1 = sizeof(&f);   // size of pointer to function
const int i2 = sizeof(f);    // error: sizeof(function)
```

□

The result is a constant of type `size_t`, an implementation-dependent unsigned integral type defined in the standard header `<stddef.h>`.

5.3.3 New

The `new` operator attempts to create an object of the *type-name* (§8.1) to which it is applied. This type must be an object type; functions cannot be allocated this way, though pointers to functions can.

> *allocation-expression:*
>> $::_{opt}$ new *placement$_{opt}$ new-type-name new-initializer$_{opt}$*
>> $::_{opt}$ new *placement$_{opt}$* (*type-name*) *new-initializer$_{opt}$*
>
> *placement:*
>> (*expression-list*)
>
> *new-type-name:*
>> *type-specifier-list new-declarator$_{opt}$*

new-declarator:
> * *cv-qualifier-list*_{opt} *new-declarator*_{opt}
> *class-name* : : * *cv-qualifier-list*_{opt} *new-declarator*_{opt}
> *new-declarator*_{opt} [*expression*]

new-initializer:
> (*initializer-list*_{opt})

■ In general, an *allocation-expression* must do three things:
   [1] Find storage for the object to be created.
   [2] Initialize that object.
   [3] Return a suitably typed pointer to the object.
Adjusting the type is purely a compile-time action. □

The lifetime of an object created by new is not restricted to the scope in which it is created. The new operator returns a pointer to the object created. When that object is an array, a pointer to its initial element is returned. For example, both new int and new int[10] return an int* and the type of new int[i][10] is int (*)[10].

■ A reference cannot be created by the *new* operator. A reference is not an object (§8.2.2, §8.4.3), so a pointer to it could not be returned by *new*. □

Where an array type (§8.2.4) is specified all array dimensions but the first must be constant expressions (§5.19) with positive values. The first array dimension can be a general *expression* even when the *type-name* is used (despite the general restriction of array dimensions in *type-name*s to *constant-expression*s (§5.19)).

This implies that an operator new() can be called with the argument zero. In this case, a pointer to an object is returned. Repeated such calls return pointers to distinct objects.

■ For example,

```
void f()
{
    char* p = new char[0];
    char* q = new char[0];

    if (p==0 || q==0) {  // allocator failed
        abort();
    }

    if (p == q) {  // impossible: 'p' must differ from 'q'
        abort();
    }
}
```

Defining a suitable *new_handler* (§15) would allow us to eliminate the tests for zero returns. □

The *type-specifier-list* may not contain const, volatile, class declarations, or enumeration declarations.

The `new` operator will call the function `operator new()` to obtain storage (§12.5). A first argument of `sizeof(T)` is supplied when allocating an object of type `T`. The *placement* syntax can be used to supply additional arguments. For example, `new T` results in a call of `operator new(sizeof(T))` and `new(2,f) T` results in a call `operator new(sizeof(T),2,f)`.

The *placement* syntax can be used only provided an `operator new()` with suitable argument types (§13.2) has been declared.

When an object of a nonclass type (including arrays of class objects) is created with operator new, the global `::operator new()` is used. When an object of a class T is created with operator new, `T::operator new()` is used if it exists (using the usual lookup rules for finding members of a class and its base classes; §10.1.1); otherwise the global `::operator new()` is used. Using `::new` ensures that the global `::operator new()` is used even if `T::operator new()` exists.

■ The reason that an array of elements of class *X* isn't allocated by an *X::operator new()* is simply that such an array isn't an *X*. This has the important side effect that *X::operator new()* really can be specialized to be an allocator for objects of class *X* and classes derived from *X*. Had *X::operator new()* been called for arrays, it would have had to be an almost general allocator with all the overheads this implies. □

■ Providing one's own *::operator new(size_t)* is a way of gaining access to every (standard) allocation operation. This can be useful in debugging, but is not recommended for general programming. The problem is that if *two* programmers make nontrivial changes to the way *::new* operates, their programs might not work as cooperating parts of a single program without special effort. □

A *new-initializer* may be supplied in an *allocation-expression*. For objects of classes with a constructor (§12.1) this argument list will be used in a constructor call; otherwise the initializer must be of the form (*expression*) or (). If present, the expression will be used to initialize the object; if not, the object will start out with an undefined value.

■ For example,

```
class complex {
    // ...
public:
    complex(double, double);
    // ...
};
```

```
void f()
{
    complex* pc = new complex(1,2);
    int* pi = new int(7);
    double* pd1 = new double();
    double* pd2 = new double;
}
```

Here, *pc* is made to point to a *complex* object with the initial value
complex(1,2), *pi* is made to point to an *int* with the value 7, and the two
pointers to *double* each initialized to point to a *double* with an undefined value.

Using empty parameters after the type in a *new* expression is simply a syntactic
convenience and has no special meaning. □

■ Note that the memory returned by *operator new()* (see §12.5 and §13.4) need
not be initialized. In this, it resembles memory allocated on the stack (automatic
storage). Only static memory has a default initial value, zero (§8.4). □

If a class has a constructor an object of that class can be created by new only if
suitable arguments are provided or if the class has a default constructor (§12.1).
Whether operator new allocates the memory itself or leaves that up to the constructor when creating an object of a class with a constructor is implementation
dependent.

■ It will, however, always be allocated without the intervention of the programmer.
Calling *operator new()* as part of the implementation of an *allocation-
expression* is the task of the implementation. □

Access and ambiguity control are done for both operator new() and the constructor; see §12.

No initializers can be specified for arrays. Arrays of objects of a class with
constructors can be created by operator new only if the class has a default constructor (§12.1). In that case, the default constructor will be called for each element of the array.

■ Providing a way of specifying arguments for the members of an array would add
complexity greater than the benefits gained. If a program absolutely must have the
elements of an array initialized to distinct values, it can often be achieved by programming a default constructor to depend on global information. This is rarely
worthwhile. □

Initialization is done only if the value returned by operator new() is
nonzero. If the value returned by the operator new() is 0 (the null pointer) the
value of the expression is 0.

The order of evaluation of the call to an operator new() to get memory and
the evaluation of arguments to constructors is undefined. It is also undefined if the
arguments to a constructor are evaluated if operator new() returns 0.

■ For example,

```
void f()
{
    int i = 1;
    complex* p = new complex(i++);

    if (p == 0) {
        // allocation failed
        // 'i' is either 1 or 2 here
        // ...
    }
    else {
        // allocation succeeded
        // 'i' is 2 here
        // ...
    }
}
```

□

In a *new-type-name* used as the operand for new, parentheses may not be used.
This implies that

```
new int(*[10])();        // error
```

is an error because the binding is

```
(new int) (*[10])();     // error
```

Objects of general type can be expressed using the explicitly parenthesized version
of the new operator. For example,

```
new (int (*[10])());
```

allocates an array of 10 pointers to functions (taking no argument and returning
int).

The *new-type-name* in an *allocation-expression* is the longest possible sequence
of *new-declarator*s. This prevents ambiguities between declarator operators &, *,
[], and their expression counterparts. For example,

```
new int*i;       // syntax error: parsed as '(new int*) i'
                 //               not as '(new int)*i'
```

The * is the pointer declarator and not the multiplication operator.

5.3.4 Delete

The delete operator destroys an object created by the new operator.

deallocation-expression:
        ::*opt* delete *cast-expression*
        ::*opt* delete [ ] *cast-expression*

The result has type void. The operand of delete must be a pointer returned by

new. The effect of applying `delete` to a pointer not obtained from the `new`
operator without a placement specification is undefined and usually harmful. Deleting a pointer with the value zero, however, is guaranteed to be harmless.

■ For example,

```
void f()
{
        int i;
        int* p = &i;
        delete p;    // error
        p = new int[10];
        p++;
        delete p;    // error
        p = 0;
        delete p;    // ok
}
```

In general, catching such bad deletions at compile time is impossible; catching them
at run time implies time and space overheads. Therefore the results of such deletions are subtle and usually disastrous. Bad deletions are usually not detected
immediately, and programs containing them are therefore among the nastiest to
debug. Almost any effort to avoid such bad deletions is worthwhile. □

The effect of accessing a deleted object is undefined and the deletion of an
object may change its value. Furthermore, if the expression denoting the object in
a `delete` expression is a modifiable lvalue, its value is undefined after the deletion.

■ For example,

```
void f()
{
        int* p = new int;
        if (p == 0) abort();
        // the value of p is not zero here
        delete p;
        // the value of p may be zero here
}
```

Implementing the `delete` operator to modify the value of a deleted pointer can be
useful for debugging by ensuring that a pointer cannot be successfully used after
being deleted. Without such modification a program might appear to function
correctly for quite a while, and the inevitable problem could be very difficult to pin-
point. □

A pointer to constant cannot be deleted.

■ The reason is that the deletion in principle modifies the object pointed to. For
example,

```
extern const char * pc; // pointer to constant

void f()
{
    delete pc;              // error: pointer to constant
    delete (char*) pc;  // I really mean it!
}
```

The purpose of prohibiting the deletion of pointers to constants is to allow program-mers to rely on *const* objects being immutable. For example,

```
void h(const int *);     // I don't modify my argument

void g(int* pi)
{
    *pi = 1;
    h(pi);
    if (*pi != 1) error("something strange happened");
}
```

Naturally, this guarantee − like all other guarantees provided by a type system − applies only as long as the type system is not deliberately or accidentally broken by explicit type conversion, aliasing, compiler errors, or hardware errors. For example, no one wants code like this squirreled away in the system:

```
void h(const int * p)   // I don't modify my argument
{
    int* q = (int*) p;
    (*q)++;                  // fooled you!
}
```

Without the restriction against deleting pointers to *const* objects the *delete* operator would have the effect of implicitly removing the *const* attribute from a pointer. No operator should have that property. □

The delete operator will invoke the destructor (if any, §12.4) for the object pointed to.

To free the storage pointed to, the delete operator will call the function operator delete(); see §12.5. For objects of a nonclass type (including arrays of class objects), the global ::operator delete() is used. For an object of a class T, T::operator delete() is used if it exists (using the usual lookup rules for finding members of a class and its base classes; §10.1.1); other-wise the global ::operator delete() is used. Using ::delete ensures that the global ::operator delete() is used even if T::operator delete() exists.

The form

     delete [ ] *cast-expression*

is used to delete arrays. The expression points to an array. The destructors (if any) for the objects pointed to will be invoked.

■ The user is required to specify when an array is deleted. The reason for this is to avoid requiring the implementation to store information specifying whether a chunk of memory allocated by *operator new()* is an array or not. This can be a minor nuisance for the user, but the alternative would imply a difference from the C object layout. This would be a serious incompatibility. In addition, the extra information required for each object allocated on the free store could easily increase the space overhead significantly. The alternative of making an array into a proper self-describing object was also rejected for C compatibility reasons; see §8.2.4.

Earlier definitions of C++ required users to specify the number of elements in the array being deleted; see §18.3. This led to clumsy code and errors, so that burden was shifted to the implementations.

Note that this implies that when *new* allocates an individual object, the size of the object must be stored somewhere. When *new* allocates an array it must in addition store the number of elements in the array. The information thus stored away is retrieved and used by the *delete* operator. □

■ Typically, the distinction between deleting an object and an array of objects is significant only when deleting objects of a class with a destructor. Then, the number of objects deleted determines the number of times the destructor must be called. Consequently, one could consider requiring the *delete[]* notation only for pointers to such classes. Classes that don't have destructors early in the development of a program, however, may have them added later. Further, a typedef naming a built-in type early in the development of a program may later be changed to refer to a class with a destructor. Consequently, making a distinction between pointers to classes with destructors and pointers to other types is asking for trouble. □

The effect of deleting an array with the plain delete syntax is undefined, as is deleting an individual object with the delete[] syntax.

■ Some trivial cases of deleting an array with the plain *delete* syntax can be detected by the compiler. For example,

```
void f()
{
    int(*p)[10] = new int[20][10];
    delete p;   // error
    delete[] p; // ok
}
```

□

■ Note that when allocating an individual object of class *X* a class specific allocator may be used. When allocating an array of X objects, the global allocator will be used. The proper use of *delete* and *delete[]* is essential for deallocation in such cases. □

■ The possibility of providing a syntax for using an overloaded *operator delete()* to match the placement syntax for *operator new()* has repeatedly been discussed. One could imagine writing code like this:

```
void* operator new(size_t, Arena*);
void operator delete(void*, Arena*);     // error

void f(Arena* a1)
{
    X* p1 = new(a1) X;
    X* p2 = new X;

    // ...

    delete(a1) p1;        // error
    delete p2;
}
```

The fundamental objection to this is that whereas in principle all necessary information is available at the point of creation of an object, hardly any is available at the
point of deletion. Even the exact type of the object pointed to is often lost at the
point of deletion. It is therefore not sensible to require the programmer to select
correctly among a variety of deletion operations. Consequently, the feature is feared
to be error prone.

A more practical answer is that the added syntax isn't needed since the problem
can be solved without it. One solution is to add a virtual function (§10.2)
my_delete() to class *X* and call that instead of using *delete* directly.

```
void* operator new(size_t, Arena*);

void f(Arena* a1)
{
    X* p1 = new(a1) X;
    X* p2 = new X;

    // ...

    p1->my_delete(a1);
    p2->my_delete(0);
}

void X::my_delete(Arena* a)
{
    this->X::~X();        // explicit call of destructor

    if (a)
        a->free((void*)this);
    else
        delete (void*)this;
}
```

The question is if such use is common enough to warrant the support of a specific
syntax. □

5.4 Explicit Type Conversion

An explicit type conversion can be expressed using either functional notation (§5.2.3) or the *cast* notation.

> *cast-expression:*
> > *unary-expression*
> > (*type-name*) *cast-expression*

The *cast* notation is needed to express conversion to a type that does not have a *simple-type-name*.

> ■ Explicit type conversion is often best avoided. Using a cast suppresses the type checking provided by the compiler and will therefore lead to surprises unless the programmer really was right. Note that a virtual function (§10.2) can often provide a type-safe alternative to casting. For example,

```
    void f1(base* p)          /* C style explicit resolution */
                              /* using a type field          */
    {
        switch (p->type_field) {
        case D:
            do_something_with_a_derived((derived*)p);
            // ...
        }
    }

    void f2(base* p)          // C++ style implicit resolution
                              // using a virtual function
    {
        p->do_something();
    }
```

> □

Types may not be defined in casts.

> ■ For example,

```
    void f(void* p)
    {
        (struct s { int a; char* c; })p;     // error
    }
```

> The reason for this restriction is that C++ relies on name equivalence (§9.1) so the resulting value couldn't be used anyway. See also §8.2.5 and §11.4. □

Any type conversion not mentioned below and not explicitly defined by the user (§12.3) is an error.

Any type that can be converted to another by a standard conversion (§4) can also be converted by explicit conversion and the meaning is the same.

A pointer may be explicitly converted to any integral type large enough to hold it. The mapping function is implementation dependent, but is intended to be unsurprising to those who know the addressing structure of the underlying machine.

A value of integral type may be explicitly converted to a pointer. A pointer converted to an integer of sufficient size (if any such exists on the implementation) and back to the same pointer type will have its original value; mappings between pointers and integers are otherwise implementation dependent.

■ For example,

```
char* f(char* p)
{
        int i = (int)p;
        return (char*)i;            // f(arg) == arg ?
}
```

Here, `f()` may or may not return a pointer to its argument. It will if and only if `sizeof(char*)<=sizeof(int)`. History shows that this is not a wise assumption to make in software that is intended to be portable. □

A pointer to one object type may be explicitly converted to a pointer to another object type (subject to the restrictions mentioned in this section). The resulting pointer may cause addressing exceptions on use if the subject pointer does not refer to an object suitably aligned in storage. It is guaranteed that a pointer to an object of a given size may be converted to a pointer to an object of the same or smaller size and back again without change. Different machines may differ in the number of bits in pointers and in alignment requirements for objects. Aggregates are aligned on the strictest boundary required by any of their constituents. A `void*` is considered a pointer to object type.

A pointer to a class B may be explicitly converted to a pointer to a class D that has B as a direct or indirect base class if an unambiguous conversion from D to B exists (§4.6, §10.1.1) and if B is not a virtual base class (§10.1). Such a cast from a base to a derived class assumes that the object of the base class is a sub-object of an object of the derived class; the resulting pointer points to the enclosing object of the derived class. If the object of the base class is not a sub-object of an object of the derived class, the cast may cause an exception.

The null pointer (0) is converted into itself.

A yet undefined class may be used in a pointer cast, in which case no assumptions will be made about class lattices (§10.1).

■ For example,

```
class S;
class T;

T* f(S* p) { return (T*)p; }
```

Here the type is changed, but the address returned is the address given as the argument. This behavior is essential for C compatibility and is usually harmless. With incautious use of multiple inheritance, however, it can lead to subtle bugs. For example, if these declarations appeared *after* the definition of `f()` or in a separate translation unit, then a well nigh undetectable error would result from the use of `f()`:

```
class A { int a; };
class S { int s; };
class T : public A, public S { int t; };
```

Had these declarations been seen, the result of calling `f()` would be to return a
pointer to the `T` object of which the `S` object pointed to by `f()`'s argument is supposed to be a base. It follows that where multiple inheritance is involved casting to
and from undefined types is best avoided. □

An object may be explicitly converted to a reference type `X&` if a pointer to that
object may be explicitly converted to an `X*`. Constructors or conversion functions
are not called as the result of a cast to a reference. Conversion of a reference to a
base class to a reference to a derived class is handled similarly to the conversion of
a pointer to a base class to a pointer to a derived class with respect to ambiguity,
virtual classes, and so on.

The result of a cast to a reference type is an lvalue; the results of other casts are
not. Operations performed on the result of a pointer or reference cast refer to the
same object as the original (uncast) expression.

■ For example,

```
void f()
{
    int i = 1;
    (float)i = 1.2;      // error
    (float&)i = 1.2;     // nonportable
}
```

Such uses of casts are often misguided. For example, on an implementation where
the size of a *float* differs from the size of an *int* this construct will not have the
effect the programmer expected.

Reference casts are mostly used to adjust the type of a reference to class objects
from a base type to a derived type or vice versa. For example,

```
class B { /* ... */ };
class D : public B { /* ... */ };

void f(B& rb)
{
    // ...
    D& rd = (D&)rb;      // I know rb refers to a D
    // ...
}
```

□

A pointer to function may be explicitly converted to a pointer to an object type
provided the object pointer type has enough bits to hold the function pointer.

■ C++ provides standard conversions from pointers to functions to *void** and explicit conversions from *void** to pointers to functions for machines that can support
such conversions. This differs from ANSI C, which prohibits any conversion
between a pointer to a function and *void**. Classic C provided explicit type

conversion between pointers to functions and pointers to *char*. It is understood that such conversions will be hard − or even impossible − to implement for some machines. It was felt that it was better to allow the conversions for the benefit of the users of architectures that can support it than to deny it because there are architectures for which the implementation is judged to be too hard. □

A pointer to an object type may be explicitly converted to a pointer to function provided the function pointer type has enough bits to hold the object pointer. In both cases, use of the resulting pointer may cause addressing exceptions, or worse, if the subject pointer does not refer to suitable storage.

■ Some machine architectures specifically prevent an address from being used for both data and code in a single program; others require a system call to change the status from data to code or vice versa. It is not reasonable to require a simple cast to perform such miracles. □

A pointer to a function may be explicitly converted to a pointer to a function of a different type. The effect of calling a function through a pointer to a function type that differs from the type used in the definition of the function is undefined. See also §4.6.

An object or a value may be converted to a class object (only) if an appropriate constructor or conversion operator has been declared (§12.3).

A pointer to member may be explicitly converted into a different pointer to member type when the two types are both pointers to members of the same class or when the two types are pointers to member functions of classes one of which is unambiguously derived from the other (§4.8).

■ There is no equivalent to *void** for pointers to members. This implies that casting of pointers to pointers to members must be used if a generic "pointer to any member of any class" is needed. For example,

```
typedef void Z::* any_ptom;

void push_ptom(any_ptom* a);
any_ptom* pop_ptom();

void f(int X::* p, double Y::* q)
{
    push_ptom((any_ptom*)(&p));
    push_ptom((any_ptom*)(&q));

    q = *(double Y::**) pop_ptom();
    p = *(int X::**) pop_ptom();
}
```

Where needed, this ugliness can be suitably disguised or encapsulated. □

A pointer to an object of a const type can be cast into a pointer to a non-const type. The resulting pointer will refer to the original object. An object of a const type or a reference to an object of a const type can be cast into a reference to a non-const type. The resulting reference will refer to the original object.

The result of attempting to modify that object through such a pointer or reference will either cause an addressing exception or be the same as if the original pointer or reference had referred a non-const object. It is implementation dependent whether the addressing exception occurs.

> ■ That is, unless the object has been stored in readonly memory the result of having cast away *const* is exactly the same as if the object had never been specified *const.* □

A pointer to an object of a volatile type can be cast into a pointer to a non-volatile type. The resulting pointer will refer to the original object. An object of a volatile type or a reference to an object of a volatile type can be cast into a reference to a non-volatile type.

5.5 Pointer-to-Member Operators

The pointer-to-member operators ->* and .* group left-to-right.

> *pm-expression:*
>   *cast-expression*
>   *pm-expression* .* *cast-expression*
>   *pm-expression* ->* *cast-expression*

The binary operator .* binds its second operand, which must be of type "pointer to member of class T" to its first operand, which must be of class T or of a class of which T is an unambiguous and accessible base class. The result is an object or a function of the type specified by the second operand.

The binary operator ->* binds its second operand, which must be of type "pointer to member of T" to its first operand, which must be of type "pointer to T" or "pointer to a class of which T is an unambiguous and accessible base class." The result is an object or a function of the type specified by the second operand.

If the result of .* or ->* is a function, then that result can be used only as the operand for the function call operator (). For example,

```
(ptr_to_obj->*ptr_to_mfct)(10);
```

calls the member function denoted by ptr_to_mfct for the object pointed to by ptr_to_obj.

> ■ Naturally, it would be possible to generalize the notion of a pointer to member to allow bound pointers, such as *ptr_to_obj->*ptr_to_mfct*, to be stored and, in general, be treated as first class objects. Doing so, however, would open vast opportunities for generalization and language extension in the general area of "what is a function and how can I call it?" and would require implementation techniques outside the realm of traditional C techniques. It was felt that restraint was in order. □

The result of an .* expression or a ->* expression is an lvalue if its second operand is an lvalue.

5.6 Multiplicative Operators

The multiplicative operators `*`, `/`, and `%` group left-to-right.

> *multiplicative-expression:*
>> *pm-expression*
>> *multiplicative-expression* `*` *pm-expression*
>> *multiplicative-expression* `/` *pm-expression*
>> *multiplicative-expression* `%` *pm-expression*

The operands of `*` and `/` must have arithmetic type; the operands of `%` must have integral type. The usual arithmetic conversions (§4.5) are performed on the operands and determine the type of the result.

The binary `*` operator indicates multiplication.

The binary `/` operator yields the quotient, and the binary `%` operator yields the remainder from the division of the first expression by the second. If the second operand of `/` or `%` is 0 the result is undefined; otherwise `(a/b)*b + a%b` is equal to `a`. If both operands are nonnegative then the remainder is nonnegative; if not, the sign of the remainder is implementation dependent.

> ■ When a division of two integers, using the `/` operator, is inexact and exactly one of the operands is negative, the result is implementation dependent. This result may be either the smallest integer greater than the algebraic quotient or the largest integer less than the algebraic quotient. Thus, for example, *-23/4* will yield either *-5* or *-6*. An implementation should specify what the result of such a division will be.
>
> Similarly, the result of the `%` operator, when the division is inexact and exactly one of the operands is negative, may be either positive or negative. An implementation should specify the sign of such an operation. In either case, the expression *(a/b)*b + a%b* must equal *a* whenever the quotient *a/b* is representable on the underlying hardware.
>
> The reason for leaving operator `%` partly unspecified is for compatibility with C and the wish to enable C++ compilers to use the arithmetic operations provided by various hardware as directly as possible. □

5.7 Additive Operators

The additive operators `+` and `-` group left-to-right. The usual arithmetic conversions (§4.5) are performed for operands of arithmetic type.

> *additive-expression:*
>> *multiplicative-expression*
>> *additive-expression* `+` *multiplicative-expression*
>> *additive-expression* `-` *multiplicative-expression*

The operands must be of arithmetic or pointer type. The result of the `+` operator is the sum of the operands. A pointer to an object in an array and a value of any integral type may be added. The result is a pointer of the same type as the original pointer, which points to another object in the same array, appropriately offset from the original object. Thus if `P` is a pointer to an object in an array, the expression

P+1 is a pointer to the next object in the array. If the resulting pointer points outside the bounds of the array, except at the first location beyond the high end of the
array, the result is undefined.

■ One can refer to an element beyond the end of an array, but it is still an error to
dereference such a pointer.

```
char a[10];
void f()
{
    char* p = &a[10];    // 'p' points one past
                         // the end of 'a'
    if (&a[9] < p)
        // ...
    *p = 999;            // error: assignment
                         // past end of array
}
```

Most implementations are incapable of detecting such errors. □

The result of the − operator is the difference of the operands. A value of any
integral type may be subtracted from a pointer, and then the same conversions
apply as for addition.

No further type combinations are allowed for pointers.

If two pointers to objects of the same type are subtracted, the result is a signed
integral value representing the number of objects separating the pointed-to objects.
Pointers to successive elements of an array differ by 1. The type of the result is
implementation dependent, but is defined as ptrdiff_t in the standard header
<stddef.h>. The value is undefined unless the pointers point to elements of the
same array; however, if P points to the last element of an array then (P+1)−1 is
P.

■ Pointer arithmetic requires a pointer to an object type. Thus the following is illegal:

```
int (*fp)()=f;
fp++;    // error: cannot increment pointer to function
```

as is this:

```
void* p;
// ...
p++;      //error: cannot increment pointer to void
```

The sizeof(void) is illegal; it logically follows that arithmetic operations on a
pointer to void are not allowed. □

5.8 Shift Operators

The shift operators << and >> group left-to-right.

> *shift-expression:*
> > *additive-expression*
> > *shift-expression* << *additive-expression*
> > *shift-expression* >> *additive-expression*

The operands must be of integral type and integral promotions are performed. The type of the result is that of the promoted left operand. The result is undefined if the right operand is negative, or greater than or equal to the length in bits of the promoted left operand. The value of E1 << E2 is E1 (interpreted as a bit pattern) left-shifted E2 bits; vacated bits are 0-filled. The value of E1 >> E2 is E1 right-shifted E2 bit positions. The right shift is guaranteed to be logical (0-fill) if E1 has an unsigned type or if it has a nonnegative value; otherwise the result is implementation dependent.

> ■ When the left operand of the >> operator has a signed type and a negative value, the result of the operation will be implementation dependent. Either a logical right shift (the most significant bits will be filled with zeros) or a signed right shift will be done, usually depending on what the target machine does most efficiently. □

5.9 Relational Operators

The relational operators group left-to-right, but this fact is not very useful; a<b<c means (a<b)<c and *not* (a<b)&&(b<c).

> *relational-expression:*
> > *shift-expression*
> > *relational-expression* < *shift-expression*
> > *relational-expression* > *shift-expression*
> > *relational-expression* <= *shift-expression*
> > *relational-expression* >= *shift-expression*

The operands must have arithmetic or pointer type. The operators < (less than), > (greater than), <= (less than or equal to), and >= (greater than or equal to) all yield 0 if the specified relation is false and 1 if it is true. The type of the result is int.

The usual arithmetic conversions are performed on arithmetic operands. Pointer conversions are performed on pointer operands. This implies that any pointer may be compared to a constant expression evaluating to 0 and any pointer can be compared to a pointer of type void* (in the latter case the pointer is first converted to void*). Pointers to objects or functions of the same type (after pointer conversions) may be compared; the result depends on the relative positions of the pointed-to objects or functions in the address space.

Two pointers to the same object compare equal. If two pointers point to non-static members of the same object, the pointer to the later declared member compares higher provided the two members not separated by an *access-specifier* label

(§11.1) and provided their class is not a union. If two pointers point to nonstatic members of the same object separated by an *access-specifier* label (§11.1) the result is undefined. If two pointers point to data members of the same union, they compare equal. If two pointers point to elements of the same array or one beyond the end of the array, the pointer to the object with the higher subscript compares higher. Other pointer comparisons are implementation dependent.

■ Comparison of pointers is guaranteed only if the pointers being compared point to elements of the same array or one beyond the end of the array. Code that depends on comparison of pointers will not be portable. For example,

```
int z[16];
int a[16];
int* zptr=z;
int* aptr=a;

if (aptr > zptr) {       // not portable
        // ...
}
```

One implementation may emit objects in the generated code in the order they appear in the source code; another may enter all declared objects in a symbol table, then step through the table emitting objects in alphabetical or some other order. The code above may execute as the programmer intends when compiled and run on one implementation, but may run differently on another implementation. The following code, on the other hand, will be portable:

```
struct s{
      int z[16];
      int a[16];
} arrays;

int* zptr=arrays.z;
int* aptr=arrays.a;

if (aptr > zptr) {       // ok
        // ...
}
```

The following illustrates another consequence of this definition of pointer comparison that may not be readily apparent:

```
static struct Array array[NUM];
static struct Array* BegPtr = array;
static struct Array* EndPtr = &array[NUM-1];
extern struct Array* TestPtr;

if (TestPtr >= BegPtr && TestPtr <= EndPtr) {
        // ...
}
```

It is probably intended here that the expression comparing *TestPtr* with *BegPtr* and with *EndPtr* will evaluate as true if and only if *TestPtr* points into *array*.

But C++ defines the result of comparison of pointers only when they point into the same array or one beyond. Thus it is not guaranteed that the expression above will be false if `TestPtr` points outside the array.

The expression may not evaluate as false on a segmented architecture with pointers that address only a single segment when `TestPtr` points to something in one segment that has the same address within its segment as a member of `array` has in another segment.

This also explains why addition, subtraction, and comparison of pointers are defined only for pointers into an array and one element beyond the end. Originally, these operations were defined only for pointers into an array. Users of machines with a nonsegmented address space developed idioms, however, that referred to the element beyond the end of the array, such as

```
int a[100];
for (int* p = a; p<&a[100]; p++) { /* ... */ }
```

On such systems addressing beyond the end of an array is harmful only in the unlikely event that an array is allocated too close to the highest address in the system. The resulting code, however, was not portable to segmented architectures unless special effort was taken. Taking that special effort was deemed feasible and worthwhile by the ANSI C committee for one element beyond *only*. Allowing further addressing beyond the end of arrays would be costly and serve few useful purposes. □

5.10 Equality Operators

> *equality-expression:*
> > *relational-expression*
> > *equality-expression* == *relational-expression*
> > *equality-expression* != *relational-expression*

The == (equal to) and the != (not equal to) operators are exactly analogous to the relational operators except for their lower precedence. (Thus a<b == c<d is 1 whenever a<b and c<d have the same truth-value.)

In addition, pointers to members of the same type may be compared. Pointer to member conversions (§4.8) are performed. A pointer to member may be compared to a constant expression that evaluates to 0.

5.11 Bitwise AND Operator

> *and-expression:*
> > *equality-expression*
> > *and-expression* & *equality-expression*

The usual arithmetic conversions are performed; the result is the bitwise AND function of the operands. The operator applies only to integral operands.

5.12 Bitwise Exclusive OR Operator

> *exclusive-or-expression:*
> *and-expression*
> *exclusive-or-expression* ^ *and-expression*

The usual arithmetic conversions are performed; the result is the bitwise exclusive OR function of the operands. The operator applies only to integral operands.

5.13 Bitwise Inclusive OR Operator

> *inclusive-or-expression:*
> *exclusive-or-expression*
> *inclusive-or-expression* | *exclusive-or-expression*

The usual arithmetic conversions are performed; the result is the bitwise inclusive OR function of its operands. The operator applies only to integral operands.

5.14 Logical AND Operator

> *logical-and-expression:*
> *inclusive-or-expression*
> *logical-and-expression* && *inclusive-or-expression*

The && operator groups left-to-right. It returns 1 if both its operands are nonzero, 0 otherwise. Unlike &, && guarantees left-to-right evaluation; moreover the second operand is not evaluated if the first operand evaluates to 0.

The operands need not have the same type, but each must have arithmetic type or be a pointer. The result is an int. All side effects of the first expression happen before the second expression is evaluated.

5.15 Logical OR Operator

> *logical-or-expression:*
> *logical-and-expression*
> *logical-or-expression* || *logical-and-expression*

The || operator groups left-to-right. It returns 1 if either of its operands is nonzero, and 0 otherwise. Unlike |, || guarantees left-to-right evaluation; moreover, the second operand is not evaluated if the first operand evaluates to nonzero.

The operands need not have the same type, but each must have arithmetic type or be a pointer. The result is an int. All side effects of the first expression happen before the second expression is evaluated.

5.16 Conditional Operator

> *conditional-expression:*
> > *logical-or-expression*
> > *logical-or-expression* ? *expression* : *conditional-expression*

Conditional expressions group right-to-left. The first expression must have arithmetic type or be a pointer type. It is evaluated and if it is nonzero, the result of the conditional expression is the value of the second expression, otherwise that of the third expression. All side effects of the first expression happen before the second or third expression is evaluated.

If both the second and the third expressions are of arithmetic type, then if they are of the same type the result is of that type; otherwise the usual arithmetic conversions are performed to bring them to a common type. Otherwise, if both the second and the third expressions are either a pointer or a constant expression that evaluates to 0, pointer conversions are performed to bring them to a common type. Otherwise, if both the second and the third expressions are references, reference conversions are performed to bring them to a common type. Otherwise, if both the second and the third expressions are void, the common type is void. Otherwise, if both the second and the third expressions are of the same class T, the common type is T. Otherwise the expression is illegal. The result has the common type; only one of the second and third expressions is evaluated.

> ■ Note that − as in all other expressions − user-defined conversions (§12.3) will be implicitly applied to bring the second and third operands to a common type if a common type cannot be found using only standard conversions. □

The result is an lvalue if the second and the third operands are of the same type and both are lvalues.

> ■ For example,
>
> ```
> void f(long x)
> {
>     int a,b;
>     x?a:b = 1;  // ok
>
>     x?x:b = 1;  // error: conversion needed to bring
>                 // 'x' and 'b' to common type
>                 // so 'x?x:b' is not an lvalue
>
>     x?1:b = 1;  // error: '1' is not an lvalue
>                 // so x?1:b' is not an lvalue
> }
> ```
>
> □

5.17 Assignment Operators

There are several assignment operators, all of which group right-to-left. All require a modifiable lvalue as their left operand, and the type of an assignment expression is that of its left operand. The result of the assignment operation is the value stored in the left operand after the assignment has taken place; the result is an lvalue.

> *assignment-expression:*
> > *conditional-expression*
> > *unary-expression assignment-operator assignment-expression*

> *assignment-operator:* one of
> > = *= /= %= += -= >>= <<= &= ^= |=

In simple assignment (=), the value of the expression replaces that of the object referred to by the left operand. If both operands have arithmetic type, the right operand is converted to the type of the left preparatory to the assignment. There is no implicit conversion to an enumeration (§7.2), so if the left operand is of an enumeration type the right operand must be of the same type. If the left operand is of pointer type, the right operand must be of pointer type or a constant expression that evaluates to 0; the right operand is converted to the type of the left before the assignment.

A pointer of type `T*const` can be assigned to a pointer of type `T*`, but the reverse assignment is illegal (§7.1.6). Objects of types `const T` and `volatile T` can be assigned to plain `T` lvalues and to lvalues of type `volatile T`; see also (§8.4).

If the left operand is of pointer to member type, the right operand must be of pointer to member type or a constant expression that evaluates to 0; the right operand is converted to the type of the left before the assignment.

Assignment to objects of a class (§9) `X` is defined by the function `X::operator=()` (§13.4.3). Unless the user defines an `X::operator=()`, the default version is used for assignment (§12.8). This implies that an object of a class derived from `X` (directly or indirectly) by unambiguous public derivation (§4.6) can be assigned to an `X`.

■ An object of a base class, however, cannot be assigned to an object of a derived class. For example,

```
struct S {
      int a;
};

struct SS : S {
      int b;
};
```

```
void f(SS xx)
{
    S x;
    x = xx;              // x.a = xx.a
    xx = x;              // error
}
```

□

A pointer to a member of class B may be assigned to a pointer to a member of class D of the same type provided D is derived from B (directly or indirectly) by unambiguous public derivation (§10.1.1).

Assignment to an object of type ''reference to T'' assigns to the object of type T denoted by the reference.

The behavior of an expression of the form E1 *op*= E2 is equivalent to E1 = E1 *op* (E2); except that E1 is evaluated only once. In += and −=, the left operand may be a pointer, in which case the (integral) right operand is converted as explained in §5.7; all right operands and all nonpointer left operands must have arithmetic type.

■ Note that operations such as += cannot be applied to variables of enumeration types since the result of + is not of an enumeration type (unless overloading has been used). For example,

```
enum E { a,b,c };
void f()
{
    E x = b;
    x += c;       // error
}
```

□

For class objects, assignment is not in general the same as initialization (§8.4, §12.1, §12.6, §12.8).

■ Assignment differs from initialization for references.

```
void f()
{
    int i = 1;
    int& r = i;   // initialization: 'r' refers to 'i'
    r = 2;        // assignment: 'i' gets the value '2'
                  // through 'r'
}
```

For arrays, only initialization is allowed.

```
char a[] = "asdf";     // initialize 'a'

void g()
{
    a = "asdf";        // error: no array assignment
}
```

For other types, the default assignment and initialization operations are identical. Assignment and initializations can be defined as separate operations for class types.
□

5.18 Comma Operator

The comma operator groups left-to-right.

> *expression:*
> > *assignment-expression*
> > *expression , assignment-expression*

A pair of expressions separated by a comma is evaluated left-to-right and the value of the left expression is discarded. All side effects of the left expression are performed before the evaluation of the right expression. The type and value of the result are the type and value of the right operand; the result is an lvalue if its right operand is.

In contexts where comma is given a special meaning, for example, in lists of actual arguments to functions (§5.2.2) and lists of initializers (§8.4), the comma operator as described in this section can appear only in parentheses; for example,

```
    f(a,  (t=3,  t+2),  c);
```

has three arguments, the second of which has the value 5.

5.19 Constant Expressions

In several places, C++ requires expressions that evaluate to an integral constant: as array bounds (§8.2.4), as `case` expressions (§6.4.2), as bit-field lengths (§9.6), and as enumerator initializers (§7.2).

> *constant-expression:*
> > *conditional-expression*

A *constant-expression* can involve only literals (§2.5), enumerators, `const` values of integral types initialized with constant expressions (§8.4), and `sizeof` expressions. Floating constants (§2.5.3) must be cast to integral types. Only type conversions to integral types may be used. In particular, except in `sizeof` expressions, functions, class objects, pointers, and references cannot be used. The comma operator and *assignment-operator*s may not be used in a constant expression.

6

Statements

This chapter discusses statements, which control the execution sequence of programs.

C++ provides statements for conditional execution (if and switch) and iteration (do, for, and while). The break, continue, return, and goto statements transfer control in a C++ program. Other statements evaluate an expression (the expression statement) or do nothing (the null statement). Statements may be grouped in { } pairs to form compound statements.

A declaration is a statement in C++; declarations are introduced in this chapter and discussed in detail in the following two chapters.

6 Statements

Except as indicated, statements are executed in sequence.

> *statement:*
> > *labeled-statement*
> > *expression-statement*
> > *compound-statement*
> > *selection-statement*
> > *iteration-statement*
> > *jump-statement*
> > *declaration-statement*

■ C++ adopts C's notion of a statement with little change. The main difference is that in C++ declarations need not be placed before statements in a block, but can be introduced where first needed. This idea and the style of programming that goes with it was inspired by Algol68. The most important use of declarations *not* at the start of a block is to postpone the introduction of a variable to the point where one has a value with which to initialize it. This use minimizes errors due to uninitialized variables. □

6.1 Labeled Statement

A statement may be labeled.

> *labeled-statement:*
> > *identifier* : *statement*
> > `case` *constant-expression* : *statement*
> > `default` : *statement*

An identifier label declares the identifier. The only use of an identifier label is as the target of a `goto`. The scope of a label is the function in which it appears. Labels cannot be redeclared within a function. A label can be used in a `goto` statement before its definition. Labels have their own name space and do not interfere with other identifiers.

Case labels and default labels may occur only in switch statements.

6.2 Expression Statement

Most statements are expression statements, which have the form

> *expression-statement:*
> > *expression*$_{opt}$ `;`

Usually expression statements are assignments or function calls. All side effects from an expression statement are completed before the next statement is executed. An expression statement with the expression missing is called a null statement; it is useful to carry a label just before the } of a compound statement and to supply a null body to an iteration statement such as `while` (§6.5.1).

6.3 Compound Statement, or Block

So that several statements can be used where one is expected, the compound statement (also, and equivalently, called ''block'') is provided.

> *compound-statement:*
> > { *statement-list*$_{opt}$ }

> *statement-list:*
> > *statement*
> > *statement-list statement*

Note that a declaration is a *statement* (§6.7).

6.4 Selection Statements

Selection statements choose one of several flows of control.

> *selection-statement:*
>   if (*expression*) *statement*
>   if (*expression*) *statement* else *statement*
>   switch (*expression*) *statement*

The *statement* in a *selection-statement* may not be a *declaration*.

■ If a declaration could be the only statement after `if` or `else`, it would introduce a name of uncertain scope and definite uselessness. For example,

```
if (i)
    int a = 7;   // error: declaration as only statement
                 // after 'if'
else
    int b = 8;   // error: declaration as only statement
                 // after 'else'
```

□

6.4.1 The `if` Statement

The expression must be of arithmetic or pointer type or of a class type for which an unambiguous conversion to arithmetic or pointer type exists (§12.3).

The expression is evaluated and if it is nonzero, the first substatement is executed. If `else` is used, the second substatement is executed if the expression is zero. The `else` ambiguity is resolved by connecting an `else` with the last encountered `else`-less `if`.

6.4.2 The `switch` Statement

The `switch` statement causes control to be transferred to one of several statements depending on the value of an expression.

The expression must be of integral type or of a class type for which an unambiguous conversion to integral type exists (§12.3). Integral promotion is performed. Any statement within the statement may be labeled with one or more case labels as follows:

> case *constant-expression* :

where the *constant-expression* (§5.19) is converted to the promoted type of the switch expression. No two of the case constants in the same switch may have the same value.

There may be at most one label of the form

> default :

within a `switch` statement.

■ A case label need not be at the highest level of scope within a switch statement. For example,

```
switch (i) {
case 1:
{
    // ...
    case 2:
    {
        // ...
        case 3:
        {
            // ...
        }
    }
}
}
```

Fortunately, people do not in general write such code. Machines, however, occasionally have good reasons for generating code like that. □

Switch statements may be nested; a `case` or `default` label is associated with the smallest switch enclosing it.

When the `switch` statement is executed, its expression is evaluated and compared with each case constant. If one of the case constants is equal to the value of the expression, control is passed to the statement following the matched case label. If no case constant matches the expression, and if there is a `default` label, control passes to the statement labeled by the default label. If no case matches and if there is no `default` then none of the statements in the switch is executed.

`case` and `default` labels in themselves do not alter the flow of control, which continues unimpeded across such labels. To exit from a switch, see `break`, §6.6.1.

Usually, the statement that is the subject of a switch is compound.

■ It does not *have* to be a compound statement, though. For example,

```
switch (i) case 1: cout << "!!!\n";
```

is simply a confusing way of saying

```
if (i == 1) cout << "!!!\n";
```

□

Declarations may appear in the *statement* of a switch-statement. It is illegal, however, to jump past a declaration with an explicit or implicit initializer unless the declaration is in an inner block that is not entered (that is, completely bypassed by the transfer of control; §6.7).

■ For example,

```
switch (i) {
    int v1 = 2;   // error: jump past initialized variable
case 1:
    int v2 = 3;
    // ...
case 2:
    if (v2 == 7) // error: jump past initialized variable
    // ...
}
```

□

This implies that declarations that contain explicit or implicit initializers must be contained in an inner block.

6.5 Iteration Statements

Iteration statements specify looping.

> *iteration-statement:*
> > while (*expression*) *statement*
> > do *statement* while (*expression*) ;
> > for (*for-init-statement* *expression*$_{opt}$; *expression*$_{opt}$) *statement*

> *for-init-statement:*
> > *expression-statement*
> > *declaration-statement*

Note that a *for-init-statement* ends with a semicolon.

The *statement* in an *iteration-statement* may not be a *declaration*.

6.5.1 The **while** Statement

In the **while** statement the substatement is executed repeatedly until the value of the expression becomes zero. The test takes place before each execution of the substatement.

The expression must be of arithmetic or pointer type or of a class type for which an unambiguous conversion to arithmetic or pointer type exists (§12.3).

6.5.2 Do statement

In the **do** statement the substatement is executed repeatedly until the value of the expression becomes zero. The test takes place after each execution of the substatement.

The expression must be of arithmetic or pointer type or of a class type for which an unambiguous conversion to arithmetic or pointer type exists (§12.3).

6.5.3 The `for` Statement

The `for` statement

$$for \ (\ for\text{-}init\text{-}statement \ expression\text{-}1_{opt} \ ; \ expression\text{-}2_{opt} \ ) \ statement$$

is equivalent to

```
for-init-statement
while ( expression-1 ) {
        statement
        expression-2 ;
}
```

except that a `continue` in *statement* will execute *expression-2* before re-evaluating *expression-1*. Thus the first statement specifies initialization for the loop; the first expression specifies a test, made before each iteration, such that the loop is exited when the expression becomes zero; the second expression often specifies incrementing that is done after each iteration. The first expression must have arithmetic or pointer type or a class type for which an unambiguous conversion to arithmetic or pointer type exists (§12.3).

Either or both of the expressions may be dropped. A missing *expression-1* makes the implied `while` clause equivalent to `while(1)`.

■ For example, a common idiom for an infinite loop is

```
for(;;) // ...
```

Similarly, loops with more than one exit point or more than one exit condition are often written like this:

```
for(;;) {
        // ...
        if ( /* ... */ ) break;
        // ...
        if ( /* ... */ ) break;
        // ...
}
```

□

If the *for-init-statement* is a declaration, the scope of the names declared extends to the end of the block enclosing the *for-statement*.

■ There is no special scope rule for a name declared in the initializing statement in a *for-statement*. This implies that the scope of such a name extends to the end of the block enclosing the *for-statement*. For example,

```
for (int i = 0; i<100; i++) {
    // ...
    break;
}

if (i<100) // 'i' is still in scope
    ;
```

The absence of a special rule implies that the same name cannot be used to control two *for* loops in the same scope.

```
for (int i = 0; i<100; i++) {
    // ...
}
for (int i = 0; i<100; i++) {   // error: 'i' defined twice
    // ...
}
```

In such cases, the second loop variable must either be renamed or not be redeclared in the *for-statement*.

On balance, it would probably have been better to introduce a special rule to limit the scope of a name introduced in the initializing statement of a *for-statement* to the *for-statement*, but much code now exists that depends on the general rule.

One could also observe that features making it easier to write large functions may be the kind of local convenience for which one pays a price in overall program structure. A major feature of the C++ class concept is that it can be used to cut the average size of functions significantly. □

6.6 Jump Statements

Jump statements unconditionally transfer control.

> *jump-statement:*
> > break ;
> > continue ;
> > return *expression*_{opt} ;
> > goto *identifier* ;

On exit from a scope (however accomplished), destructors (§12.4) are called for all constructed class objects in that scope that have not yet been destroyed. This applies to both explicitly declared objects and temporaries (§12.2).

6.6.1 The break Statement

The break statement may occur only in an *iteration-statement* or a switch statement and causes termination of the smallest enclosing *iteration-statement* or switch statement; control passes to the statement following the terminated statement, if any.

6.6.2 The `continue` Statement

The `continue` statement may occur only in an *iteration-statement* and causes control to pass to the loop-continuation portion of the smallest enclosing *iteration-statement*, that is, to the end of the loop. More precisely, in each of the statements

```
while (foo) {          do {                   for (;;) {
    // ...                 // ...                 // ...
contin: ;              contin: ;              contin: ;
}                      } while (foo);          }
```

a `continue` not contained in an enclosed iteration statement is equivalent to `goto contin`.

6.6.3 The `return` Statement

A function returns to its caller by the `return` statement.

A return statement without an expression can be used only in functions that do not return a value, that is, a function with the return value type `void`, a constructor (§12.1), or a destructor (§12.4). A return statement with an expression can be used only in functions returning a value; the value of the expression is returned to the caller of the function. If required, the expression is converted, as in an initialization, to the return type of the function in which it appears. This may involve the construction and copy of a temporary object (§12.2). Flowing off the end of a function is equivalent to a return with no value; this is illegal in a value-returning function.

■ Note that returning a value of a class with a default constructor is *not* equivalent to returning no value.

```
class X {
    // ...
public:
    X();
};

X f()
{
    // ...
    return;      // error: return value expected
}

X g()
{
    // ...
    return X(); // ok
}
```

□

6.6.4 The goto Statement

The goto statement unconditionally transfers control to the statement labeled by
the identifier. The identifier must be a label (§6.1) located in the current function.

6.7 Declaration Statement

A declaration statement introduces a new identifier into a block; it has the form

> *declaration-statement:*
> > *declaration*

If an identifier introduced by a declaration was previously declared in an outer
block, the outer declaration is hidden for the remainder of the block, after which it
resumes its force.

Any initializations of auto or register variables are done each time their
declaration-statement is executed. Destruction of local variables declared in the
block is done on exit from the block (§6.6). Destruction of auto variables defined
in a loop is done once per iteration. For example, here the Index j is created and
destroyed once each time round the i loop:

```
for (int i = 0; i<100; i++)
    for (Index j = 0; j<100; j++) {
        // ...
    }
```

Transfer out of a loop, out of a block, or back past an initialized auto variable
involves the destruction of auto variables declared at the point transferred from
but not at the point transferred to.

It is possible to transfer into a block, but not in a way that causes initializations
not to be done. It is illegal to jump past a declaration with an explicit or implicit
initializer unless the declaration is in an inner block that is not entered (that is,
completely bypassed by the transfer of control) or unless the jump is from a point
where the variable has already been initialized. For example,

```
void f()
{
    // ...
    goto lx;      // error: jump past initializer
    // ...
ly:
    X a = 1;
    // ...
lx:
    goto ly;      // ok, jump implies destructor
                  // call for 'a'
}
```

■ C has no such restriction. Typically, that is no advantage to the programmer since it simply allows code that unintentionally depends on undeclared variables. This alone would not have been reason enough for C++ to disallow a valid C construct. In C++, however, the destruction of a variable that has not been constructed is usually a disaster and must be avoided. Since destructor calls are implicit, even the case where a variable is never used on a path where its initialization was bypassed would end in disaster and must be outlawed.

One might have allowed jumping past variables without destructors and not past variables with destructors. This would, however, have broken the principle that there should be no fundamental differences in the use of user-defined and built-in types, with only the doubtful benefit of allowing a traditional class of errors. □

An `auto` variable constructed under a condition is destroyed under that condition and cannot be accessed outside that condition. For example,

```
if (i)
    for (int j = 0; j<100; j++) {
        // ...
    }
if (j!=100)      // error: access outside condition
    // ...
;
```

■ After all, *i* might have been *0*. □

Initialization of a local object with storage class `static` (§7.1.1) is done the first time control passes through its declaration (only). Where a `static` variable is initialized with an expression that is not a *constant-expression*, default initialization to 0 of the appropriate type (§8.4) happens before its block is first entered.

■ This makes recursive and mutually recursive function calls used in the initializers well-defined. Consider this beauty:

```
int foo(int i)
{
    static int s = foo(2*i);     // recursive  call
    return i+1;
}
```

A first call of *foo, foo(3)* will yield the result *4* and leave *foo*'s *s* with the value 7. The reason is that in the second call of *foo()*, *s* is considered initialized even though it has not yet been updated with the value in the first call of *foo*. These semantics can be implemented by a simple first time switch. □

The destructor for a local `static` object will be executed if and only if the variable was constructed. The destructor must be called either immediately before or as part of the calls of the `atexit()` functions (§3.4). Exactly when is undefined.

6.8 Ambiguity Resolution

There is an ambiguity in the grammar involving *expression-statement*s and *declaration*s: An *expression-statement* with a function-style explicit type conversion (§5.2.3) as its leftmost subexpression can be indistinguishable from a *declaration* where the first *declarator* starts with a (. In those cases the *statement* is a *declaration*.

To disambiguate, the whole *statement* may have to be examined to determine if it is an *expression-statement* or a *declaration*. This disambiguates many examples. For example, assuming T is a *simple-type-name* (§7.1.6),

```
T(a)->m = 7;        // expression-statement
T(a)++;             // expression-statement
T(a,5)<<c;          // expression-statement

T(*e)(int);         // declaration
T(f)[];             // declaration
T(g) = { 1, 2 };    // declaration
T(*d)(double(3));   // declaration
```

The remaining cases are *declaration*s. For example,

```
T(a);               // declaration
T(*b)();            // declaration
T(c)=7;             // declaration
T(d),e,f=3;         // declaration
T(g)(h,2);          // declaration
```

The disambiguation is purely syntactic; that is, the meaning of the names, beyond whether they are *type-name*s or not, is not used in the disambiguation.

■ Note that a simple lexical lookahead can help a parser disambiguate most cases. Consider analyzing a *statement* consisting of a sequence of tokens as follows:

    type-name (*d-or-e*) *tail*

Here, *d-or-e* must be a *declarator*, an *expression*, or both for the statement to be legal. This implies that *tail* must be a semicolon, something that can follow a parenthesized *declarator* or something that can follow a parenthesized *expression*, that is, an *initializer*, const, volatile, (, [, or a postfix or infix operator.

The general cases cannot be resolved without backtracking, nested grammars or similar advanced parsing strategies. In particular, the lookahead needed to disambiguate this case is not limited.

In a parser with backtracking the disambiguating rule can be stated very simply:
[1] If it looks like a *declaration*, it is; otherwise
[2] if it looks like an *expression*, it is; otherwise
[3] it is a syntax error.
A user can explicitly disambiguate cases that appear obscure. For example,

```
void f()
{
    auto int (*p) ();    // explicitly declaration
    (void) int (*p) ();  // explicitly expression-statement
    0, int (*p) ();      // explicitly expression-statement
    (int (*p) ());       // explicitly expression-statement
    int (*p) ();         // resolved to declaration
}
```

□

A slightly different ambiguity between *expression-statement*s and *declaration*s is resolved by requiring a *type-name* for function declarations within a block (§6.3). For example,

```
void g()
{
    int f();    // declaration
    int a;      // declaration
    f();        // expression-statement
    a;          // expression-statement
}
```

Declarations

A declaration introduces one or more names into a program and specifies how those names are to be interpreted. A declaration can specify a storage class, type, and linkage for an object or function. It can also provide the definition of a function or an initial value for an object. A declaration can give a name to a constant (enumeration declaration), declare a new type, or specify a synonym for a type. Inline functions, const, volatile, and the provision of type-safe linkage are discussed.

7 Declarations

Declarations specify the interpretation given to each identifier; they do not necessarily reserve storage associated with the identifier (§3.1). Declarations have the form

> *declaration:*
> > *decl-specifiers*$_{opt}$ *declarator-list*$_{opt}$;
> > *asm-declaration*
> > *function-definition*
> > *linkage-specification*

The declarators in the *declarator-list* (§8) contain the identifiers being declared. Only in function definitions (§8.3) and function declarations may the *decl-specifiers* be omitted. Only when declaring a class (§9) or enumeration (§7.2), that is, when the *decl-specifier* is a *class-specifier* or *enum-specifier,* may the *declarator-list* be empty. *asm-declaration*s are described in §7.3, and *linkage-specification*s in §7.4. A declaration occurs in a scope (§3.2); the scope rules are summarized in §10.4.

7.1 Specifiers

The specifiers that can be used in a declaration are

> *decl-specifier:*
> > *storage-class-specifier*
> > *type-specifier*
> > *fct-specifier*
> > *template-specifier*
> > `friend`
> > `typedef`

> *decl-specifiers:*
> > *decl-specifiers*_{*opt*} *decl-specifier*

■ Most declarations introduce a name. The exception is a declaration of an unnamed bit-field in a structure (§9.6).

```
struct s {
    // ...
    int :2;      // two bit field
    // ...
};
```

Unnamed fields are occasionally used for padding to match an externally imposed layout and therefore need no name. Leaving the name out of other declarations is an error. For example,

```
static char;    // error: name expected
extern int;     // error: name expected
```

The name introduced need not be the name of an object or a function.

```
class C;        // introduce a class name
typedef int I;  // introduce a synonym for 'int'
```

□

The longest sequence of *decl-specifier*s that could possibly be a type name is taken as the *decl-specifiers* of a *declaration*. The sequence must be self-consistent as described below. For example,

```
typedef char* Pc;
static Pc;                    // error: name missing
```

Here, the declaration `static Pc` is illegal because no name was specified for the static variable of type `Pc`. To get a variable of type `int` called `Pc`, the *type-specifier* `int` must be present to indicate that the *typedef-name* `Pc` is the name being (re)declared, rather than being part of the *decl-specifier* sequence. For example,

```
void f(const Pc);        // void f(char*const)
void g(const int Pc);    // void g(const int)
```

Note that since `signed`, `unsigned`, `long`, and `short` by default imply `int`, a *typedef-name* appearing after one of those specifiers must be the name being (re)declared. For example,

```
void h(unsigned Pc);        // void h(unsigned int)
void k(unsigned int Pc);    // void k(unsigned int)
```

■ Note that the subtleties to do with whether an identifier is a use of a name of a type or a redefinition of that name stems from the ability to leave the name of a type out of a declaration and have it default to *int* (§7.1.6). If in doubt, don't use implicit *int*s. □

7.1.1 Storage Class Specifiers

The storage class specifiers are

> *storage-class-specifier:*
>> `auto`
>> `register`
>> `static`
>> `extern`

The `auto` or `register` specifiers can be applied only to names of objects declared in a block (§6.3) and for formal arguments (§8.3). The `auto` declarator is almost always redundant and not often used; one use of `auto` is to distinguish a *declaration-statement* from an *expression-statement* (§6.2) explicitly.

■ The compiler knows that

> `int  (*p)[5];`

is the declaration of a pointer to an array of five integers, but decorating the declaration with a redundant *auto* may help a human reader.

> `auto int  (*p)[5];`

It might also help the human writer who does not wish to be a language lawyer. □

A `register` declaration is an `auto` declaration, together with a hint to the compiler that the variables declared will be heavily used. The hint may be ignored and in most implementations it will be ignored if the address of the variable is taken.

■ Unlike C, C++ allows taking the address of an object declared to have storage class *register*. The following, therefore, is legal C++ but not legal C:

> ```
> register i;
> int* ip = &i;    // C++, but not C
> ```

If such a sequence appears, the object must be allocated in storage for which an address can be represented.

One reason for this difference is that compiler technology has progressed to the point where the `register` hint is often more trouble than it is worth. Another reason is that in C++ variables are often objects of classes with associated operations. Leaving `register` as more than a simple hint to the compiler could hinder both portability and optimization. □

An object declaration is a definition unless it contains the `extern` specifier and has no initializer (§3.1).

A definition causes the appropriate amount of storage to be reserved and any appropriate initialization (§8.4) to be done.

The `static` and `extern` specifiers can be applied only to names of objects and functions and to anonymous unions.

■ In particular,

```
static class X {                    // error
      int a;
      // ...
};

typedef static int sint;            // error
```

are illegal. □

There can be no `static` function declarations within a block, nor any `static` or `extern` formal arguments. Static class members are described in (§9.4); `extern` cannot be used for class members.

A name specified `static` has internal linkage.

■ The word "static" has two basic meanings in C and C++. One is "allocated once at a fixed address" (as opposed to allocated on the stack once per function call); the other is "local" (as in local to a translation unit or "in class scope"). These two meanings interact and frequently cause confusion. □

Objects declared `const` have internal linkage unless they have previously been given external linkage. A name specified `extern` has external linkage unless it has previously been given internal linkage. A file scope name without a *storage-class-specifier* has external linkage unless it has previously been given internal linkage and provided it is not declared `const`. For a nonmember function an `inline` specifier is equivalent to a `static` specifier for linkage purposes (§3.3). All linkage specifications for a name must agree. For example,

```
static char* f(); // f() has internal linkage
char* f()          // f() still has internal linkage
      { /* ... */ }

char* g();         // g() has external linkage
static char* g()   // error: inconsistent linkage
      { /* ... */ }
```

```
static int a;     // 'a' has internal linkage
int a;            // error: two definitions

static int b;     // 'b' has internal linkage
extern int b;     // 'b' still has internal linkage

int c;            // 'c' has external linkage
static int c;     // error: inconsistent linkage

extern int d;     // 'd' has external linkage
static int d;     // error: inconsistent linkage
```

■ These rules for the use of *extern* and *static* and declarations without explicit *extern* or *static* are the strictest possible given existing code and the ANSI C rules. The weak specification of *extern* and *static* in the original specification of C led to serious differences among C dialects. This became a major source of confusion and portability problems. People who find the C++ rules overly strict are encouraged to remember that. We have even more sympathy with people who find the C++ rules not quite strict enough, but encourage them to remember that every tightening of the rules breaks somebody's code. □

The name of an undefined class can be used in an `extern` declaration. Such a declaration, however, cannot be used before the class has been defined. For example,

```
struct S;
extern S a;
extern S f();
extern void g(S);

void h()
{
    g(a);         // error: S undefined
    f();          // error: S undefined
}
```

7.1.2 Function Specifiers

Some specifiers can be used only in function declarations.

> *fct-specifier:*
>   `inline`
>   `virtual`

The `inline` specifier is a hint to the compiler that inline substitution of the function body is to be preferred to the usual function call implementation. The hint may be ignored. For a nonmember function `inline` specifier also gives the function default internal linkage (§3.3).

■ Inlining does not affect the meaning of a function call. In this, inlining differs
from macro expansion. An inline function has the usual function definition syntax
and obeys all the usual scope and type checking rules. Inlining is simply a different
implementation technique for function calls. Instead of generating code transferring
control and passing arguments to a single copy of the function's code, a suitably
modified copy of the function's code replaces the call. Inlining saves the time
needed for the transfer of control (both there and back again) including the time
needed to save and restore registers, copy arguments, and so on. Once inlined, the
code of a function becomes available to optimizers that would otherwise not optimize across a function call boundary.

Note that arguments may have to be copied to avoid changing the meaning of a
function call even when inlining is used.

For comparison, consider the following roughly equivalent pair of a macro and
an inline function:

```
double old_a;
#define DBL(a)  ((old_a=a),((a)+(a)))
inline int dbl(int a) { old_a = a; return a+a; }
```

The most obvious difference is that the function has the usual function definition
syntax and has its type defined. It can be used like this

```
void f(int* pi, char* pc)
{
    double old_a = 7;    // hides global 'old_a'
    // ...
    old_a = dbl(*pi++);
    old_a = dbl(pc);        // error: argument type mismatch
}
```

and the correct call will expand to something like

```
int tmp;
old_a = ( (tmp=*pi++), (::old_a=tmp), (tmp+tmp));
```

The temporary *tmp* is introduced to ensure that the argument expression is evaluated
only once and that the variable *old_a* used in *dbl()* is bound to the global variable of that name.

Consider, in contrast,

```
void f(int* pi, char* pc)
{
    double old_a = 7;    // hides global 'old_a'
    // ...
    old_a = DBL(*pi++);
    old_a = DBL(pc);        // errors on expansion
}
```

macro-expands into

```
void f(int* pi, char* pc)
{
    double old_a = 7;     // hides global 'old_a'
    // ...
    old_a = ((old_a=*pi++),((*pi++)+(*pi++)));
    old_a = ((old_a=pc),((pc)+(pc)));      // error
}
```

merrily evaluating the argument expression three times per call and referring to the local copy of *old_a*. The second expansion caused two compiler errors: one for adding pointers and one for assigning a *char** to a *double*. Neither will seem particularly obvious to a programmer who simply called *DBL()*.

Sometimes the behavior of the macro is just what is needed, but often the differences from the behavior of functions cause time consuming surprises to the programmer. The property of macros that is most often useful – compared with inline functions – is their ability to operate on any type of argument. This advantage can be partially offset by the use of virtual functions (§10.2) and templates (§14). Templates also partially offset the advantage that occasionally can be gained from macros with arguments that are not expressions. □

■ Consider when to specify an inline function. Since inlining is purely an optimization, it should be used only when the benefit in run-time or space outweighs the costs and inconveniences imposed by its use.

For all but the simplest functions, the time spent in a call is dominated by the time it takes to execute the function and not the cost of calling it. This implies that the saving from inlining any but the simplest functions is minimal. Further, there can be a space cost from inlining; if the size of the code generated by inlining is larger than the code used in the function call sequence, a net loss of space is incurred. This can be noticeable when a function is called in many places. On the other hand, the code generated for a really minuscule function can be smaller than the function call sequence, so one can achieve a gain in time *and* space. The ideal candidate for inlining is a function that does something really simple such as returning a value, incrementing a value, or calling another function. Such functions proliferate where data hiding is used. For example,

```
class account {
    int sum;
    // ...
public:
    int balance() { return sum; }
    int withdraw(int x) { return sum-=x; }
    // ...
};
```

Such tiny functions are obvious candidates for inlining. A useful rule of thumb is that inline functions consisting of one or two simple expressions are good candidates for inlining.

There are functions for which inlining is a guaranteed win. That is, they decrease the size of the generated code *and* increase the execution speed even on machines with fast, compact function calls. This is the kind of function that simply

performs type conversions so the expanded code for the function is just a call to
another function decorated with a few type conversions. For example,

```
class pXvector : public pvector {
    // ...
    X& operator[](int i)
        { return (X&) pvector::operator[](i); }
};
```

Note that inlining isn't a panacea. It can easily be overused. For example, the
definition of an inline function has to be available for inlining to be done. This
implies that all callers of an inline function must be recompiled if its definition
changes; the usual function call implementation protects users against that. Occasionally, it can also be a problem that inlining exposes implementation details in
header files where every user can read them. □

■ Note that the order of evaluation of actual arguments to functions is undefined
(§5.2.2). In particular, an inline expansion is not required to preserve the order of
evaluation of actual arguments that the implementation would have produced for an
out-of-line function call. Since one call of a function in a program may be inlined
while another call is handled by the normal function call mechanism this can lead to
two calls of the same function with identical actual arguments yielding different
results. Relying on the order of evaluation of function arguments is ill-advised. □

■ As stated, a compiler is free to ignore the hint to inline a function. It is necessary
to allow a compiler to ignore that hint. Determining whether a function can be
inlined or not is in general not possible. Consider, for example, an inline function
that either calls itself recursively or returns based on the result of an input operation.

```
#include <iostream.h>

inline void f()
{
    char ch = 0;
    if (cin>>ch && ch!='q') f();
}
```

Naturally, when not all invocations of a function are expanded inline, a callable version of the function must be generated. Further, such a version must be generated if
the address of an inline function is taken. A call of an inline function through a
pointer to function typically results in a noninlined call.

Ordinary calls may be generated for inline functions for more mundane reasons.
For example,

- An inline function was too large for inlining to be worthwhile.
- An inline function was recursive.
- An inline function was invoked in a program before it was defined.
- An inline function was invoked twice within an expression.
- An inline function contained a loop, a switch, or a *goto*.

Limitations on inlining will vary from implementation to implementation. The
limitations above are the ones found in the original C++ implementation. It is easy
to do better.

The original C++ implementation limited inlining to at most one call of a single inline function per expression . This simple technique avoids trouble with recursion and — most important — minimizes the use of temporary variables so that inlining can be used on machines with limited stack space.

What is worthwhile to inline depends critically on the application, the C++ implementation, and the hardware on which the application is to run. One could imagine a machine for which inlining was never worthwhile because function call was blindingly fast. It is also easy to imagine a machine for which certain forms of inlining are unusually important. For example, on a machine with special hardware for vector operations outlining a function because it contained a loop might be exactly the wrong thing to do since the loop might be much less expensive than a function call. Implementers should, of course, always be sensitive to the needs of their users, but it is probably worthwhile to pay special attention to uses of inlining. □

■ One might claim that a clever enough compiler could do as well or better without the `inline` hint. This was, after all, the argument used to make `register` (just) a hint. First, `inline` already is a hint. Its only semantic effect is to give the function a particularly weak form of internal linkage — the peculiarity is that an inline member function is not allowed to have two different definitions in two different translation units (§3.3). Second, it was a distinct advantage that C allowed the programmer to provide the `register` hint. For almost fifteen years a compiler "smart enough" to make `register` redundant was generally not available. On many machines, it still isn't. Where such a compiler is not available, a good programmer can occasionally achieve significant performance improvements by explicit use of `register`. We see no reason for inlining to be considered radically different. In fact, inlining could be a nastier problem for a compiler than register allocation because good inlining in the absence of the source text of the function to be inlined can be very difficult. Also, without a mechanism like `inline` for explicitly making the source text available to the compiler, the source text of the key functions — the smallest and most frequently used functions from standard libraries — will typically not be available to the compiler. □

A function (§5.2.2, §8.2.5) defined within the declaration of a class is `inline` by default.

An inline member function must have exactly the same definition in every compilation in which it appears.

■ The intent of this rule is to prevent inlining from being a legitimate way of proliferating definitions of what appears to be a single member function. A compiler that relies exclusively on completely separate compilation cannot catch such errors; compilation systems relying on information stored between compilations can.

Since this manual does not define the way programs are stored, the definition of "exactly the same" is nontrivial and the enforcement of this constraint is often difficult; see also §10.8c. □

A class member function need not be explicitly declared `inline` in the class declaration to be inline. When no `inline` specifier is used, linkage will be external unless an `inline` definition appears before the first call.

```
class X {
public:
    int f();
    inline int g();   // X::g() has internal linkage
    int h();
};

void k(X* p)
{
    int i = p->f();   // now X::f() has external linkage
    int j = p->g();
    // ...
}

inline int X::f()    // error: called before defined
                     // as inline
{
    // ...
}

inline int X::g()
{
    // ...
}

inline int X::h()    // now X::h() has internal linkage
{
    // ...
}
```

■ These rules were formed to serve the needs of people defining classes. There was a strong wish to be able to specify that small, heavily used member functions be expanded inline, as well as insistence that the *inline* specification itself is an implementation detail which does not belong in the necessarily class declaration.

Because C++ is typically compiled by a one pass compiler there is the problem of what to do if a function is first declared, then called, and finally defined as an inline. Four choices were feasible.

[1] Require *inline* in the declaration.
[2] Disallow declaring a member function *inline* after calling it.
[3] Decide that the function has external linkage at the call point.
[4] Don't decide about linkage until the end of the compilation.

Option [2] was chosen because code like this was deemed harmless and essential:

```
class X {
public:
    int f();
    int g();
};
```

```
int h(X* p) { return p->f(); }   // call X::f()
// no call of X::g()

inline int X::f()   // error: defined inline
                    // after being called
{
    // ...
}

inline int X::g()   // ok
{
    // ...
}
```

Option [3] would imply that a definition of the function with external linkage is laid down when the definition is seen, even though it is *inline*. This would not be convenient because sequences of a declaration without an *inline* specifier, followed by a call, followed by a definition with an *inline* specifier occur commonly in classes appearing in header files, which may typically be included in several separate compilations. The result would be frequent linkage clashes of function definitions. Option [4] was deemed to require too many postponed decisions to accommodate one pass compilation.

Note that an inline function is required to have exactly one definition. It is therefore illegal to define an inline function with different inline versions in separate compilations (§3.3).

There is no equivalent special rule for nonmember functions. For example,

```
extern f();
inline f() { /* ... */ }        // error
```

is an error because *inline* implies *static* and

```
extern f();
static f() { /* ... */ }        // error
```

is an error (§7.1.1). □

The *virtual* specifier may be used only in declarations of nonstatic class member functions within a class declaration; see §10.2.

7.1.3 The **typedef** Specifier

Declarations containing the *decl-specifier* *typedef* declare identifiers that can be used later for naming fundamental or derived types. The *typedef* specifier may not be used in a *function-definition* (§8.3).

> *typedef-name:*
> > *identifier*

Within the scope (§3.2) of a *typedef* declaration, each identifier appearing as part of any declarator therein becomes syntactically equivalent to a keyword and names the type associated with the identifier in the way described in §8. A *typedef-name* is thus a synonym for another type. A *typedef-name* does not introduce a new type the way a class declaration (§9.1) does. For example, after

```
typedef int MILES, *KLICKSP;
```

the constructions

```
MILES distance;
extern KLICKSP metricp;
```

are all legal declarations; the type of distance is int; that of metricp is "pointer to int."

A typedef may be used to redefine a name to refer to the type to which it already refers – even in the scope where the type was originally declared. For example,

```
typedef struct s { /* ... */ } s;
typedef int I;
typedef int I;
typedef I I;
```

■ A name introduced by a *typedef* occupies the same name space as other identifiers (except statement labels – see §6.1) and (except for allowing multiple definitions as described above) obeys the usual scope rules. Thus, for example,

```
typedef long I;
long I;          // error: I redefined

void f()
{
    int I;       // ok: hides the type name 'I'
}
```

□

An unnamed class defined in a typedef gets its typedef name as its name. For example,

```
typedef struct { /* ... */ } S; // the struct is named S
```

■ This ensures that the struct has a name that can be used for linkage. This style of declaration is common in C programs where the name of a structure cannot be used as a type name except when prefixed by the keyword *struct*. Allowing it in C++ avoids a compatibility problem.

A cleaner C++ alternative is

```
struct S { /* ... */ };
```

□

A typedef may not redefine a name of a type declared in the same scope to refer to a different type. For example,

```
class complex { /* ... */ };
typedef int complex;     // error: redefinition
```

Similarly, a class may not be declared with the name of a type declared in the same scope to refer to a different type. For example,

```
typedef int complex;
class complex { /* ... */ };   // error: redefinition
```

A *typedef-name* that names a class is a *class-name* (§9.1). The synonym may not be used after a `class`, `struct`, or `union` prefix and not in the names for constructors and destructors within the class declaration itself. For example,

```
struct S {
    S();
    ~S();
};

typedef struct S T;

S a = T();       // ok
struct T * p;    // error
```

■ Consider also,

```
struct S;
typedef struct S T;
struct T { /* ... */ }; // error

struct S {
    S();
    T();           // member function: warn
    ~T();          // error
    ~S();          // ok
};

S::T() { /* ... */ }      // ok
```

□

■ Similarly, a *typedef-name* that names an enumeration may not be used after the *enum* prefix.

Note that a type name, declared in a *typedef* or class declaration, may be combined with the *const* and *volatile* specifiers in another declaration; it may not be combined with another type name. Thus given

```
typedef int I;
```

the following are legal:

```
const I ci = 12;     // ci is const int
volatile I vi;       // vi is volatile int
```

but these are not accepted:

```
short I shi;        // error: can't combine type specifiers
unsigned I ui;      // error: can't combine type specifiers
```

□

■ The `typedef` specifier may not be used for a *function-definition* but it may be used in a function declaration (§8.2.5). For example,

```
typedef int (*PF)(char*);
typedef void* F(unsigned);

PF pf1;                 // int (*pf1)(char*)
F* pf2;                 // void* (*pf2)(unsigned)
F f;                    // void* f(unsigned)
F h { /* ... */ }       // syntax error
```

□

7.1.4 The `template` Specifier

The `template` specifier is used to specify families of types or functions; see §14.

7.1.5 The `friend` Specifier

The `friend` specifier is used to specify access to class members; see §11.4.

7.1.6 Type Specifiers

The type-specifiers are

> *type-specifier:*
> > *simple-type-name*
> > *class-specifier*
> > *enum-specifier*
> > *elaborated-type-specifier*
> > `::` *class-name*
> > `const`
> > `volatile`

The words `const` and `volatile` may be added to any legal *type-specifier* in the declaration of an object. Otherwise, at most one *type-specifier* may be given in a declaration. A `const` object may be initialized, but its value may not be changed thereafter. Unless explicitly declared `extern`, a `const` object does not have external linkage and must be initialized (§8.4; §12.1). An integer `const` initialized by a constant expression may be used in constant expressions (§5.19). Each element of a `const` array is `const` and each nonfunction, nonstatic member of a `const` class object is `const` (§9.3.1).

■ Adding *const* to a declaration ensures that an object to which the *const* is applied cannot have its value changed through an expression involving the name being declared unless an explicit type conversion is used to remove the ''constness'' − and possibly even not then. It is worth remembering, however, that there may be other ways of referring to the object and that explicit type casting is possible; *const* does *not* simply mean ''store in readonly memory'' nor does it mean ''compile-time constant.''

Fundamentally, saying *const* obliges and enables the compiler to prevent accidental updates of the value of an object using a specific name. For example,

```
int i = 1;
const int* p = &i;   // 'i' cannot be updated through 'p'
void f()
{
    i++;                 // ok
}
```

Consider also,

```
void g()
{
    (*(int*)p)++;    // ok
}
```

Casting away *const* is generally ill advised since it violates a guarantee making a program much harder to understand and debug. It can also be hazardous. This variant, for example, may fail:

```
const int i = 1;
const int* p = &i;   // 'i' cannot be updated through 'p'

void h()
{
    (*(int*)p)++;    // may be ok, may be run-time error
}
```

since *i* might have been put in readonly memory. □

A const object of a type that does not have a constructor or a destructor may be placed in readonly memory. The effect of a write operation on any part of such an object is either an addressing exception or the same as if the object had been non-const.

■ This implies that most *const* objects of C++ style class types may not be placed in readonly memory, whereas most *const* objects of built-in types and C style structures may. The purpose of this distinction is to allow the use of readonly memory for large tables, while still enabling ''constness'' for class objects to be defined by the programmer through the definition of *const* member functions (§9.3).

Note that since in most practical machine architectures memory cannot be made ''readonly'' during program execution, an object can be placed in readonly memory only if it is initialized by a value that can be determined at compile time. For example,

```
const one = 1;   // can go in readonly memory
f(int i)
{
    const two = i;      // cannot go in readonly memory
    // ...
}
```

□

■ In C++, the default linkage of a *const* object is internal. In ANSI C, the default storage class of a *const* object is *extern*. Naturally, explicitly declaring a *const* object *extern* will provide behavior equivalent to ANSI C, as in the following:

```
extern const MIN = -1;
```

Also, C++ requires a *const* object to be explicitly initialized; ANSI C does not.
    The significance of these differences is that C++ declarations such as

```
const pi = 3;     // :-)
```

can appear in header files that are included in many compilations and that in C++ *const*s of suitable types can appear in constant expressions.

```
const tblsize = 256;
short gtbl[tblsize];
```

This implies that simple *const*s such as

```
const int MIN = -1;
```

can be used as an alternative to the more traditional C

```
#define MIN -1
```

and

```
enum { MIN = -1 };
```

□

There are no implementation-independent semantics for volatile objects; volatile is a hint to the compiler to avoid aggressive optimization involving the object because the value of the object may be changed by means undetectable by a compiler. Each element of a volatile array is volatile and each nonfunction, nonstatic member of a volatile class object is volatile (§9.3.1).

■ Objects that are accessed by code involved in concurrent activities are obvious candidates for being declared *volatile*. For example,
    −   an object accessible to a signal handler,
    −   an object used for memory mapped I/O.
For example, an aggressive optimizer might consider optimizing this:

```
char c = ireg[3].data;   // skip character
c = ireg[3].data;
```

into this:

```
char c = ireg[3].data;
```

on noticing that the same object was assigned from the same location twice without using the assigned value.

Unless the programmer tells the compiler, there really is no way for it to know that *ireg* is a device register and that its member *data* is "magically" refilled with a new value each time it is read. A declaration

```
class ioregister {
    // ...
    volatile int data;
    // ...
};

ioregister ireg[16];
```

will give the compiler the information it needs to avoid being too clever. □

If the *type-specifier* is missing from a declaration, it is taken to be int.

■ As mentioned in §7.1 this can lead to confusion. □

simple-type-name:
    complete-class-name
    qualified-type-name
    char
    short
    int
    long
    signed
    unsigned
    float
    double
    void

At most one of the words long or short may be specified together with int. Either may appear alone, in which case int is understood. The word long may appear together with double. At most one of the words signed and unsigned may be specified together with char, short, int, or long. Either may appear alone, in which case int is understood. The signed specifier forces char objects and bit-fields to be signed; it is redundant with other integral types.

*class-specifier*s and *enum-specifier*s are discussed in §9 and §7.2, respectively.

elaborated-type-specifier:
    class-key class-name
    class-key identifier
    enum *enum-name*

class-key:
```
class
struct
union
```

If an *identifier* is specified, the *elaborated-type-specifier* declares it to be a *class-name*; see §9.1.

If defined, a name declared using the `union` specifier must be defined as a union. If defined, a name declared using the `class` specifier must be defined using the `class` or `struct` specifier. If defined, a name declared using the `struct` specifier must be defined using the `class` or `struct` specifier.

■ Requiring consistency in the use of *class* and *struct* is pointless and could even lead to confusion since they can be used to define completely equivalent classes. For example,

```
class S {
    int i;
public:
    void f();
};
```

can be replaced by

```
struct S {
private:
    int i;
public:
    void f();
};
```

without any effect whatsoever. □

Names of nested types (§9.7) can be qualified by the name of their enclosing class:

qualified-type-name:
> *typedef-name*
> *class-name* :: *qualified-type-name*

complete-class-name:
> *qualified-class-name*
> :: *qualified-class-name*

qualified-class-name:
> *class-name*
> *class-name* :: *qualified-class-name*

A name qualified by a *class-name* must be a type defined in that class or in a base class of that class. As usual, a name declared in a derived class hides members of that name declared in base classes; see §3.2.

7.2 Enumeration Declarations

An enumeration is a distinct integral type (§3.6.1) with named constants. Its name becomes an *enum-name*, that is, a reserved word within its scope.

> *enum-name:*
> > *identifier*

> *enum-specifier:*
> > enum *identifier$_{opt}$* { *enum-list$_{opt}$* }

> *enum-list:*
> > *enumerator*
> > *enum-list , enumerator*

> *enumerator:*
> > *identifier*
> > *identifier = constant-expression*

The identifiers in an *enum-list* are declared as constants, and may appear wherever constants are required. If no enumerators with = appear, then the values of the corresponding constants begin at zero and increase by one as the declaration is read from left to right. An enumerator with = gives the associated identifier the value indicated; subsequent identifiers without initializers continue the progression from the assigned value. The value of an enumerator must be an int or a value that can be promoted to int by integral promotion (§4.1).

The names of enumerators must be distinct from those of ordinary variables and other enumerators in the same scope.

■ For example,

```
enum color { red, orange, yellow, green, blue };

enum fruit {
    apple,
    pear,
    orange,  // error: 'orange' redefined
    kiwi
};

enum bird {
    emu,
    dodo,
    ostrich,
    kiwi     // error: 'kiwi' redefined
             // (even though fruit::kiwi == bird::kiwi)
};

int emu;        // error: 'emu' redefined
```

□

The values of the enumerators need not be distinct. An enumerator is considered defined immediately after it and its initializer, if any, has been seen. For example,

```
enum { a, b, c=0 };
enum { d, e, f=e+2 };
```

defines a, c, and d to be 0, b and e to be 1, and f to be 3.

Each enumeration defines an integral type that is different from all other integral types. The type of an enumerator is its enumeration. The value of an enumerator or an object of an enumeration type is converted to an integer by integral promotion (§4.1). For example,

```
enum color { red, yellow, green=20, blue };
color col = red;
color* cp = &col;
if (*cp == blue) // ...
```

makes color an integral type describing various colors, and then declares col as an object of that type, and cp as a pointer to an object of that type. The possible values of an object of type color are red, yellow, green, blue; these values can be converted to the int values 0, 1, 20, and 21. Since enumerations are distinct types, objects of type color may be assigned only values of type color. For example,

```
color c = 1;     // error: type mismatch,
                 // no conversion from int to color

int i = yellow;  // ok: yellow converted to int value 1
                 // integral promotion
```

See also §18.3.

■ Naturally, one can explicitly cast to an enumeration. There is no guarantee, however, that the resulting value will be one of the enumerators and the value stored can be implementation dependent. For example,

```
color c2 = color(i);  // explicitly cast int 'i' to color
color c3 = color(600);
i = c3;
```

The value of i after the assignment need not be 600. If color is represented as a single byte, which is not unlikely, the value of i will be quite different.

Appearances to the contrary, there are no operations (except assignment) defined on enumerations; variables and constants of enumeration types are converted into integers before arithmetic is done. For example,

```
enum bit { one=1, two=2, four=4, eight=8 };

void f(bit b1, bit b2)
{
    bit aa = b1|b2;   // error: cannot convert int into bit
    bit bb = b1+b2;   // error: cannot convert int into bit
    bit cc = b1;
    cc++;             // error: cannot convert int into bit
}
```

The reason arithmetic and logical operations are not defined for enumerations is that the results of such operations often are not among the values defined for the enumerators. For example, in the call *f(two,four)*, *b1|b2* and *b1+b2* both get the *int* value *6* and the enumeration *bit* has no such value. Similarly, *cc++* causes *1* to be added to the integer value of *b1* – in this case *2* – yielding the integer value *3*. Fortunately, an integer cannot be assigned back into *cc* without an explicit cast. □

Enumerators defined in a class (§9) are in the scope of that class and can be referred to outside member functions of that class only by explicit qualification with the class name (§5.1). The name of the enumeration itself is also local to the class (§9.7). For example,

```
class X {
public:
    enum direction { left='l', right='r' };
    int f(int i)
        { return i==left ? 0 : i==right ? 1 : 2; }
};

void g(X* p)
{
    direction d;          // error: 'direction' not in scope
    int i;
    i = p->f(left);       // error: 'left' not in scope
    i = p->f(X::right);   // ok
    // ...
}
```

7.3 Asm Declarations

An asm declaration has the form

> *asm-declaration:*
>   asm (*string-literal*) ;

The meaning of an `asm` declaration is implementation dependent. Typically it is used to pass information through the compiler to an assembler.

7.4 Linkage Specifications

Linkage (§3.3) between C++ and non-C++ code fragments can be achieved using a *linkage-specification*:

> *linkage-specification:*
>> extern *string-literal* { *declaration-list$_{opt}$* }
>> extern *string-literal declaration*

> *declaration-list:*
>> *declaration*
>> *declaration-list declaration*

The *string-literal* indicates the required linkage. The meaning of the *string-literal* is implementation dependent. Linkage to a function written in the C programming language, "C", and linkage to a C++ function, "C++", must be provided by every implementation. Default linkage is "C++". For example,

```
complex sqrt(complex);     // C++ linkage by default
extern "C" {
    double sqrt(double);   // C linkage
}
```

■ Linkage specifications are used both to declare functions and objects defined in some other language and to declare C++ functions with linkage that makes them usable from other languages. For example,

```
extern "C" double sqrt(double d)
{
    // C++ code
}
```

It might be best to think of a linkage string as indicating a linkage convention rather than a language. Different languages may share linkage conventions. □

Linkage specifications nest. A linkage specification does not establish a scope. A *linkage-specification* may occur only in *file* scope (§3.2).

■ For example,

```
void f()
{
    extern "C" double frand();  // error: local linkage
                                //        specification
    // ...
}
```

The reason for the restriction was partly to simplify the language rules by not having to specify the meaning of multiple linkage specifications in separate scopes. The primary reason, however, was that in our experience local declarations like the one above were a major source of linkage problems. Far too often, the type specified locally was simply wrong. Typically, it had been right when written and on the system for which it was written − then the code was ported or the part of the system it referred to changed. Orthogonality and generality did not seem to be sufficient reasons to extend the language to support a major source of maintenance problems. □

A *linkage-specification* for a class applies to nonmember functions and objects declared within it. A *linkage-specification* for a function also applies to functions and objects declared within it. A linkage declaration with a string that is unknown to the implementation is an error.

If a function has more than one *linkage-specification*, they must agree; that is, they must specify the same *string-literal*. A function declaration without a linkage specification may not precede the first linkage specification for that function. A function may be declared without a linkage specification after an explicit linkage specification has been seen; the linkage explicitly specified in the earlier declaration is not affected by such a function declaration.

> ■ Allowing a declaration without a linkage declaration to follow a declaration with a linkage specification allows us to localize the linkage specifications in header files and to convert programs easily, leaving (redundant) local declarations untouched. For example,

```
extern "C" double sqrt(double); // from standard header

// ancient function:
double myfunction(double arg1, double arg2)
{
    extern double sqrt(double);
    // ...
}

double sqrt(double d)
{
    // spiffy new version of sqrt()
    // written in C++
}
```

> □

At most one of a set of overloaded functions (§13) with a particular name can have C linkage. See §7.4.

Linkage can be specified for objects. For example,

```
extern "C" {
    // ...
    _iobuf _iob[_NFILE];
    // ...
    int _flsbuf(unsigned,_iobuf*);
    // ...
}
```

Functions and objects may be declared `static` within the { } of a linkage specification. The linkage directive is ignored for such a function or object. Otherwise, a function declared in a linkage specification behaves as if it was explicitly declared `extern`. For example,

```
extern "C" double f();
static double f();        // error
```

is an error (§7.1.1). An object defined within an

```
extern "C" { /* ... */ }
```

construct is still defined (and not just declared).

■ This implies that

```
extern "C" { /* ... */ }
```

can be used without changing the semantics of the enclosed object definitions, but it
has the peculiar effect that the declarations

```
extern "C" {
    int a1;
}

extern "C" int a2;
```

are *not* equivalent. Here *a1* is defined and *a2* only declared. □

■ Since functions with different linkage may have different calling conventions, a
linkage specification may have a major effect on pointers to functions. In particular,
C++ functions that do not have the ellipsis in their argument type may use a more
efficient calling sequence than has traditionally been used for C functions. For
example, this defines a function with C linkage taking a pointer to a function with
C++ linkage as its argument:

```
typedef int (*CPPF)(int);
extern "C" void func(CPPF fp);
```

The opposite case, a function with C++ linkage taking a function with C linkage as
its argument can be declared like this:

```
extern "C" typedef int (*CF)(int);
void func(CF fp);
```

One could imagine extending the linkage concept to be an integral part of the type
system, take part in overloading resolution, and so on. Doing so, however, would
bloat C++ compilers with all kinds of features for "foreign language" calls and
object conversion rules; see §7.4, §7.1c. □

Linkage from C++ to objects defined in other languages and to objects defined
in C++ from other languages is implementation and language dependent. Only
where the object layout strategies of two language implementations are similar
enough can such linkage be achieved.

When the name of a programming language is used to name a style of linkage
in the *string-literal* in a *linkage-specification*, it is recommended that the spelling
be taken from the document defining that language, for example, Ada (not ADA)
and FORTRAN (not Fortran).

■ A linkage specification does not affect the semantics of the function or object given special linkage; that is, a function given *"C"* linkage doesn't suddenly get C type checking rules and a variable of type *char** given *"Pascal"* doesn't suddenly acquire a length field somewhere. The obvious temptation to overload the linkage notation with all kinds of implementation-dependent meaning should almost always be resisted in the interest of portability. □

Commentary

The following sections discuss how one might use and implement a type-safe linkage scheme.

7.1c Linkage Specifications

As mentioned in §7.4, an implementation must provide linkage to C++ (which is the default) and linkage to C. Some implementations will extend the linkage specification mechanism to other languages: Fortran, Ada, Pascal, and so on. The *extern* specifier must be used not only for functions written in other languages to be called from a C++ program, but also when foreign linkage is to be generated for a C++ function that is to be called from another language. For example,

```
extern "C" {
        // C++ declarations for C functions to be
        // called from C++ and for C++ functions to
        // be called from C go here
}
extern "Ada" {
        // C++ declarations for Ada functions to be
        // called from C++ and for C++ functions to
        // be called from Ada go here
}
```

One obvious way of designing foreign linkage would be to build knowledge of the types and calling conventions of foreign languages into a C++ compiler. For example, a C++ compiler might convert zero-terminated C++ strings into Pascal strings with a length prefix at the invocation of a function with Pascal linkage and use call by reference when calling a function with Fortran linkage, convert a C++ object into a roughly equivalent Smalltalk object, and so on.

There are significant disadvantages to this approach, however.

- The complexity and speed of a C++ compiler would be adversely affected.
- Two implementations might extend C++ with a linkage specification to the same language, say Fortran, in different ways, with the effect that identical

C++ programs have subtly different behaviors on different implementations.
–   Unless an extension is widely available and accepted, programs that use it
    will not be portable.
Linkage from C++ to another language will usually be best done by a simple
linkage convention augmented with library routines and rules for argument passing,
format conversion, and so on.   This approach will avoid building knowledge of
foreign-language-calling conventions into C++ compilers.   C++ provides facilities
that ought to make implementing this approach simpler than it would be from most
other languages.   Reference arguments can be used to handle Fortran argument
passing, for example, and a constructor for a Pascal string type taking a C style
string can be written easily.

7.1.1c Sharing Header Files with C

The *extern* specifier, intended to ease the integration of C++ into multilanguage
systems, allows a programmer to give a set of functions C linkage with only a single linkage specification.   This is particularly useful when standard C headers are to
be used.   Given an ANSI C header containing, for example,

```
extern double sqrt(double);
extern double cos(double);
// ...
```

one can trivially modify it for use from C++, as follows:

```
extern "C" {

extern double sqrt(double);
extern double cos(double);
// ...


}
```

Unfortunately, this creates a C++ header that cannot be included in a C program.
Sharing with C can be achieved by conditional compilation (§16).

```
#ifdef __cplusplus
extern "C" {
#endif

extern double sqrt(double);
extern double cos(double);
// ...

#ifdef __cplusplus
}
#endif
```

The macro __cplusplus is defined by every C++ compiler (§16.10).
    If the C header cannot or should not be changed, the *extern* specification can

surround the *#include*, in a separate C++ header file. The C++ version of *math.h* might look like this:

```
extern "C" {
#include <math.h>
}
```

Most C functions used in C++ programs come from well-defined C libraries, for which there are − or ought to be − header files. Therefore, ideally, linkage specifications must be added only to header files.

7.1.2c Converting C Programs

Converting C programs and C++ programs from older implementations that didn't provide C linkage specifications to use type-safe linkage yielded two interesting observations. The first was that most declarations of C functions scattered in C++ programs were either redundant (because the function had already been declared in a header file) or at least potentially incorrect (because they differed from their corresponding declarations in the header files for some commonly used system).

The second observation was that introducing linkage specifications revealed errors in programs − even in programs that had been considered correct for years. The process is reminiscent of running *lint* on an old C program. Most nontrivial programs converted to the new linkage convention contained inconsistent function declarations. Many declarations found in programs were simply wrong. That is, they differed from the function definitions. This was sometimes caused by sloppiness, for example, when a programmer declared a function

```
f(int, ...);
```

to quiet the compiler instead of looking up the type of the second argument. A more common cause was that a header file had changed since the function declaration was put in the program so the local declaration didn't match any more.

Some programmers try to get around the requirement for explicit C linkage specifications by enclosing entire programs in linkage directives. This might be considered a reasonable way of converting old C++ code with minimal effort if it did not require every program that calls a function from such a program to also use the C linkage, thereby forfeiting the benefits of argument type checking. Further, the limitation that at most one of a set of overloaded functions can have C linkage (§7.4) usually defeats this way of converting a program if any of its functions are overloaded.

7.2c Type-safe Linkage

As C++ is defined, all declarations and all uses of variables, functions, and other identifiers must adhere to the type rules. It is *not* specified how this consistency is to be achieved in an environment with separate compilation.

Ideally, that problem is left for the linker to solve. A linker has access to all the code (in object code form), whereas the compiler has access to only a small part of a program at a time. So the obvious solution is to decorate all names emitted from the compiler to the linker with their types and let the linker do the checking.

Unfortunately, linkers are usually rather low-level programs with limited notions of type, they differ dramatically from system to system, and they are among the hardest programs in a system to change (because everyone depends on them).

Consequently, C tried to ensure the consistency of separately compiled programs by controlling the information given to the compiler in header files. This approach works fine up to a point, but does involve extra-linguistic mechanisms, is usually error-prone, and can be costly because of the need to have other programs (in addition to the linker and the compiler) know about the detailed structure of a program.

Here, we will describe an alternative approach that involves using traditional linkers to do type checking by encoding type information in function names.

7.2.1c Function Name Encoding

Originally designed to implement overloading of functions, name encoding is now a common technique for providing type-safe linkage. With function overloading, multiple instances of functions with the same name appear in C++ source code. Naturally, only one instance of a function with any given name can appear in the object code, and it must be possible to determine which instance of an overloaded function is to be invoked for each call. This can be done by encoding the signature of a function (the types of its arguments and of what class, if any, it is a member) within the name used in the generated code. This section presents one scheme for function name encoding.

The encoding scheme described here uses both upper- and lower-case characters; a slightly different encoding would be needed for implementations that lack case distinction in linker names.

If two C++ implementations for the same system use different calling sequences or in other ways are not link compatible it would be unwise to use identical encodings of type signatures. Such implementations might agree on using encodings that differ by a single character where incompatibilities exist (only). For example, one might use a 'G' instead of the regular 'F' to indicate a function. Preserving the overall encoding scheme would be valuable to tool builders.

A function name is encoded by appending its signature to its name. A double underscore (_ _) separates the string representing the function name as it appears in the C++ source code from the function's encoded signature, so using names with embedded sequences of underscores, like a_ _b_ _c, in a C++ program is not recommended.

The basic types are encoded as follows:

type	encoding
void	v
char	c
short	s
int	i
long	l
float	f
double	d
long double	r
...	e

A global function name is encoded by prefixing the signature with the character F. Thus `f(int,double,...)` becomes `f__Fide`. The function `f()` is equivalent to `f(void)`, so it becomes `f__Fv`.

The name of a class is encoded as the length of the name followed by the name itself. An argument of type x, for a class x, will be encoded as `1x` and an argument of type rec, for a class rec, will be encoded as `3rec`. A qualified name such as `Outer::Inner` is encoded by a 'Q' (for "qualified") followed by a single digit indicating the number of qualifications followed by the names. Thus `Outer::Inner` becomes `Q25Outer5Inner`.

class	notation	encoding
simple	Complex	7Complex
qualified	X::YY	Q21X2YY

A member function, which is translated to an ordinary function with the object for which it is invoked (its `this` pointer) as an additional first argument (§9.3.1), is differentiated from a function whose first argument is of a class type by encoding the type of the `this` pointer before the F. Thus, `rec::update(double)` becomes `update__3recFd` and `x::f(int)` becomes `f__1xFi`, but `f(x,int)` becomes `f__F1xi`.

A constructor for class x taking no arguments, `x()`, would be encoded as `__ct__1xFv`, and the destructor, `~x()`, would be `__dt__1xFv`.

Type modifiers are encoded as follows:

modifier	encoding
unsigned	U
const	C
volatile	V
signed	S

`f(unsigned)` becomes `f__FUi`. If more than one modifier is used, the modifiers are encoded in alphabetical order; `f(signed const char)`, which is

equivalent to *f(const signed char)*, becomes *f__FCSc*.
The type declarators are encoded as follows:

type	notation	encoding
pointer	*	P
reference	&	R
array	[10]	A10_
function	()	F
pointer to member	S::*	M1S

f(char)* becomes *f__FPc*. The order of declarators and modifiers affects the meaning of a declaration (§8), so *f(const char* arg)* (*arg* is a pointer to a *char* constant) becomes *f__FPCc* and *f(char* const arg)* (*arg* is a constant pointer to *char*) becomes *f__FCPc*.

The function return type, as well as the argument types, is encoded for an argument that is a pointer to function type. The encoded return type appears after the argument types, preceded by a single underscore. For example, *f(int (*)(char*))* becomes *f__FPFPc_i*.

To shorten encodings, repeated types in an argument list need not be repeated in full in the name encoding; instead, a reference to the first occurrence of the type in the argument list can be used. For example, *f(complex,complex)* could be encoded as *f__F7complexT1*, where *T1* is short for "same type as the first argument." Similarly, *f(record,record,record)*, could be encoded as *f__F6recordN21*, where *N21* stands for "the next two arguments are the same type as the first."

Function names encoded as described here can be many characters long. Implementations that depend on a linker that limits the length of an identifier will have to modify this encoding scheme. One way to shorten function names would be to store, in the last two characters in the generated name, a hash code representing the truncated characters. If a 45-character name is generated on a system with a 31-character limit, for example, the last 16 characters can be replaced by a two-character hash code, yielding a 31-character name.

Naturally, encoding signatures into identifiers of limited length loses information about the argument types. If the lost type information was that which made the overloaded functions unique, name collisions will occur. Experience has shown, however, that 31 characters is usually enough to produce distinct names in real programs. Further, a proper linker will detect and report name clashes caused by the hash coding.

The names of operator functions are encoded like this:

operator	encoding	operator	encoding
*	__ml	/	__dv
%	__md	+	__pl
-	__mi	<<	__ls
>>	__rs	==	__eq
!=	__ne	<	__lt
>	__gt	<=	__le
>=	__ge	&	__ad
|	__or	^	__er
&&	__aa	||	__oo
!	__nt	~	__co
++	__pp	--	__mm
=	__as	->	__rf
+=	__apl	-=	__ami
*=	__amu	/=	__adv
%=	__amd	<<=	__als
>>=	__ars	&=	__aad
|=	__aor	^=	__aer
,	__cm	->*	__rm

operator	encoding
() (function call)	__cl
[] (subscripting)	__vc
constructor	__ct
destructor	__dt
operator new()	__nw
operator delete()	__dl
operator T()	__op<signature of T>

7.2.2c Decoding Function Names

Function name encoding allows object code to have distinct names for functions that share the same name in the C++ source code and enables type-safe linkage, but what happens when the linker detects an error or when the programmer tries to use a symbolic debugger? A linker that doesn't understand the C++ compiler's name encoding scheme will report errors using the names found in the object code; on most systems, a debugger written for C can be used on the object code generated for a C++ program and it will correctly refer to the C++ source code, but it will use the encoded names found in the object code.

C++ users will want a linker that reports errors using the function names that appear in their source code, as well as a debugger that reverses the encoding on output and accepts names as they appear in the C++ source on input. Further, a C++ implementation should ideally provide a name decoder for debugger writers and others who deal directly with object code.

If no function name decoder is available, programmers may need to understand the encoding scheme used by their C++ implementation. As an interim measure, a filter can be provided for processing linker error messages. This output was produced by such a filter:

```
C++ symbol mapping:

PathListHead::~PathListHead()     __dt__12PathListHeadFv
Path::operator&(Path&)            __ad__4PathFR4Path
Path::first()                     first__4PathFv
Path::last()                      last__4PathFv
Path::findpath(String&)           findpath__4PathFR6String
Path::fullpath()                  fullpath__4PathFv
```

Here, encoded and unencoded names of undefined functions are shown side by side to help users of tools that haven't been converted to understand C++ encoded names.

7.3c Limitations

Types of variables are not encoded in their names, nor are the return types of functions encoded. This makes it impossible to catch errors like these:

```
// file 1:
extern int a;
int f() { return a++; }

// file 2:
float a;
extern float f();
```

The reason for letting these errors go undetected is that changing the name encoding scheme so that they would be caught would cause other errors that are caught under the current scheme to go undetected. Consider encoding variable types and function return types. Using X to designate "return type" and a slightly modified example, we would get

```
// file 1:
int a;                           // a__i
int f() { return a++; }          // f__FXi

// file 2:
float a;                         // a__f
float f() { return a = 1.0; }    // f__FXf
```

Now there are two different objects called a and two different functions, with the same argument list, called f. This is not legal C++ and it is correctly rejected by current linkers under the name encoding scheme described here. Changing the encoding scheme to include encoding of variable types and return types, however, would cause this error to be undetected.

Handling all inconsistencies − thus making a C++ implementation 100% type-safe − would require either linker support or a mechanism (an environment) allowing the compiler access to information from separate compilations.

8

Declarators

A declarator declares a single object, function, or type, within a declaration. The syntax for declarators, including pointers, references, pointers to members, arrays, functions, and types, is explained, as well as how to initialize a declarator in a declaration.

8 Declarators

The *declarator-list* appearing in a declaration is a comma-separated sequence of declarators, each of which may have an initializer.

>   *declarator-list:*
>   *init-declarator*
>   *declarator-list* , *init-declarator*

>   *init-declarator:*
>   *declarator initializer*$_{opt}$

The two components of a *declaration* are the specifiers (*decl-specifiers*; §7.1) and the declarators (*declarator-list*). The specifiers indicate the fundamental type, storage class, or other properties of the objects and functions being declared. The declarators specify the names of these objects and functions and (optionally) modify the type with operators such as * (pointer to) and ( ) (function returning). Initial values can also be specified in a declarator; initializers are discussed in §8.4 and §12.6.

Declarators have the syntax

declarator:
>   *dname*
>   *ptr-operator declarator*
>   *declarator* (*argument-declaration-list*) *cv-qualifier-list*$_{opt}$
>   *declarator* [*constant-expression*$_{opt}$]
>   (*declarator*)

ptr-operator:
>   * *cv-qualifier-list*$_{opt}$
>   & *cv-qualifier-list*$_{opt}$
>   *complete-class-name* :: * *cv-qualifier-list*$_{opt}$

cv-qualifier-list:
>   *cv-qualifier cv-qualifier-list*$_{opt}$

cv-qualifier:
>   const
>   volatile

dname:
>   *name*
>   *class-name*
>   ~ *class-name*
>   *typedef-name*
>   *qualified-type-name*

A *class-name* has special meaning in a declaration of the class of that name and when qualified by that name using the scope resolution operator :: (§12.1, §12.4).

8.1 Type Names

To specify type conversions explicitly, and as an argument of sizeof or new, the name of a type must be specified. This is done with a *type-name*, which is syntactically a declaration for an object or function of that type that omits the name of the object or function.

type-name:
>   *type-specifier-list abstract-declarator*$_{opt}$

type-specifier-list:
>   *type-specifier type-specifier-list*$_{opt}$

abstract-declarator:
>   *ptr-operator abstract-declarator*$_{opt}$
>   *abstract-declarator*$_{opt}$ (*argument-declaration-list*) *cv-qualifier-list*$_{opt}$
>   *abstract-declarator*$_{opt}$ [*constant-expression*$_{opt}$]
>   (*abstract-declarator*)

It is possible to identify uniquely the location in the *abstract-declarator* where the identifier would appear if the construction were a declarator in a declaration. The named type is then the same as the type of the hypothetical identifier. For example,

```
int                    // int i
int *                  // int *pi
int *[3]               // int *p[3]
int (*)[3]             // int (*p3i)[3]
int *()                // int *f()
int (*)(double)        // int (*pf)(double)
```

name respectively the types "integer," "pointer to integer," "array of 3 pointers to integers," "pointer to array of 3 integers," "function taking no arguments and returning pointer to integer," and "pointer to function taking a `double` argument and returning an integer."

8.1.1 Ambiguity Resolution

The ambiguity arising from the similarity between a function-style cast and a declaration mentioned in §6.8 can also occur in the context of a declaration. In that context, it surfaces as a choice between a function declaration with a redundant set of parentheses around an argument name and an object declaration with a function-style cast as the initializer. Just as for statements, the resolution is to consider any construct that could possibly be a declaration a declaration. A declaration can be explicitly disambiguated by a nonfunction-style cast or a = to indicate initialization. For example,

```
struct S {
    S(int);
};

void foo(double a)
{
    S x(int(a));        // function declaration
    S y((int)a);        // object declaration
    S z = int(a);       // object declaration
}
```

8.2 Meaning of Declarators

A list of declarators appears after a (possibly empty) list of *decl-specifiers* (§7.1). Each declarator contains exactly one *dname*; it specifies the identifier that is declared. Except for the declarations of some special functions (§12.3, §13.4) a *dname* will be a simple *identifier*. An `auto`, `static`, `extern`, `register`, `friend`, `inline`, `virtual`, or `typedef` specifier applies directly to each *dname* in a *declarator-list*; the type of each *dname* depends on both the *decl-specifiers* (§7.1) and its *declarator*.

Thus, a declaration of a particular identifier has the form

        T D

where T is a type and D is a declarator. In a declaration where D is an unadorned
identifier the type of this identifier is T.

    In a declaration where D has the form

        (D1)

the type of D1 is the same as that of D. Parentheses do not alter the type of the
embedded *dname*, but they may alter the binding of complex declarators.

    ■ Declarators are intended to allow expressing many types with only a few syntactic
elements.

operator	meaning
*	pointer
: : *	pointer to member
&	reference
[ ]	array
( )	function

In addition, each operator may be suffixed by *const*, *volatile*, or a combination
of both.

    The declarator syntax of C − and therefore of C++ − is widely recognized as
being unnecessarily hard to read and write.

    The fundamental problem is that the notation is not linear, but mirrors the
expression syntax which is based on precedences. For example, "pointer to a vector
of 10 pointers to functions taking an *int* argument and returning a pointer to a
char" is easy to say and easy to draw on a blackboard. It is not easy to write or
even read in C++. The use of typedefs (§7.1.3) is strongly recommended for all nontrivial types. For example,

```
        typedef char* F(int);    // F is the type
                                 // functions taking an int
                                 // argument and returning
                                 //a pointer to a char

        typedef F* A[10];        // A is the type array of 10
                                 // pointers to Fs

        A* p;                    // p is a pointer of the horribly
                                 // long type mentioned in the
                                 // paragraph above
```

    □

8.2.1 Pointers

In a declaration T D where D has the form

       ★ *cv-qualifier-list$_{opt}$* D1

the type of the contained identifier is ''... *cv-qualifier-list* pointer to T.'' The *cv-qualifiers* apply to the pointer and not to the object pointed to.

For example, the declarations

```
const ci = 10, *pc = &ci, *const cpc = pc;
int i, *p, *const cp = &i;
```

declare `ci`, a constant integer; `pc`, a pointer to a constant integer; `cpc`, a constant pointer to a constant integer; `i`, an integer; `p`, a pointer to integer; and `cp`, a constant pointer to integer. The value of `ci`, `cpc`, and `cp` cannot be changed after initialization. The value of `pc` can be changed, and so can the object pointed to by `cp`. Examples of legal operations are

```
i = ci;
*cp = ci;
pc++;
pc = cpc;
pc = p;
```

Examples of illegal operations are

```
ci = 1;       // error
ci++;         // error
*pc = 2;      // error
cp = &ci;     // error
cpc++;        // error
p = pc;       // error
```

Each is illegal because it would either change the value of an object declared `const` or allow it to be changed through an unqualified pointer later.

`volatile` specifiers are handled similarly.

See also §5.17 and §8.4.

There can be no pointers to references (§8.2.2) or pointers to bit-fields (§9.6).

■ When a *const* or *volatile* type specifier appears in a declaration, it modifies the immediately following declarator, or, in the declaration of a *const* member function (§9.3), the function's *this* pointer (§9.3.1). Thus

```
const char* step[3] = { "left", "right", "hop" };
```

declares an array of pointers to *chars* that are *const*. The pointers can be changed; the *chars* pointed to cannot.

```
step[2] = "skip";    // ok: changes pointer to const char
step[2][1] = 'i';    // error: can't change const char
```

Had the intention been to declare an array of *const* pointers to *chars*, the following would have been correct:

```
char* const step[3] = { "left", "right", "hop" };
```

Here, the *chars* pointed to can be changed; the pointers cannot.

```
step[2] = "skip";      // error: can't change const pointer
step[2][1] = 'i';       // ok: changes char pointed to
                        // by const pointer
```

To declare an array of *const* pointers to *const chars*, the following would be used:

```
const char* const step[3] = { "left", "right", "hop" };
```

Neither the pointers nor the *chars* to which they point may be changed.

```
step[2] = "skip";      // error: can't change const pointer
step[2][1] = 'i';      // error: can't change const char
```

□

8.2.2 References

In a declaration T D where D has the form

    & *cv-qualifier-list*$_{opt}$ D1

the type of the contained identifier is ''... *cv-qualifier-list* reference to T.''   The type void& is not permitted.

For example,

```
void f(double& a) { a += 3.14; }
// ...
    double d = 0;
    f(d);
```

declares a to be a reference argument of f so the call f(d) will add 3.14 to d.

```
int v[20];
// ...
int& g(int i) { return v[i]; }
// ...
g(3) = 7;
```

declares the function g() to return a reference to an integer so g(3)=7 will assign 7 to the fourth element of the array v.

```
struct link {
    link* next;
};

link* first;
```

```
void h(link*& p)  // 'p' is a reference to pointer
{
    p->next = first;
    first = p;
    p = 0;
}

void k()
{
        link* q = new link;
        h(q);
}
```

declares p to be a reference to a pointer to `link` so `h(q)` will leave q with the value 0. See also §8.4.3.

There can be no references to references, no references to bit-fields (§9.6), no arrays of references, and no pointers to references. The declaration of a reference must contain an *initializer* (§8.4.3) except when the declaration contains an explicit `extern` specifier (§7.1.1), is a class member (§9.2) declaration within a class declaration, or is the declaration of an argument or a return type (§8.2.5); see §3.1.

8.2.3 Pointers to Members

In a declaration T D where D has the form

       complete-class-name :: *   *cv-qualifier-list$_{opt}$* D1

the type of the contained identifier is "... *cv-qualifier-list* pointer to member of class *complete-class-name* of type T."

For example,

```
class X {
public:
    void f(int);
    int a;
};

int X::* pmi = &X::a;
void (X::* pmf)(int) = &X::f;
```

declares pmi and pmf to be a pointer to a member of X of type `int` and a pointer to a member of X of type `void(int)`, respectively. They can be used like this:

```
X obj;
//...
obj.*pmi = 7;    // assign 7 to an integer
                 // member of obj
(obj.*pmf)(7);   // call a function member of obj
                 // with the argument 7
```

Note that a pointer to member cannot point to a static member of a class (§9.4). See also §5.5 and §5.3.

   ■ See the commentary at the end of this chapter for a discussion of pointers to members. □

8.2.4 Arrays

In a declaration T D where D has the form

>   D1 [*constant-expression*_{opt}]

then the contained identifier has type ''... array of T.'' If the *constant-expression* (§5.19) is present, it must be of integral type and have a value greater than 0. The constant expression specifies the number of elements in the array. If the constant expression is N, the array has N elements numbered 0 to N−1.

   An array may be constructed from one of the fundamental types (except `void`), from a pointer, from a pointer to member, from a class, from an enumeration, or from another array.

   When several ''array of'' specifications are adjacent, a multidimensional array is created; the constant expressions that specify the bounds of the arrays may be omitted only for the first member of the sequence. This elision is useful for function arguments of array types, and when the array is external and the definition, which allocates storage, is given elsewhere. The first *constant-expression* may also be omitted when the declarator is followed by an *initializer-list* (§8.4). In this case the size is calculated from the number of initial elements supplied (§8.4.1).

   The declaration

```
float fa[17], *afp[17];
```

declares an array of `float` numbers and an array of pointers to `float` numbers. The declaration

```
static int x3d[3][5][7];
```

declares a static three-dimensional array of integers, with rank 3×5×7. In complete detail, x3d is an array of three items; each item is an array of five arrays; each of the latter arrays is an array of seven integers. Any of the expressions x3d, x3d[i], x3d[i][j], x3d[i][j][k] may reasonably appear in an expression.

   When an identifier of array type appears in an expression, except as the operand of `sizeof` or `&` or used to initialize a reference (§8.4.3), it is converted into a pointer to the first member of the array. Because of this conversion, arrays are not modifiable lvalues. Except where it has been declared for a class (§13.4.5), the subscript operator `[]` is interpreted in such a way that E1[E2] is identical to `*((E1)+(E2))`. Because of the conversion rules that apply to `+`, if E1 is an array and E2 an integer, then E1[E2] refers to the E2-th member of E1. Therefore, despite its asymmetric appearance, subscripting is a commutative operation.

   A consistent rule is followed for multidimensional arrays. If E is an *n*-

dimensional array of rank $i \times j \times \cdots \times k$, then E appearing in an expression is converted to a pointer to an $(n-1)$-dimensional array with rank $j \times \cdots \times k$. If the $*$ operator, either explicitly or implicitly as a result of subscripting, is applied to this pointer, the result is the pointed-to $(n-1)$-dimensional array, which itself is immediately converted into a pointer.

For example, consider

```
int x[3][5];
```

Here x is a 3×5 array of integers. When x appears in an expression, it is converted to a pointer to (the first of three) five-membered arrays of integers. In the expression x[i], which is equivalent to *(x+i), x is first converted to a pointer as described; then x+i is converted to the type of x, which involves multiplying i by the length of the object to which the pointer points, namely five integer objects. The results are added and indirection applied to yield an array (of five integers), which in turn is converted to a pointer to the first of the integers. If there is another subscript the same argument applies again; this time the result is an integer.

It follows from all this that arrays in C++ are stored row-wise (last subscript varies fastest) and that the first subscript in the declaration helps determine the amount of storage consumed by an array but plays no other part in subscript calculations.

■ The C notion of an array – which C++ has adopted without change – is very low-level. Together with the pointer concept and the rules for converting an array to a pointer it provides a mechanism that closely models the memory and address concept of traditional hardware. This concept is simple, general, and potentially maximally efficient.

As a low-level concept, it also suffers the following major limitations:
[1] An array is of fixed size with its size fixed at compile time.
[2] An array is one-dimensional; talking about multidimensional arrays in C is simply referring to a conventional use of arrays of arrays.
[3] An array is not self-describing; that is, given a pointer to an array there is no information available to determine the array's size.
The last property means that passing pointers to arrays is inherently dangerous.

Suggestions have been made about how to improve the C array concept to make it "higher level" by removing any or all of the limitations listed above. They all suffer from the flaw that in making the notion of an array "higher level," they remove some of the low-level properties that make the C array/pointer notion such a powerful tool for building higher level abstractions. Rather than repairing the C array/pointer concept, one ought to use it to build higher level abstractions. Self-describing, range checking arrays or the yet more powerful associative arrays are obvious candidates for user-defined types built from arrays (see §14.2). The C++ concepts of class, operator overloading, and templates support these notions. □

8.2.5 Functions

In a declaration T D where D has the form

>   D1 (*argument-declaration-list*) *cv-qualifier-list*$_{opt}$

the contained identifier has the type "... *cv-qualifier-list*$_{opt}$ function taking arguments of type *argument-declaration-list* and returning T."

>> *argument-declaration-list:*
>>>   *arg-declaration-list*$_{opt}$ $\cdots$ $_{opt}$
>>>   *arg-declaration-list* , ...

>> *arg-declaration-list:*
>>>   *argument-declaration*
>>>   *arg-declaration-list* , *argument-declaration*

>> *argument-declaration:*
>>>   *decl-specifiers declarator*
>>>   *decl-specifiers declarator* = *expression*
>>>   *decl-specifiers abstract-declarator*$_{opt}$
>>>   *decl-specifiers abstract-declarator*$_{opt}$ = *expression*

If the *argument-declaration-list* terminates with an ellipsis, the number of arguments is known only to be equal to or greater than the number of argument types
specified; if it is empty, the function takes no arguments. The argument list
(void) is equivalent to the empty argument list. Except for this special case
void may not be an argument type (though types derived from void, such as
void*, may). Where legal, ", ..." is synonymous with "...". The standard header <stdarg.h> contains a mechanism for accessing arguments passed
using the ellipsis. See §12.1 for the treatment of array arguments.

> ■ Declaring f(...) may be useless, however, since there is no established portable
> way of accessing arguments to a function without at least one argument before the
> ellipsis. □

A single name may be used for several different functions in a single scope; this
is function overloading (§13). All declarations for a function taking a given set of
arguments must agree exactly both in the type of the value returned and in the
number and type of arguments; the presence or absence of the ellipsis is considered
part of the function type. Argument types that differ only in the use of typedef
names or unspecified argument array bounds agree exactly.

> ■ In particular f(int[]) and f(int*) are the same function. □

The return type and the argument types, but not the default arguments (§8.2.6), are
part of the function type. A *cv-qualifier-list* can be part of a declaration or definition of a nonstatic member function, and of a pointer to a member function; see
§9.3.1. It is part of the function type.

Functions cannot return arrays or functions, although they can return pointers and references to such things. There are no arrays of functions, although there may be arrays of pointers to functions.

Types may not be defined in return or argument types.

■ For example,

```
void f(struct S { int a, b; } arg)   // error
{
    // ...
}
```

The reason to prohibit this is that C++ relies on name equivalence and since *S* would be in the scope of *f()* the only legal calls of *f()* would be from within *f()* itself. The restriction on return types applies for the same reason.

```
enum E { A,B,C } f()   // error
{
    // ...
}
```

In C, these declarations are legal – if poor style – and potentially usable because C relies on structural equivalence in places. □

The *argument-declaration-list* is used to check and convert actual arguments in calls and to check pointer-to-function and reference-to-function assignments and initializations.

■ Since the point of declaration is after the complete declarator (§3.2) some pretty weird declarations can be written.

```
typedef int I;
void f()
{
    extern I I(I a);    // int I(int a);
    int i = I(1);       // call the function
}
```

Naturally, this is best avoided, though roughly equivalent examples can occur naturally when program fragments written separately are combined.

The definition of point of declaration also ensures that this example is illegal:

```
int f(int a = f(0));    // error: call of undeclared
                        // function 'f'
```

□

An identifier can optionally be provided as an argument name; if present in a function declaration, it cannot be used since it immediately goes out of scope; if present in a function definition (§8.3), it names a formal argument. In particular, argument names are also optional in function definitions and names used for an argument in different declarations and the definition of a function need not be the same.

The declaration

```
int i,
    *pi,
    f(),
    *fpi(int),
    (*pif)(const char*, const char*);
```

declares an integer i, a pointer pi to an integer, a function f taking no arguments
and returning an integer, a function fpi taking an integer argument and returning a
pointer to an integer, and a pointer pif to a function which takes two pointers to
constant characters and returns an integer. It is especially useful to compare the
last two. The binding of *fpi(int) is *(fpi(int)), so the declaration sug-
gests, and the same construction in an expression requires, the calling of a function
fpi, and then using indirection through the (pointer) result to yield an integer. In
the declarator (*pif)(const char*, const char*), the extra parentheses
are necessary to indicate that indirection through a pointer to a function yields a
function, which is then called.

The declaration

```
fseek(FILE*, long, int);
```

declares a function taking three arguments of the specified types. Since no return
value type is specified it is taken to be int (§7.1.6). The declaration

```
printf(const char* ...);
```

declares a function that can be called with varying number and types of arguments.
For example,

```
printf("hello world");
printf("a=%d b=%d", a, b);
```

It must always have a value, however, that can be converted to a const char* as
its first argument.

    ■ Argument names are optional in function declarations (and in a function definition
for arguments not used in the function). For example, a declaration for a function
pow might appear as

```
double pow(double x, double y);
```

or as

```
double pow(double, double);
```

    Sometimes it is useful to omit an argument name. A function may have extra
unused arguments − either to allow for a need envisioned for the future, or because
the function has changed so that it no longer requires an argument but not all the
calls have been changed or the header file containing the declaration hasn't been
changed yet. To prevent inappropriate use, a programmer may leave these unnamed.

    Alternatively, well-chosen names may be used to document unused arguments, as
in this example:

```
int f(int reserved_for_future_use);
int g(int no_longer_used);
```

Including argument names in function declarations allows for better documentation because the documenter can refer to an argument by name, rather than as "the second argument." □

8.2.6 Default Arguments

If an expression is specified in an argument declaration this expression is used as a default argument. All subsequent arguments must have default arguments supplied in this or previous declarations of this function. Default arguments will be used in calls where trailing arguments are missing. A default argument cannot be redefined by a later declaration (not even to the same value). A declaration may add default arguments, however, not given in previous declarations.

The declaration

```
point(int = 3, int = 4);
```

declares a function that can be called with zero, one, or two arguments of type int. It may be called in any of these ways:

```
point(1,2);  point(1);  point();
```

The last two calls are equivalent to point(1,4) and point(3,4), respectively.

■ The *point* function could equivalently have been declared like this:

```
point(int,int);
point(int, int = 4);
point(int = 3, int);
```

but, *not* like this:

```
point(int,int);
point(
    int = 3,    // error: default argument not at end
    int
);
point(int, int = 4);
```

or like this:

```
point(int,int);
point(int, int = 4);
point(
    int = 3,
    int = 4  // error: redefinition of default argument
);
```

C++ prohibits the obvious call syntax and semantics for calling *point()* given a default value for only the first argument, which would be

```
point(,3);        // syntax error
```

It was felt that having empty arguments significant was not only too subtle, but also
seriously decreased the opportunities for detecting errors; an extra comma in an
argument list is not an unusual result of bad typing or sloppy editing. □

■ One useful way of thinking about default arguments is as a shorthand for defining
a set of overloaded functions. For example, instead of writing

```
point(int = 3, int = 4);
```

we might have written

```
point (int,int);
inline point(int a) { return point(a,4); }
inline point() { return point(3,4); }
```

This is a plausible and general way of implementing default arguments. □

Default argument expressions have their names bound and their types checked
at the point of declaration, and are evaluated at each point of call. In the following
example, g will be called with the value f(2):

```
int a = 1;
int f(int);
int g(int x = f(a)); // default argument: f(::a)

void h() {
    a = 2;
    {
        int a = 3;
        g();            // g(f(::a))
    }
}
```

Local variables may not be used in default argument expressions. For example,

```
void f()
{
    int i;
    extern void g(int x = i);    // error
    // ...
}
```

Note that default arguments are evaluated before entry into a function and that
the order of evaluation of function arguments is implementation dependent. Consequently, formal arguments of a function may not be used in default argument
expressions. Formal arguments of a function declared before a default argument
expression are in scope and may hide global and class member names. For example,

```
int a;
int f(int a, int b = a);    // error: argument 'a'
                            // used as default argument
typedef int I;
int g(int I, int b = I(2)); // error: 'int' called
```

Similarly, the declaration of `X::mem1()` in the following example is illegal because no object is supplied for the nonstatic member `X::a` used as an initializer.

```
class X {
    int a;
    static b;
    mem1(int i = a); // error: nonstatic member 'a'
                     // used as default argument
    mem2(int i = b); // ok
};
```

The declaration of `X::mem2()` is legal, however, since no object is needed to access the static member `X::b`. Classes, objects, and members are described in §9.

■ Note that in a declaration of an object or function qualified by a class name default arguments are analyzed in the scope defined by the class name. For example,

```
int a;

class Y {
    static int a;
    f(int = a); // Y::a
    g(int);
};

Y::g(int x = a)          // Y::a
{
    // ...
}
```

□

A default argument is not part of the type of a function.

```
int f(int = 0);

void h()
{
    int j = f(1);
    int k = f();                // fine, means f(0)
}

int (*p1)(int) = &f;
int (*p2)() = &f;      // error: type mismatch
```

An overloaded operator (§13.4) cannot have default arguments.

■ Note that the usual scope rules apply to function declarations, so a function declaration in an inner scope hides a declaration of the same function in an enclosing scope. This implies that one cannot in an inner scope add default arguments to default arguments specified in the enclosing scope.

```
point(int, int = 4);
int p2(int = 3);

void f()
{
    extern point(
        int = 3,  // error: default argument not at end
        int
    );
    extern int p2(int = 4);      // ok
    // ...
}
```

□

■ Early versions of C++ allowed multiple default initializers for a single argument, as long as they were equivalent. Defining "equivalent" proved problematic, however. A programmer might reasonably consider the initializers for *x* here to be equivalent:

```
int f(int x = 1+3);
int f(int x = 2*2);          // error: two initializers for x
```

Now consider these initializers for *y*:

```
void g(float y = 1.333333333);
void g(float y = 4/3);     // error: two initializers for y
```

Are they equivalent?

One might propose that default initializations be considered equivalent if they are lexically identical, but doing so would make

```
void h(int a = f());
```

different from

```
void h(int a = f() + 0);      // error: two initializers
```

Further, it would require the two declarations

```
void j(char* p = "asdf");
void j(char* p = "asdf");     // error: two initializers
```

to match. This would be difficult to do on implementations where multiple occurrences of the same string do not share storage (whether two strings have the same address is implementation dependent − §2.5.4).

Allowing multiple occurrences of equivalent argument initializers would render the semantics of the language dependent on the implementation of constant expression evaluation. Allowing nontrivial equivalences (especially of expressions whose type is not integral) demands complexity in the constant expression evaluator which is not otherwise required by the language. Thus C++ no longer allows multiple default initializers for an argument. □

8.3 Function Definitions

Function definitions have the form

> *function-definition:*
> > *decl-specifiers$_{opt}$ declarator ctor-initializer$_{opt}$ fct-body*

> *fct-body:*
> > *compound-statement*

The *declarator* in a *function-definition* must contain a declarator with the form

> D1 (*argument-declaration-list*) *cv-qualifier-list$_{opt}$*

as described in §8.2.5.

The formal arguments are in the scope of the outermost block of the *fct-body*.

A simple example of a complete function definition is

```
int max(int a, int b, int c)
{
    int m = (a > b) ? a : b;
    return (m > c) ? m : c;
}
```

Here int is the *decl-specifiers*; max(int a, int b, int c) is the *declarator*; { /* ... */ } is the *fct-body*.

A *ctor-initializer* is used only in a constructor; see §12.1 and §12.6.

A *cv-qualifier-list* can be part of a nonstatic member function declaration, non-static member function definition, or pointer to member function only; see §9.3.1. It is part of the function type.

Note that unused formal arguments need not be named. For example,

```
void print(int a, int)
{
    printf("a = %d\n",a);
}
```

■ This is useful for reserving a space in the argument lists. This way future needs can be served without affecting the interface. Leaving the name out clearly states that the argument is not intended to be used, thus suppressing helpful compiler warnings to that effect. □

■ A function may change the value of its arguments. Such changes propagate back to the caller only if the argument is of a non-const reference type. Alternatively, a function can change values through pointers. For example,

```
void f(int i, int* p, int& r, const int& rc)
{
    i++;       // increment local copy only
    p++;       // increment local copy of pointer only
    (*p)++;    // increment object pointed to
    r++;       // increment actual argument
    rc++;      // error: actual argument considered constant
}
```

In early versions of C++ where temporaries were allowed as initializers for non-*const* references the increment *r++* might have affected only the temporary used as the argument and not the actual argument. This was a trap that caused subtle errors. Hence the change in the rules; see §8.4.3; □

■ There is only one guaranteed way of accessing arguments passed using the ... mechanism. The standard header file *<stdarg.h>* as specified for ANSI C will provide declarations that can be used by a function that does not know the number or types of its arguments when it is compiled. A familiar example of such a function is C's *printf*.

The *<stdarg.h>* header will declare the following:

– the type *va_list* used to represent variable argument lists.
– the macro

> *void va_start(va_list ap, lastarg);*

where *lastarg* is the last named parameter in the variable argument list. *va_start* must be called before the unnamed arguments are accessed; invoking *va_start* initializes *ap* to point to the first of the unnamed arguments.

– the macro

> *type va_arg(va_list ap, type);*

where *type* is the type of the next argument in the argument list. After *va_start* has been invoked, each invocation of *va_arg* will yield a value of type *type* from the argument list and will modify *ap* to point to the next argument.

– the macro or function

> *void va_end(va_list ap);*

va_end must be called after the arguments have been accessed and before the function returns.

The following example, which defines a function *numprint* to print an integer or floating point value given a *printf*-style format specification, shows how a variable-length argument list might be used:

```
#include <stdio.h>
#include <stdarg.h>

void numprint(char* format ...)
{
    va_list ap;

    va_start(ap, format);      // initialize ap


    for (char* p=format; *p; p++) {
        if (*p == '%') {
            switch (*++p) {
            case 'd':
                int ival=va_arg(ap, int);
                printf("%d", ival);
                break;
            case 'f':
                double dval=va_arg(ap, double);
                printf("%f", dval);
                break;
            }
        }
        else printf("%c",*p);
    }

    va_end(ap);                 // must call to clean up
}
```

C++ allows the declaration *f(...)* even though there is no guaranteed way of accessing the actual arguments from within the definition of *f()*. The intent was to provide an equivalent to C's completely unchecked function call. Don't use it.

People who are used to programming with implementations of Classic C where arguments are passed as a contiguous region of storage will look for ways of passing an argument list from a function specified with ... to another without copying or determining the number of actual arguments. For example,

```
void another_handler(const char* ...);

void some_error_handler(const char* format ...)
{
    // ...
    another_handler(format);    // not portable
    exit(99);
}
```

This is not portable in C or C++. Some implementations will pass some or all arguments in registers or special storage thus violating the assumption that arguments are passed in a contiguous region of storage. To do this portably, the *va_list* type and the macros from *<stdarg.h>* must be used. For example,

```
#include <stdarg.h>
void real_handler(const char*, va_list);

void my_error_handler(const char* format ...)
{
    // ...
    va_list ap;
    va_start(ap,format);
    real_handler(format,ap);    // portable
    va_end(ap);
    exit(99);
}
```

Naturally, *real_handler()* must in turn use the *va_arg()* macro to read its arguments. For example,

```
#include <stdarg.h>

void real_handler(const char* format, va_list ap)
{
    // assume that 'format' tells us that
    // three arguments, a char*, an int, and a double,
    // are passed - in that order - by the va_list 'ap'

    char* p = va_arg(ap, char*);    // read a char*
    int i = va_arg(ap,int);         // read an int
    double d = va_arg(ap,double);   // read a double
    // ...
}
```

The *<stdarg.h>* facility is a descendent of Andrew Koenig's *<varargs.h>* facility and its use is very similar. □

8.4 Initializers

A declarator may specify an initial value for the identifier being declared.

> *initializer:*
>> = *assignment-expression*
>> = { *initializer-list* $_{,opt}$ }
>> (*expression-list*)

> *initializer-list:*
>> *assignment-expression*
>> *initializer-list* , *assignment-expression*
>> { *initializer-list* $_{,opt}$ }

■ There are clearly too many notations for initialization, but each seems to serve a particular style of use well. The =*{initializer-list,opt}* notation was inherited from C and serves well for the initialization of data structures and arrays. For example,

```
struct Conf {
    char* month;
    int year;
    char* location;
} cpp[] = {
    "November", 1987, "Santa Fe",
    "October", 1988, "Denver",
    "November", 1989, "Tyngsboro",
    "April", 1990, "San Francisco"
};
```

The =*expression* notation also comes from C and is most natural for initializing simple variables, especially variables of arithmetic or pointer type. For example,

```
int i = 1;
complex z = complex(2.3,4);
char* p = "No.4.Op29";
```

The (*expression-list*) notation for initialization came from Simula and seems best when one is creating objects of types that do not fit the arithmetic mold. For example,

```
Vector v(100);  // vector of 100 integers
Task ring_monitor("monitor",1024,SHARED);
```

Rewriting the last two sets of examples shows the style difference.

```
int i(1);
complex z(2.3,4);
char* p("No.4.Op29");

Vector v = 100;          // vector of 100 integers
Task ring_monitor = Task("monitor",1024,SHARED);
```

Semantically there is little difference, but notation does matter and people will differ on aesthetics and develop a variety of styles. See also §8.2.4, §12.6. □

Automatic, register, static, and external variables may be initialized by arbitrary expressions involving constants and previously declared variables and functions.

```
int f(int);
int a = 2;
int b = f(a);
int c(b);
```

A pointer of type const T*, that is, a pointer to constant T, can be initialized with a pointer of type T*, but the reverse initialization is illegal. Objects of type T can be initialized with objects of type T independently of const and volatile modifiers on both the initialized variable and on the initializer. For example,

```
int a;
const int b = a;
int c = b;

const int* p0 = &a;
const int* p1 = &b;
int* p2 = &b;          // error: makes a pointer to
                       // nonconst point to a const

int *const p3 = p2;
int *const p4 = p1;    // error: makes a pointer to
                       // nonconst point to a const
const int* p5 = p1;
```

The reason for the two errors is the same: had those initializations been allowed
they would have allowed the value of something declared const to be changed
through an unqualified pointer.

Default argument expressions are more restricted; see §8.2.6.

Initialization of objects of classes with constructors is described in §12.6.1.
Copying of class objects is described in §12.8. The order of initialization of static
objects is described in §3.4 and §6.7.

Variables with storage class static (§3.5) that are not initialized are guaranteed
to start off as 0 converted to the appropriate type. So are members of static class
objects. The initial values of automatic and register variables that are not initialized are undefined.

When an initializer applies to a pointer or an object of arithmetic type, it consists of a single expression, perhaps in braces. The initial value of the object is
taken from the expression; the same conversions as for assignment are performed.

Note that since () is not an initializer,

```
X a();
```

is not the declaration of an object of class X, but the declaration of a function taking no argument and returning an X.

An initializer for a static member is in the scope of the member's class. For
example,

```
int a;

struct X {
    static int a;
    static int b;
};

int X::a = 1;
int X::b = a;    // X::b = X::a
```

■ The qualification $X::$ externs the scope of X for the duration of the declaration. This ensures that a means $X::a$ and not $::a$. This is exactly what happens when a member function is declared outside its class declaration. For example,

```
int a;

class Y {
        int a;
        int f();
};

int Y::f() { return a; }     // return Y::a not ::a
```

□

See §8.2.6 for initializers used as default arguments.

8.4.1 Aggregates

An *aggregate* is an array or an object of a class (§9) with no constructors (§12.1), no private or protected members (§11), no base classes (§10), and no virtual functions (§10.2). When an aggregate is initialized the *initializer* may be an *initializer-list* consisting of a brace-enclosed, comma-separated list of initializers for the members of the aggregate, written in increasing subscript or member order. If the aggregate contains subaggregates, this rule applies recursively to the members of the subaggregate. If there are fewer initializers in the list than there are members of the aggregate, then the aggregate is padded with zeros of the appropriate types.
For example,

```
struct S { int a; char* b; int c; };
S ss = { 1, "asdf" };
```

initializes `ss.a` with 1, `ss.b` with "asdf", and `ss.c` with 0.
An aggregate that is a class may also be initialized with an object of its class or of a class publicly derived from it (§12.8).
Braces may be elided as follows. If the *initializer-list* begins with a left brace, then the succeeding comma-separated list of initializers initializes the members of the aggregate; it is erroneous for there to be more initializers than members. If, however, the *initializer-list* or a subaggregate does not begin with a left brace, then only enough elements from the list are taken to account for the members of the aggregate; any remaining members are left to initialize the next member of the aggregate of which the current aggregate is a part.
For example,

```
int x[] = { 1, 3, 5 };
```

declares and initializes `x` as a one-dimensional array that has three members, since no size was specified and there are three initializers.

```
float y[4][3] = {
    { 1, 3, 5 },
    { 2, 4, 6 },
    { 3, 5, 7 },
};
```

is a completely-bracketed initialization: 1, 3, and 5 initialize the first row of the array y[0], namely y[0][0], y[0][1], and y[0][2]. Likewise the next two lines initialize y[1] and y[2]. The initializer ends early and therefore y[3] is initialized with zeros. Precisely the same effect could have been achieved by

```
float y[4][3] = {
    1, 3, 5, 2, 4, 6, 3, 5, 7
};
```

The last (rightmost) index varies fastest (§8.2.4).

The initializer for y begins with a left brace, but the one for y[0] does not, therefore three elements from the list are used. Likewise the next three are taken successively for y[1] and y[2]. Also,

```
float y[4][3] = {
    { 1 }, { 2 }, { 3 }, { 4 }
};
```

initializes the first column of y (regarded as a two-dimensional array) and leaves the rest 0.

Initialization of arrays of objects of a class with constructors is described in §12.6.1.

The initializer for a union with no constructor is either a single expression of the same type, or a brace-enclosed initializer for the first member of the union. For example,

```
union u { int a; char* b; };

u a = { 1 };
u b = a;
u c = 1;                    // error
u d = { 0, "asdf" };        // error
u e = { "asdf" };           // error
```

There may not be more initializers than there are members or elements to initialize. For example,

```
char cv[4] = { 'a', 's', 'd', 'f', 0 };   // error
```

is an error.

8.4.2 Character Arrays

A `char` array (whether signed or unsigned) may be initialized by a *string-literal*; successive characters of the string initialize the members of the array. For example,

```
char msg[] = "Syntax error on line %s\n";
```

shows a character array whose members are initialized with a string. Note that because '`\n`' is a single character and because a trailing '`\0`' is appended, `sizeof(msg)` is 25.

There may not be more initializers than there are array elements. For example,

```
char cv[4] = "asdf";   // error
```

is an error since there is no space for the implied trailing '`\0`'.

■ In this, C++ differs from ANSI C, where the example is allowed and is intended to be a convenience to the programmer. □

8.4.3 References

A variable declared to be a `T&`, that is "reference to type `T`" (§8.2.2), must be initialized by an object of type `T` or by an object that can be converted into a `T`. For example,

```
void f()
{
    int i;
    int& r = i;  // 'r' refers to 'i'
    r = 1;       // the value of 'i' becomes 1
    int* p = &r; // 'p' points to 'i'
    int& rr = r; // 'rr' refers to what 'r' refers to,
                 // that is, to 'i'
}
```

A reference cannot be changed to refer to another object after initialization.

■ This means that references are not first class citizens in C++. In a very real sense a reference is not an object. Sometimes, like `r` above for example, a reference can be optimized out of existence.

It would be easy to make references into "proper objects" in C++. This would require either that there be two sets of operations on references (one referring to the reference itself, the other referring through the reference to whatever it refers) or that operators have their meanings subtly dependent on their operands. Simula uses the former approach, Algol68 the latter. For C++ the former approach would require at least twelve new operators to match `&` (address of), `++` (prefix and postfix), `−−` (prefix and postfix), `=`, `==`, `!=`, `<`, `>`, `<=`, and `>=`. The latter approach seemed too subtle for C++.

Since C already had pointers that are first class citizens and proper objects, we decided to leave C++ references without pointer-like operations and let users express things that require pointer-like behavior using a pointer type.

A consequence of references not being objects is that there can be no arrays of references. A declaration of an array of references seems to make sense. For example,

```
int a, b;
int& v[] = { a, b };     // error: no arrays of references
```

Using such an array, however, would be most problematic. Unless several fundamental rules of the language are changed, accessing it would imply the existence of pointers to references. By definition `v[1]` means `*(v+1)`, and we would have thus created a pointer to a reference. □

Note that initialization of a reference is treated very differently from assignment to it.

■ Initialization is an operator that operates on the reference itself, whereas assignment – like every other operation – operates through the reference on the object referred to. □

Argument passing (§5.2.2) and function value return (§6.6.3) are initializations.

■ By far the major use of references in C++ is for passing arguments and for returning values. In the former case arguments of some type `const T&` act as an efficient alternative to call by value and in the latter case references are used to allow function calls on the left side of assignments. □

The initializer may be omitted for a reference only in an argument declaration (§8.2.5), in the declaration of a function return type, in the declaration of a class member within its class declaration (§9.2), and where the `extern` specifier is explicitly used. For example,

```
int& r1;          // error: initializer missing
extern int& r2;   // ok
```

If the initializer for a reference to type `T` is an lvalue of type `T` or of a type derived (§10) from `T` for which `T` is an accessible base (§4.6), the reference will refer to the initializer; otherwise, if and only if the reference is to a `const` an object of type `T` will be created and initialized with the initializer. The reference then becomes a name for that object. For example,

```
double d = 1.0;

double& rd = d;          // rd refers to 'd'
const double& rcd = d;   // rcd refers to 'd'

double& rd2 = 1;         // error: type mismatch
const double& rcd2 = 1;  // rcd2 refers to temporary
                         // with value '1'
```

■ The distinction between references to *const*s and references to non- *const*s is a major change from earlier definitions of C++. The distinction was made to eliminate a major source of errors and surprises. Earlier, all references could be initialized to refer to temporary objects so all the initializations above were legal.

Naturally, this feature will be faded out of implementations slowly, to avoid breaking working code. □

A reference to a volatile T can be initialized with a volatile T or a plain T but not a const T. A reference to a const T can be initialized with a const T or a plain T or something that can be converted into a plain T but not a volatile T. A reference to a plain T can be initialized only with a plain T.

The lifetime of a temporary object created in this way is the scope in which it is created (§3.5).

■ Note that *char* is a type that differs from both *signed char* and *unsigned char*, so in

```
char c = 'c';
char& rc = c;
const signed char& rsc = c;
const unsigned char& ruc = c;
```

rsc and ruc will each be initialized to a temporary, even though the representation of plain *char* will be identical to one of the explicit varieties. Had *const* been left out of the declarations of *rsc* and *ruc*, both initializations would have been errors. The initialization of rc does not require the use of a temporary.

This rule follows the same logic as the rule for pointers to the different flavors of *char* (§3.6.1). □

Note that a reference to a class B can be initialized by an object of a class D provided B is an accessible and unambiguous base class of D (in that case a D is a B); see §4.7.

Commentary

8.1c Pointers to Members

As initially defined, the C++ language provided no way of expressing the concept of a pointer to a member of a class (§9.2). When a pointer to a member function (§9.3) was needed, in an error handling function for example, users had to subvert the language's type checking.

The type of a nonmember function, *int f(char*)*, for example, is *int (char*)*, and a pointer to such a function is of type *int (*) (char*)*.

Pointers to nonmember functions can be declared and used like this:

```
void f(char*);   // declare function

f("Hello!");     // call

void (*pf)(char*);        // declare pointer to function

(*pf)("Goodbye!");        // call through pointer
```

Consider a trivial class for which the member function *f* and object *i* are declared, and an object *s* of that class, declared as follows:

```
struct S {
    int f(char*);
    int i;
};
int S::f(char*) { /* ... */ }
S s;
```

One can take the address of the member *i* in the object *s*, as follows:

```
int* ip = &s.i;          // ip points to s's member i
```

The notation for pointer to member of class *S* is *S::** (§8.2.3) and the notation for taking the address of a member of a class *S* is *&S::*. Thus one can take the address of a member *i* in class *S* as follows:

```
int S::* sip = &S::i;   // sip gets offset of 'i' in an S
```

Note that *&s.i* yields the address of *i* in the specific object *s*, whereas *&S::i* yields a representation of *i*'s relative position in all objects of class *S* (§5.3).

It is not legal to take the address of a member that doesn't have a name. For example,

```
class X { public: int a[2]; };
int X::*ai = &X::a[1];    // error: can't take address
                          // of unnamed member
```

In a definition the member function *f* of class *S* declared above appears as

```
int S::f(char*) { /* ... */ }
```

The type of *S::f* is now expressed as *int S::(char*)*. That is, "member of *S* that is a function taking a *char** argument and returning an *int*." A pointer to such a function is of type *int (S::*)(char*)*. One can now write

```
// declare and initialize pointer to member function
int (S::*pmf)(char*) = &S::f;

S s_var;
// call function through pointer for the object s_var
int j = (s_var.*pmf)("hello");
```

The syntax isn't the most readable one can imagine. It is, however, consistent with the C declarator syntax.

A pointer to member function can be called through a pointer to an object, as follows:

```
S* p;
// call function through pointer for the object *p
int k = (p->*pmf)("goodbye");
```

A virtual function (§10.2) can be called through a pointer to an object. Consider the following code:

```
struct B {
    virtual vf();
};

struct D : B {
    vf();
};


int f2(B* pb, int (B::*pbf)())
{
    // call virtual function pointed to
    // by pbf for object that pb points to
    return (pb->*pbf)();
}


void f1()
{
    D d;

    // call f2 and pass pointer to derived object
    // and pointer to virtual function in base class
    int i = f2(&d, &B::vf);
}
```

In *f2*, as called by *f1* shown here, *D::vf()* will be invoked. Naturally, the implementation looks in *d*'s table of virtual functions exactly as it would for a call to a virtual function identified by name rather than by a pointer.

8.1.1c Pointers to Static Members

Pointers to static members are ordinary pointers (§3.6.2). Thus the pointer to member syntax is not used with static members. The address of a static member is taken with the pointer syntax for nonmember objects. Similarly, a pointer that points to a static member is dereferenced as an ordinary pointer.

8.1.2c Implementation of Pointers to Members

Pointers to members must be implemented in a way that is consistent with the layout of class objects and the implementation of inheritance. In particular, since it is possible to have a pointer to a virtual function, the implementation of pointers to members depends on the way virtual base classes are represented and on the way virtual function call is implemented. The explanation below assumes the object and virtual table layout described in §10.2c and §10.10c.

This implies that pointers to members are implemented as structures holding relative positions in objects and indexes into virtual function tables. Thus, examining the value of a pointer to a member will not necessarily reveal a machine address. It is recommended that the reader understand the implementation of multiple inheritance with virtual base classes and virtual functions before reading this section (see §10.2c, §10.3c, §10.5c, §10.6c, §10.7c, §10.8c, and §10.10c).

The simplest implementation of a pointer to a nonstatic data member is simply the offset of the member in an object of the class type (the layout of class objects is described in §10.2c). Consider

```
class X {
public:
    int mem1;
    int mem2;
};

int X::*pm = &X::mem2;
```

If class *X* is laid out in memory such that *mem2* is offset four bytes from the start of an *X* object, then the value stored in *pm* could be *4*. To allow the representation of a null pointer to member to be *0*, however, a better choice is *5*; that is, the offset plus *1*.

Implementation of pointers to nonstatic member functions is more complicated since more information needs to be retained to call through the pointer successfully. A pointer to a nonstatic, nonvirtual function member must contain the following:

–   the offset, *delta*, of the *this* pointer appropriate for the class (possibly a base class) for which the function is defined (§10.2c, §10.3c), and
–   the address of the function.

A pointer to a nonstatic virtual function must contain

–   the offset of the *this* pointer,
–   the offset of the pointer to the class's virtual function table (the offset of its *vptr*) (§10.7c, §10.8c), and

  − the index of the function in the virtual function table.

Pointers to nonstatic member functions can be implemented as follows:

```
typedef int (*vptr) ();

class Ptr_to_mem_func {
public:
    short delta;   // offset of 'this' pointer
    short index;   // index into vtbl
    vptr faddr;    // address of nonvirtual function
    short v_off;   // offset of vptr
};
```

Note that the logical implementation for the virtual function table is an array of pointer to member functions.

Because a pointer to member function can point to either a virtual or a nonvirtual function, its implementation needs either the address of the nonvirtual function or the offset of the *ptr*, but not both. Thus the layout of *Ptr_to_mem_func* can be optimized as follows:

```
class Ptr_to_mem_func {
public:
    short delta;           // offset of 'this' pointer
    short index;           // index into vtbl
    union {
        vptr faddr;        // for nonvirtual function
        short v_off;       // for virtual function
    };
};
```

An index can never be negative, so the *index* field is used to determine whether the object is a pointer to a virtual or a nonvirtual member function. If *index* has a negative value, the object is a pointer to a nonvirtual member function and the *faddr* field contains the address of the function. If *index* has a positive value, the object is a pointer to a virtual member function and the *v_off* field contains the offset of the *vptr* in the class for which the function pointed to is defined. Consider

```
class B1 {
    int i;
public:
    int B1f();
    int virtual B1vf1();
    int virtual B1vf2();
};
```

```
class B2 {
     int i,j,k;
public:
     int B2f();
     int virtual B2vf1();
};


class D : public B1, public B2 { };

int (D::*pmf1)() = &D::B1f;
int (D::*pmf2)() = &D::B2f;
int (D::*pmf3)() = &D::B1vf2;
int (D::*pmf4)() = &D::B2vf1;
```

If base and derived classes are laid out as described in §10, then the pointers to
member functions will be declared and initialized to the equivalent of the following:

```
Ptr_to_mem_func pmf1 =
{
     0,             // B1 is the first base class
     -1,            // indicates a nonvirtual function
     &B1::B1f       // address of function
};


Ptr_to_mem_func pmf2 =
{
     8,             // offset of B2 part of a D object
     -1,            // indicates a nonvirtual function
     &B2::B2f       // address of function
};


Ptr_to_mem_func pmf3 =
{
     0,             // B1 is the first base class
     2,             // index of B1vf2 in B1's vtbl
     4              // offset of B1's vptr
};


Ptr_to_mem_func pmf4 =
{
     8,             // offset of B2 part of a D object
     1,             // index of B2vf1 in B2's vtbl
     12             // offset of B2's vptr
};
```

Naturally, the declaration

```
int (D::*pmf0)() = 0;
```

produces the equivalent to the following initialization:

```
Ptr_to_mem_func pmf0 = {0, 0, 0};
```

9

Classes

A *class* is a user-defined type. A class declaration specifies the representation of objects of the class and the set of operations that can be applied to such objects. This chapter presents the syntax and semantics for simple classes.

The definition of both `static` and non-`static` members is discussed, and the scope rules involving classes and functions − including local and nested classes containing member functions − are described. The mechanisms for controlling the layout of class objects, for conforming to externally imposed formats, and for maintaining compatibility with C layouts (`structs`, `unions` and bit-fields) are presented.

The commentary at the end of this chapter discusses C++'s facilities for expressing interfaces and how design decisions in this area affect compile-time, run-time, and space efficiencies. Derived classes (that is, inheritance), access control, and special member functions are discussed in the next three chapters.

9   Classes

A class is a type. Its name becomes a *class-name* (§9.1), that is, a reserved word within its scope.

> *class-name:*
> > *identifier*

*Class-specifier*s and *elaborated-type-specifier*s (§7.1.6) are used to make *class-name*s. An object of a class consists of a (possibly empty) sequence of members.

> *class-specifier:*
> > *class-head* { *member-list$_{opt}$* }

class-head:

>>*class-key identifier$_{opt}$ base-spec$_{opt}$*
>>*class-key class-name base-spec$_{opt}$*

class-key:

```
class
struct
union
```

The name of a class can be used as a *class-name* even within the *member-list* of the class specifier itself.

■ For example,

```
class link { link* next; };
```

Note that classes may be unnamed. An unnamed class cannot have constructors (§12.1) or destructors (§12.4) and cannot be passed as an argument or returned as a value (since it does not have a name that would allow a matching formal argument or a return value to be declared). □

A *class-specifier* is commonly referred to as a class declaration. A class is considered defined when its *class-specifier* has been seen even though its member functions are in general not yet defined.

■ Except for historical reasons, a class declaration would have been called a class definition. □

Objects of an empty class have a nonzero size.

■ This implies that objects of an empty class can be allocated and have distinct addresses. For example,

```
class empty {}; // class with no members

empty e1, e2;
empty* p1 = &e1;

void f()
{
    if (p1 == &e2) error("impossible");
}
```

Empty classes can be used as place holders during program development. In particular, an empty class is sometimes used as a base class (§10) where the programmer suspects that two classes have something in common, but hasn't yet determined exactly what. □

■ Nameless classes can be used (only) to declare singleton objects. For example,

```
struct {
    // ...
} global;
```

Such objects cannot be passed as arguments except by suppressing type checking using the ellipsis (§8.2.5). A nameless class cannot have a constructor (§12.1) or a destructor (§12.4). Typically, if a class is useful it represents some concept and since that will have a name it would be only natural to name the class. A major use of the unnamed class syntax is the C construct

```
typedef struct { /* ... */ } mystruct;
```

that is equivalent to the C++ construct

```
struct mystruct { /* ... */ };
```

□

Class objects may be assigned, passed as arguments to functions, and returned by functions (except objects of classes for which copying has been restricted; see §12.8). Other plausible operators, such as equality comparison, can be defined by the user; see §13.4.

■ "Class" is the key concept of C++. A class is a user-defined type. The class is the unit of data hiding and encapsulation (§11.1). The class is the mechanism supporting data abstraction by allowing representation details to be hidden and accessed exclusively through a set of operations defined as part of the class (§9.3, §11.4). Polymorphism is supported through classes with virtual functions (§10.2). The class provides a unit of modularity. In particular, a class with only static members (§9.4) provides a facility akin to what is called a "module" in many languages: a named collection of objects and functions in their own name space. □

A structure is a class declared with the *class-key* struct; its members and base classes (§10) are public by default (§11). A union is a class declared with the *class-key* union; its members are public by default and it holds only one member at a time (§9.5).

■ Thus the C++ class concept can be seen as a generalization of the C notion of a structure or − looking at it the other way − the C concept of a structure is a simple variant of the C++ class concept. In particular, C structures do not support member functions of any kind. Having a C struct be a simple variant of a C++ class has important implications for cooperation between C and C++ programs. The layout of structures that are both C and C++ is identical, so such structures can be shared freely between C and C++ programs without space or time overheads caused by conversion or translation. Even for classes using features not available to C, the correspondence between the C++ class layout and an equivalent C structure layout is usually obvious so that sharing can be trivially achieved. See, for example §10.1c. □

9.1 Class Names

A class declaration introduces a new type. For example,

```
struct X { int a; };
struct Y { int a; };
X a1;
Y a2;
int a3;
```

declares three variables of three different types. This implies that

```
a1 = a2;        // error: Y assigned to X
a1 = a3;        // error: int assigned to X
```

are type mismatches, and that

```
int f(X);
int f(Y);
```

declare an overloaded (§13) function f() and not simply a single function f() twice. For the same reason,

```
struct S { int a; };
struct S { int a; };  // error, double definition
```

is an error because it defines S twice.

■ In other words, C++ relies on name equivalence, *not* on structural equivalence of types. In this it differs from ANSI C – if not from Classic C – that explicitly allows a form of structural equivalence between separately compiled program fragments. □

A class declaration introduces the class name into the scope where it is declared and hides any class, object, function, or other declaration of that name in an enclosing scope (§3.2). If a class name is declared in a scope where an object, function, or enumerator of the same name is also declared the class can be referred to only using an *elaborated-type-specifier* (§7.1.6). For example,

```
struct stat {
    // ...
};

stat gstat;             // use plain 'stat' to
                        // define variable

int stat(struct stat*); // redefine 'stat' as function
```

```
void f()
{
    struct stat* ps;     // 'struct' prefix needed
                         // to name struct stat
    // ...
    stat(ps);            // call stat()
    // ...
}
```

■ This apparently spurious overloading mechanism exists to accommodate programs relying on the C notion of separate name spaces for structure names and other names. It does so without seriously compromising the C++ notion that the name of a class is the name of a type that obeys the usual scope rules and can be used without a special prefix (*struct*, or *union*, for example) telling the compiler that it is the name of a class. □

■ Note that this kind of name overloading can lead to ambiguities. Consider having both a constructor and a function of the same name.

```
class X {
    // ...
    X(int);
};

void X(int);
```

Any use of *X(int)* is ambiguous.

```
X(1);    // error: constructor or global function called?
```

Having both a function and a conversion function can cause exactly the same problem.

```
class XX { /* ... */ };

class YY {
    // ...
    operator XX();
};

void XX(YY);
```

Any use of *XX(YY)* is ambiguous.

```
YY a;
XX(a);  // error: global function call or
        // conversion of 'a' to an XX?
```

□

An *elaborated-type-specifier* with a *class-key* used without declaring an object or function introduces a class name exactly like a class declaration but without defining a class. For example,

```
struct s { int a; };

void g()
{
    struct s;    // hide global struct 's'
    s* p;        // refer to local struct 's'
    struct s { char* p; };   // declare local struct 's'
}
```

Such declarations allow declaration of classes that refer to each other. For example,

```
class vector;

class matrix {
    // ...
    friend vector operator*(matrix&, vector&);
};

class vector {
    // ...
    friend vector operator*(matrix&, vector&);
};
```

Declaration of friends is described in §11.4, operator functions in §13.4. If a class mentioned as a friend has not been declared its name is entered in the same scope as the name of the class containing the friend declaration (§11.4).

■ For example,

```
class X {
    friend class Y;     // 'Y' is in enclosing scope
};

Y* p;   // 'Y' is in global scope because 'X' is
```

☐

An *elaborated-type-specifier* (§7.1.6) can also be used in the declarations of objects and functions. It differs from a class declaration in that if a class of the elaborated name is in scope the elaborated name will refer to it. For example,

```
struct s { int a; };

void g()
{
    struct s* p = new s;     // refer to global 's'
    p->a = 1;
}
```

A name declaration takes effect immediately after the *identifier* is seen. For example,

```
class A * A;
```

first specifies A to be the name of a class and then redefines it as the name of a
pointer to an object of that class. This means that the elaborated form `class A`
must be used to refer to the class. Such artistry with names can be confusing and
is best avoided.

A *typedef-name* (§7.1.3) that names a class is a *class-name*; see also §7.1.3.

■ A nickname can be used to avoid problems caused by there being no effective way
of making a class name local to a single compilation short of using local (§9.8) or
nested classes (§9.7). Instead of declaring the class name *static*, as one could do
for an object name, one can choose a name for the class that is almost certain not to
clash with any other class name. Having done that, the typedef can be used to provide a conveniently short name for use in the code. For example,

```
class long_name_that_will_not_clash_with_anything;

class long_name_that_will_not_clash_with_anything {
        // ...
};

typedef long_name_that_will_not_clash_with_anything X;

// from now on we'll just call it 'X'
```

□

9.2 Class Members

> *member-list:*
> > *member-declaration member-list*$_{opt}$
> > *access-specifier : member-list*$_{opt}$
>
> *member-declaration:*
> > *decl-specifiers*$_{opt}$ *member-declarator-list*$_{opt}$;
> > *function-definition* ;$_{opt}$
> > *qualified-name* ;
>
> *member-declarator-list:*
> > *member-declarator*
> > *member-declarator-list* , *member-declarator*
>
> *member-declarator:*
> > *declarator pure-specifier*$_{opt}$
> > *identifier*$_{opt}$: *constant-expression*
>
> *pure-specifier:*
> > = 0

A *member-list* may declare data, functions, classes, enumerations (§7.2), bit-fields (§9.6), friends (§11.4), and type names (§7.1.3, §9.1). A *member-list* may also contain declarations adjusting the access to member names; see §11.3. A member may not be declared twice in the *member-list*. The *member-list* defines the full set of members of the class. No member can be added elsewhere.

■ This means that

```
class X {
    int i;
    int i;   // error: redefinition
    int j;
};

int X::k;        // error: attempt to define member
                 // outside class declaration
```

exhibits two errors.

The rule against double declarations also applies to function members:

```
class Y {
    f();
    f() { /* ... */ }   // error: redeclaration
};
```

□

Note that a single name can denote several function members provided their types are sufficiently different (§13).

■ Note that a name cannot denote both a function and a data member.

```
class Y {
    int f();
    int f;       // error
};
```

This could be made to work but only at the expense of a major complication of the overloading resolution rules. Consider

```
struct Z {
    int f();
    int (*f)(); // error
};

void g(Z* p)
{
    p->f();           // would have been ambiguous
}
```

The same restriction against overloading nonfunction names applies to nonmember objects. For example,

```
int glob();
int (*glob)();                // error
```

```
void h()
{
    glob();        // would have been ambiguous
}
```

□

Note that a *member-declarator* cannot contain an *initializer* (§8.4). A member can be initialized using a constructor; see §12.1.

A member may not be `auto`, `extern`, or `register`.

The *decl-specifiers* can be omitted in function declarations only. The *member-declarator-list* can be omitted only after a *class-specifier*, an *enum-specifier*, or *decl-specifiers* of the form `friend` *elaborated-type-specifier*. A *pure-specifier* may be used only in the declaration of a virtual function (§10.2).

Members that are class objects must be objects of previously declared classes. In particular, a class `cl` may not contain an object of class `cl`, but it may contain a pointer or reference to an object of class `cl`.

■ Since a class is defined immediately after the closing brace (`}`) has been seen the following is allowed:

```
struct Y {
    int i;
} m1, m2 = { sizeof(Y) }, m3 = m2;
```

Before the end of the declaration of a class, its name can be used only where its size need not be known. For example,

```
class X {
    X();
    X* p;
    X& r;
    static X a; // a declaration; NOT a definition
    X f();
    void g(X);
    int h() { return sizeof(X); }
};
```

It may look as if the definition of `X::h()` uses the size of `X` before the end of the declaration of `X`, but because definitions of inline functions are not type checked until after the complete class declaration has been seen (§9.3.2), that is not the case.

Consider also

```
class Z {
    int i;
    enum { e = sizeof(Z); };       // error: Z undefined
    int f(int i=sizeof(Z));        // error: Z undefined
    int g(int i=sizeof(Z)) {}      // error: Z undefined

    void h(int i) { i=sizeof(Z); } // ok
    Z() : i(sizeof(Z)) {}          // ok
};
```

□

When an array is used as the type of a nonstatic member all dimensions must be specified.

■ In particular, the old C trick of declaring a structure with an empty array as its last member − and later using that array to access space beyond the end of the object − is illegal.

```
struct trick {
        // some members
        char v[];    // error
        char& access(int i)
        {
                return v[i]; // access beyond the end of object
        }
};
```

One practical reason for this restriction is that this trick (in any of its many forms) causes chaos where derived classes and virtual functions are used. In particular, the pointer to the table of virtual functions is often placed at the end of an object. Thus,

```
struct trick {
        virtual f();
        char v[];    // error
        char& access(int i)
        {
                return v[i]; // access beyond the end of object
        }
};
```

would leave that pointer as the first four characters of *trick::v*.

Note that similar tricks involving access beyond the end of an array are equally suspect in relying on undefined behavior (§5.9). A safer alternative is

```
struct ok {
        // some members
        ok(int s) : sz(s), v(new char[s]) { }

        char* v;
        unsigned sz;

        char& access(int i)
        {
                return v[i]; // ok
        }
};
```

□

A simple example of a class declaration is

```
struct tnode {
    char tword[20];
    int count;
    tnode *left;
    tnode *right;
};
```

which contains an array of twenty characters, an integer, and two pointers to similar structures. Once this declaration has been given, the declaration

```
tnode s, *sp;
```

declares s to be a tnode and sp to be a pointer to a tnode. With these declarations, sp->count refers to the count member of the structure to which sp points; s.left refers to the left subtree pointer of the structure s; and s.right->tword[0] refers to the initial character of the tword member of the right subtree of s.

Nonstatic data members of a class declared without an intervening *access-specifier* are allocated so that later members have higher addresses within a class object. The order of allocation of nonstatic data members separated by an *access-specifier* is implementation dependent (§11.1). Implementation alignment requirements may cause two adjacent members not to be allocated immediately after each other; so may requirements for space for managing virtual functions (§10.2) and virtual base classes (§10.1); see also §5.4.

    ■ See also §11.1. □

A function member (§9.3) with the same name as its class is a constructor (§12.1). A static data member, enumerator, member of an anonymous union, or nested type may not have the same name as its class.

9.3 Member Functions

A function declared as a member (without the friend specifier; §11.4) is called a member function, and is called using the class member syntax (§5.2.4). For example,

```
struct tnode {
    char tword[20];
    int count;
    tnode *left;
    tnode *right;
    void set(char*, tnode* l, tnode* r);
};
```

Here set is a member function and can be called like this:

```
void f(tnode n1, tnode n2)
{
    n1.set("abc",&n2,0);
    n2.set("def",0,0);
}
```

The definition of a member function is considered to be within the scope of its class. This means that (provided it is nonstatic §9.4) it can use names of members of its class directly. A static member function can use only the names of static members, enumerators, and nested types directly. If the definition of a member function is lexically outside the class declaration, the member function name must be qualified by the class name using the : : operator. For example,

```
void tnode::set(char* w, tnode* 1, tnode* r)
{
    count = strlen(w)+1;
    if (sizeof(tword)<=count)
        error("tnode string too long");
    strcpy(tword,w);
    left = 1;
    right = r;
}
```

The notation tnode::set specifies that the function set is a member of and in the scope of class tnode. The member names tword, count, left, and right refer to members of the object for which the function was called. Thus, in the call n1.set("abc",&n2,0), tword refers to n1.tword, and in the call n2.set("def",0,0) it refers to n2.tword. The functions strlen, error, and strcpy must be declared elsewhere.

■ Member functions are sometimes referred to as "*methods*." This terminology comes from Smalltalk, where calling a member function is referred to as "*sending a message*." The analogy is not exact because of the reliance on static type checking in C++; the analogy between methods and member functions is somewhat more accurate for virtual functions (§10.2). Similarly, the Smalltalk phrase "*instance variable*" is sometimes used to mean data member. □

Members may be defined (§3.1) outside their class declaration if they have already been declared but not defined in the class declaration; they may not be redeclared. See also §3.3. Function members may be mentioned in friend declarations after their class has been defined.

■ Why can't functions be added to a class after the end of the class declaration? If this were allowed, a user could gain access to a class simply by declaring an additional function.

```
class X {
      int a;        // accessible only by X::f()
public:
      f();
};

int X::hijack()
{
      return a++; // error: 'hijack' not a member of X
}
```

This would, in particular, invalidate the desirable property that a C++ class contains the complete list of functions that can use private members. This property is important for debugging and for understanding a program in general. A class declaration is the complete specification of the interfaces provided by a class. If it were possible to add functions later this would not be the case. Similarly, it is not possible to specify properties of a class, such as what base classes and members it has, before the class declaration itself. For example,

```
class circle : public shape;     // error

void f(circle* p)
{
        // use shape attributes of 'p'
}
```

See also §11.4. Allowing such techniques is technically feasible, but undesirable since it would require both the compiler and the programmer to keep track of partially specified classes.

If a function is explicitly declared *friend* (§7.1.5), it is not a member of the class in which the *friend* declaration occurs, though it may be a member of some other class. Member functions may be explicitly declared *inline* (§9.3), *static* (§7.1.1), or *virtual* (§9.3). They have external linkage by default and may not be explicitly declared *extern*.

```
class C {
      friend f1();        // declare global f1() to be a friend
      friend C2::f1();    // declare C2::f1() to be a friend
      inline f2();
      static f3();
      virtual f5();
      inline virtual f6();
      extern f7();        // error: 'extern' member
};
```

□

Each member function that is called must have exactly one definition in a program.

■ Only an *inline* member function can be defined in several translation units, and even then it is illegal to provide different definitions in different translation units. Allowing that would have opened the possibility of operations on a given object changing their meaning as the object was passed along from function to function. Worse, for virtual inline functions it would lead to the requirement that each object could potentially carry around its own table of virtual functions so that identical operations on objects of (apparently) identical types would have different meanings. This is an unacceptable corruption of the notion of a type. □

The effect of calling a nonstatic member function (§9.4) of a class X for something that is not an object of class X is undefined.

■ For example,

```
((X*)0)->f();
```

is not guaranteed to work. In particular, this will not work for virtual functions on any implementation since the information needed to find the appropriate virtual function for an object of type X is not found at location 0. Even for nonvirtual functions, one should expect this trick to fail eventually because specialized C++ implementations might assume something about the contents of objects even when calling nonvirtual functions. In particular, one might expect implementations instrumented for debugging, interpreters, and implementations supporting dynamic loading to be sensitive to "housekeeping" information placed in the objects by the compiler.

Naturally, this trick would work only if $f()$ either checks its *this* pointer before accessing any members or never uses any member of the object for which it was called. In the latter case, the function should have been declared *static* (§9.4). □

9.3.1 The `this` Pointer

In a nonstatic (§9.3) member function, the keyword `this` is a pointer to the object for which the function is called.

■ This means that within a member function of a class X, a member of a class X can be equivalently referred to as *mem* and *this->mem*. This equivalence is rarely used explicitly, but consider the following:

```
class X {
    int a;
public:
    X(int a) { this->a = a; }
};
```

The most common explicit use of *this* is in linked list manipulations where *this* is added to the representation of some list. □

■ In many languages, notably Smalltalk, the equivalent construct for identifying the object for which a function is invoked is called *self*. □

■ The simplest way to implement a call to a member function is for a compiler to transform it into an ordinary function call in the generated code. A pointer to the object for which the member function is called − its *this* pointer − is needed.

Given a class A, a call to the member function $A::f$, for example,

```
A* pa;
pa->f(2);
```

could be transformed into

```
f(pa,2);          // generated code
```

This implies that calling a C++ member function does not incur run-time overheads compared to a C function call. In particular, since a call of a member function may cross a protection boundary (as defined by the access rules of a class; see §11) the access control mechanisms do not imply a run-time cost. On some machine architectures, the efficiency of the code generated for member function calls can be improved if the compiler passes the `this` pointer in a register. □

The type of `this` in a member function of a class X is X `*const` unless the member function is declared `const` or `volatile`; in those cases, the type of `this` is const X `*const` and volatile X `*const`, respectively. A function declared `const` and `volatile` has a `this` with the type const volatile X `*const`. See also §18.3.3. For example,

```
struct s {
    int a;
    int f() const;
    int g() { return a++; }
    int h() const { return a++; } // error
};

int s::f() const { return a; }
```

The `a++` in the body of `s::h` is an error because it tries to modify (a part of) the object for which `s::h()` is called. This is not allowed in a const member function where `this` is a pointer to const, that is, `*this` is a const.

A const member function (that is, a member function declared with the const qualifier) may be called for const and non-const objects, whereas a non-const member function may be called only for a non-const object. For example,

```
void k(s& x, const s& y)
{
    x.f();
    x.g();
    y.f();
    y.g();          // error
}
```

The call `y.g()` is an error because `y` is const and `s::g()` is a non-const member function that could (and does) modify the object for which it was called.

Similarly, only volatile member functions (that is, a member function declared with the volatile specifier) may be invoked for volatile objects. A member function can be both const and volatile.

■ In early implementations of C++, *this* was non-*const*, and assignment to *this* in constructors and destructors had special meaning; see §18.3. The techniques relying on assignment to *this* proved error-prone and have been replaced by user-defined free store management through class specific *operator new()* and *operator delete()* functions (§12.5). □

Constructors (§12.1) and destructors (§12.4) may be invoked for a const or volatile object. Constructors (§12.1) and destructors (§12.4) cannot be declared const or volatile.

9.3.2 Inline Member Functions

A member function may be defined (§8.3) in the class declaration, in which case it is inline (§7.1.2). Defining a function within a class declaration is equivalent to declaring it inline and defining it immediately after the class declaration; this rewriting is considered to be done after preprocessing but before syntax analysis and type checking of the function definition. Thus

```
int b;
struct x {
      char* f() { return b; }
      char* b;
};
```

is equivalent to

```
int b;
struct x {
      char* f();
      char* b;
};
```

```
inline char* x::f() { return b; } // moved
```

Thus the b used in x::f() is X::b and not the global b.

■ Note that this "rewriting" is a semantic notion and not a prescription for a particular implementation.

This rewriting rule implies that an inline function may refer to members declared lexically after it in the class declaration. This allows even mutually recursive functions to be written without forward declarations.

```
class X {
    void f() { g(); }
    void g() { f(); }
};
```

This is desirable, because the rule against double declarations of class members (§9.2) prevents forward declarations from being used.

```
class X {
    void g();
    void f() { g(); }
    void g() { f(); }  // error: double declaration of 'g'
};
```

   □

   Member functions can be defined even in local or nested class declarations where this rewriting would be syntactically illegal. See §9.8 for a discussion of local classes and §9.7 for a discussion of nested classes.

9.4 Static Members

A data or function member of a class may be declared static in the class declaration. There is only one copy of a static data member, shared by all objects of the class in a program. A static member is not part of objects of a class. Static members of a global class have external linkage (§3.3). The declaration of a static data member in its class declaration is *not* a definition. A definition is required elsewhere; see also §18.3.

   ■ This implies that one can declare static members of a class without having access to its definition. For example,

```
class X;

class Y {
public:
    static class X sx;
    // ...
};
```

A static data member is a separate object. In particular, a static member is not *const* just because some object of the class of which it is a static member is *const*.

```
class X { /* ... */ };

const Y a;
Y b;

void f(X& xx)
{
        Y::sx = xx;      // ok
}
```

   □

   A static member function does not have a this pointer so it can access non-static members of its class only by using . or ->. A static member function cannot be virtual. There cannot be a static and a nonstatic member function with the same name and the same argument types.

Static members of a local class (§9.8) have no linkage and cannot be defined outside the class declaration. It follows that a local class cannot have static data members.

A static member mem of class cl can be referred to as cl::mem (§5.1), that is, independently of any object. It can also be referred to using the . and -> member access operators (§5.2.4). When a static member is accessed through a member access operator, the expression on the left side of the . or -> is not evaluated. The static member mem exists even if no objects of class cl have been created. For example, in the following, run_chain, idle, and so on exist even if no process objects have been created:

```
class process {
    static int no_of_processes;
    static process* run_chain;
    static process* running;
    static process* idle;
    // ...
public:
    // ...
    int state();
    static void reschedule();
    // ...
};
```

and reschedule can be used without reference to a process object, as follows:

```
void f()
{
    process::reschedule();
}
```

Static members of a global class are initialized exactly like global objects and only in file scope. For example,

```
void process::reschedule() { /* ... */ };
int process::no_of_processes = 1;
process* process::running = get_main();
process* process::run_chain = process::running;
```

Static members obey the usual class member access rules (§11) except that they can be initialized (in file scope).

The type of a static member does not involve its class name; thus the type of process :: no_of_processes is int and the type of &process :: reschedule is void(*)().

■ The use of the word *static* to indicate that a member of a class is not associated with an individual object of a class (and not replicated in each object) parallels the use of the word *static* to indicate that only one copy of a local variable is to be used for all calls of a function. For data members, this means that the member has the storage class *static* (§3.5); it still has external linkage (§3.3), though.

The purpose of *static* members is to reduce the need for global variables by providing alternatives that are local to a class. A *static* member function or variable acts as a global for members of its class without affecting the rest of a program. In particular, its name does not clash with the names of global variables and functions or with the names of members of other classes. The association between the *static* members and their class is explicit and obvious, whereas the use of global variables and functions for similar purposes is neither. □

■ One could consider allowing initializers for data members within a class declaration. For example,

```
class X {
        static int x1 = 1;              // error
        static const int x2 = 2;        // error
        static int x3 = sqrt(2);        // error
        static const int x4 = sqrt(2);  // error
        // ...
};
```

The problem is that class declarations typically appear in header files, so a declaration like the one above will be seen by a compiler many times while compiling a multifile program. Especially when dealing with general initializers, it is important that there is exactly one definition of an object in a program. Allowing examples like the ones above would complicate separate compilation.

Allowing examples, such as *X::x1* above, where the complications are minor would introduce a complication into the language that does not seem to provide benefits commensurate with the confusion it would cause by allowing initializers for member declarations in a few selected cases. Also, many such special cases can be handled by using an enumerator instead of a *const*.

```
class Y {
    enum { y1 = 1 };  // Y::y1 is the constant 1
};
```

□

9.5 Unions

A union may be thought of as a structure whose member objects all begin at offset zero and whose size is sufficient to contain any of its member objects. At most one of the member objects can be stored in a union at any time. A union may have member functions (including constructors and destructors), but not virtual (§10.2) functions. A union may not have base classes. A union may not be used as a base class.

■ Since a union is fundamentally a low-level construct for saving storage, there seems little reason to support the derived class mechanisms for it. Consider, for example, allowing a union as a base class. How would the overriding of virtual functions (§10.2) be handled? Two members of the union may have completely different sets of virtual functions. □

An object of a class with a constructor or a destructor or a user-defined assignment operator (§13.4.3) cannot be a member of a union. A union can have no `static` data members.

■ It would do no good to be able to define a union member function *virtual* since a union cannot be a base class.

The rule against unions of classes with constructors or destructors can be a nuisance, especially when dealing with software − such as YACC − that requires the use of unions. The rule is necessary, though, because member functions for a class that has constructors usually rely on being invoked on objects that have been correctly constructed. In particular, the invocation of assignment operators and destructors on something that has not been correctly constructed will usually cause a disaster.

Where necessary, one can separate the representation of a class from its operations using a derived class (§10) like this:

```
struct Xrep { // traditional C structure
              // can be put in a union
    // data members only
};

class X : private Xrep { // C++ class with functions
                         // maintaining proper consistency
                         // of the representation
    // constructors, destructors, ...
};
```

Naturally, this technique must be used with care, but doing so in stylized tools like YACC is quite feasible. □

A union of the form

```
union { member-list } ;
```

is called an anonymous union; it defines an unnamed object (and not a type). The names of the members of an anonymous union must be distinct from other names in the scope in which the union is declared; they are used directly in that scope without the usual member access syntax (§5.2.4). For example,

```
void f()
{
    union { int a; char* p; };
    a = 1;
    // ...
    p = "Jennifer";
    // ...
}
```

Here a and p are used like ordinary (nonmember) variables, but since they are union members they have the same address.

A global anonymous union must be declared `static`.

■ Suppose no storage class specifier were required for a global anonymous union. What should be its linkage? Making it *internal* would make global anonymous unions differ from all other variables. If the default were *external*, an implementation would have to ensure that each member name match only the same name in an identical anonymous union. This could be difficult and might become either a bottleneck for portability or a source of incompatibilities between implementations. Requiring that a global anonymous union be explicitly declared static allows the language to provide global anonymous unions without having the user worry about surprising side effects. □

An anonymous union may not have `private` or `protected` members (§11). An anonymous union may not have function members.

■ Note that ordinary unions may have member functions. In particular, constructors can be most useful for defining suitable initialization for a union. For example,

```
union u {
    int i;
    char c;
    char* p;
    u(int ii) { i = ii; }
    u(char cc) { c = cc; }
    u(char* pp) { p = pp; }
};

u u1 = 1;        // u1.i = 1
u u2 = '1';      // u2.c = '1'
u u3 = "1";      // u3.p = "1"
```

Ordinary unions may have also have private members.

```
union u {
private:
    int a;
public:
    char* p;
    // ...
};
```

This is not assumed to be a very important or useful feature. It is simply easier to allow it than to disallow it. □

A union for which objects or pointers are declared is not an anonymous union. For example,

```
union { int aa; char* p; } obj, *ptr = &obj;
aa = 1;          // error
ptr->aa = 1;   // ok
```

The assignment to plain `aa` is illegal since the member name is not associated with any particular object.

Initialization of unions that do not have constructors is described in §8.4.1.

9.6 Bit-Fields

A *member-declarator* of the form

> *identifier*$_{opt}$: *constant-expression*

specifies a bit-field; its length is set off from the bit-field name by a colon. Allocation of bit-fields within a class object is implementation dependent. Fields are packed into some addressable allocation unit. Fields straddle allocation units on some machines and not on others. Alignment of bit-fields is implementation dependent. Fields are assigned right-to-left on some machines, left-to-right on others.

An unnamed bit-field is useful for padding to conform to externally-imposed layouts. As a special case, an unnamed bit-field with a width of zero specifies alignment of the next bit-field at an allocation unit boundary.

An unnamed field is not a member and cannot be initialized.

A bit-field must have integral type (§3.6.1). It is implementation dependent whether a plain (neither explicitly signed nor unsigned) int field is signed or unsigned. The address-of operator & may not be applied to a bit-field, so there are no pointers to bit-fields. Nor are there references to bit-fields.

■ The layout of bit-fields is highly implementation dependent, and it is wise not to make any assumptions about it unless absolutely necessary. In particular, bit-fields are often used to specify access to memory locations where the underlying hardware assigns special meaning to different bits. For example, consider the memory used for I/O control in a machine with memory mapped I/O or words set aside for the interrupt system. Such use is inherently implementation dependent.

To enable such use, an implementation must carefully document how the layout of structures is done. In particular, for bit-fields a user needs to know whether a plain *int* bit-field is *signed* or *unsigned* and whether bit-fields are allocated from high-order to low-order bit or from low-order to high-order bit in a word. In general, how an implementation treats a plain bit-field will depend on what operations the target hardware does most efficiently.

Further, an implementation should specify how a bit-field that does not fit adjacent to a previously allocated field in a suitably sized and aligned storage unit will be handled. Consider

```
struct bits {
    int b1: 24;
    int b2: 16;
    int b3: 24;
};
```

On a machine with 32-bit words that allocates from low-order to high-order, the object might be allocated in adjacent words, like this:

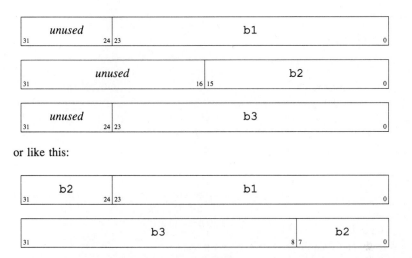

or like this:

Unlike ANSI C, which restricts bit-fields to *int*, *signed int*, or *unsigned int*, C++ allows a bit-field to be of any integral type. That is, a bit-field may be *char*, *short*, *int*, *long*, any of their signed and unsigned varieties, or an enumeration type.

People often try to use bit-fields to save space. Such efforts are often naive and can lead to waste of space instead. Using a two bit field instead of an eight bit *char* is a saving only if one can find other small fields to pack into that *char*. Even packing several small data items into a single word rather than using several words can be a loss in both run-time and space. On many machines a byte or a word is the smallest amount of memory that can be accessed without extra overhead. Extracting a bit-field may involve extra cycles and more often than not also extra instructions. Saving a byte of memory for storing an object may be more than offset by having to store and execute an extra instruction to extract the field from the smallest directly addressable unit of memory in which the object is allocated. □

9.7 Nested Class Declarations

A class may be declared within another class. A class declared within another is called a *nested* class. The name of a nested class is local to its enclosing class. The nested class is in the scope of its enclosing class. Except by using explicit pointers, references, and object names, declarations in a nested class can use only type names, static members, and enumerators from the enclosing class.

```
int x;
int y;

class enclose {
public:
    int x;
    static int s;

    class inner {

        void f(int i)
        {
            x = i;    // error: assign to enclose::x
            s = i;    // ok: assign to enclose::s
            ::x = i;  // ok: assign to global x
            y = i;       // ok: assign to global y
        }

        void g(enclose* p, int i)
        {
            p->x = i;   // ok: assign to enclose::x
        }

    };
};

inner* p = 0;    // error 'inner' not in scope
```

■ The rules for nested classes mark a change from earlier versions of C++, and the rule that class names obey exactly the same rules as other names is not compatible with C. For example,

```
struct X {
    struct Y { /* ... */ };
};

struct Y a;      /* C, but not C++ */
X::Y b;          // C++, but not C
```

The reason for the change was that the lack of proper name scope nesting was causing absurdities. In C, a `struct` cannot have member functions and thus does not need to establish a scope. In C++ on the other hand, the `class` is the focus of programming and the context for writing the most critical code. The C rule left a class as an incomplete scoping mechanism. This prevented C++ programmers from maintaining locality within a class, which became intolerable. It is still not clear whether a coherent set of scope rules for C++ could be designed based on the C rule that a struct is not a scope. It *is* clear, however, that such a set of rules would be so complicated that even expert C++ programmers would be unable to predict reliably the meanings of nontrivial examples involving nested or local functions.

The current rules for nested classes are a reversion to the original (prerelease) definition of C++. They are also easier to implement than any rules based on the C rule. ☐

■ Note that simply declaring a class nested in another does not mean that the enclosing class contains an object of the enclosed class. Nesting expresses scoping, not containment of sub-objects. ☐

Member functions of a nested class have no special access to members of an enclosing class; they obey the usual access rules (§11). Member functions of an enclosing class have no special access to members of a nested class; they obey the usual access rules. For example,

```
class E {
    int x;

    class I {
        int y;
        void f(E* p, int i)
        {
            p->x = i;    // error: E::x is private
        }
    };

    int g(I* p)
    {
        return p->y;    // error: I::y is private
    }
};
```

Member functions and static data members of a nested class can be defined in the global scope. For example,

```
class enclose {
    class inner {
        static int x;
        void f(int i);
    };
};

typedef enclose::inner ei;
int ei::x = 1;

void enclose::inner::f(int i) { /* ... */ }
```

Like a member function, a friend function defined within a class is in the lexical scope of that class; it obeys the same rules for name binding as the member functions (described above and in §10.4) and like them has no special access rights to members of an enclosing class or local variables of an enclosing function (§11).

■ For example,

```
int a;

class enclose {
public:
    int x;
    static y;
    class inner {
        int a;
        static b;

        friend void f(inner* p, int i)
        {
            p->a = i;
            a = 2;   // error: inner::a is not static
            b = 1;   // ok: inner::b is static
            x = 4;   // error: enclose::x is not static
            y = 3;   // ok: enclose::y is static
        }

        friend void g(inner*, int);
    };
};

void g(enclose::inner* p , int i)
{
    p->a = i;
    a = 2;   // ok: assign to ::a
    b = 1;   // error: inner::b is not in scope
    x = 3;   // error: enclose::x is not in scope
    y = 4;   // error: enclose::y is not in scope

    enclose::x = 3;   // error: enclose::x is not static
    enclose::y = 4;   // ok: enclose::y is static
}
```

□

9.8 Local Class Declarations

A class can be declared within a function definition; such a class is called a *local* class. The name of a local class is local to its enclosing scope. The local class is in the scope of the enclosing scope. Declarations in a local class can use only type names, static variables, `extern` variables and functions, and enumerators from the enclosing scope. For example,

```
int x;
void f()
{
    static int s ;
    int x;
    extern int g();

    struct local {
        int h() { return x; }    // error: 'x' is auto
        int j() { return s; }    // ok
        int k() { return ::x; }  // ok
        int l() { return g(); }  // ok
    };
    // ...
}

local* p = 0;    // error: 'local' not in scope
```

■ Allowing reference to the enclosing function's automatic variables would imply the introduction of nested functions. □

An enclosing function has no special access to members of the local class; it obeys the usual access rules (§11). Member functions of a local class must be defined within their class definition. A local class may not have static data members.

■ These restrictions allow the language not to introduce a notation for defining static members and functions outside the declaration of a local class. Enabling such declarations would only encourage the writing of complicated local classes. □

9.9 Local Type Names

Type names obey exactly the same scope rules as other names. In particular, type names defined within a class declaration cannot be used outside their class without qualification. For example,

```
class X {
public:
    typedef int I;
    class Y { /* ... */ };
    I a;
};

I b;      // error
Y c;      // error
X::Y d;   // ok
```

The following rule limits the context sensitivity of the rewrite rules for inline functions and for class member declarations in general. A *class-name* or a *typedef-name* or the name of a constant used in a type name may not be redefined in a class declaration after being used in the class declaration, nor may a name that is not a *class-name* or a *typedef-name* be redefined to a *class-name* or a *typedef-name* in a class declaration after being used in the class declaration. For example,

```
typedef int c;
enum { i = 1 };

class X {
    char v[i];
    int f() { return sizeof(c); }
    char c;                 // error: typedef name
                            // redefined after use
    enum { i = 2 };         // error: 'i' redefined after
                            // use in type name 'char[i]'
};

typedef char* T;

struct Y {
    T a;
    typedef long T; // error: T already used
    T b;
};
```

■ One might consider resolving the examples above by stating unequivocally that class member names are always to be preferred over global names when interpreting class members, thus resolving *X::f()* to return *sizeof(char)* and *T* to *long*. If that were done, would the following be considered acceptable?

```
typedef char* T;

class Z {
    int f() { T a = 1; return 1; }
    typedef int T;        // illegal: a ''what if'' example
};
```

Note that if the declaration of *Z* is allowed, but not the declaration of *Y*, the following absurdity results:

```
typedef char* T;

class Z {
    T f1();         // error
    int f2() { T a = 1; return 1; }      // ok
    T f3() { T a; return a; } // error AND ok
    typedef int T;        // illegal: a ''what if'' example
};
```

The more restrictive rule was adopted to minimize confusion. A compiler might be able to unravel reliably examples like the one above if suitable rules were adopted, but people would not. □

■ The scope rules for type names are identical to those for other names. Here are some examples:

```
typedef int T2;

struct S2 {
    struct Y {
        typedef char T2;
        T2 b;    // a char
    };
    typedef long T2;
    T2 c;         //a long
};

T2 a;    // an int

typedef int T3;

struct S3 {
    struct T3 { }; // ok
    T3 a, b;
} x;

x.a = x.b;   // legal
T3 t;        // legal, means int t;
t = x.a;     // error: 't' is an int
             // and 'x.a' is a S3::T3
```

□

Commentary

9.1c Interfaces

C++ provides a single declaration for a class that acts as the interface to both users and implementers of the member functions. There is no direct support for the notions of "interface definition" and "implementation module." This implies that the size of every object is known to the compiler. This in turn implies that a C++ program requires recompilation whenever changes are made to the *private* or *protected* parts, even though such changes apparently affect only the implementer of a class and not its users.

The reason for this is to allow the use of genuine automatic, static, and member variables; that is, to be able to allocate and manipulate objects directly rather than through a pointer. The benefits of this − over the alternative approach pioneered by Simula that allocates objects that are not of built-in types on the free store − are significant in both run-time and space. For example,

```
#include <complex.h>

void f()
{
    complex x = 2;
    complex y = x+3;
    // ...
}
```

Here *x* and *y* are allocated on the stack (saving memory management operations) and operations on these variables (for example, the plus operation above) are easily inlined to manipulate the representation of the objects directly.

The C++ solution also implies a minimal space overhead. For example,

```
class rectangle {
    complex top_left;
    complex bottom_right;
};
```

A *rectangle* requires exactly the space for two complex numbers, say four words. Had an indirection been required, a rectangle would have required a minimum of two additional words for the two indirections. Unless sophisticated optimizations were applied, three extra words would be needed for free store ''housekeeping'' (one in each complex object and one in the rectangle itself). The indirection needed to represent a local variable of type *rectangle* would complete the doubling of the size. Declaring a local variable of type *rectangle* would also imply three allocation and three deallocation operations − compared to zero for C++.

Having objects be free of compiler-generated ''housekeeping'' information unless such information is essential greatly helps the passing of information between C++ and other languages such as C and Fortran. In particular, passing pointers to data structures is trivial.

Allocation of objects on the free store can lead not only to inefficiency, but also − in languages where the indirection is implicit − to a noticeable discontinuity in the semantics of assignment. Built-in types have copy semantics (that is, if *a* and *b* are *int*s, *a=b* copies the value of *b* into *a*) whereas user-defined types have pointer semantics (that is, if *a* and *b* are of a user-defined type such as *complex*, *a=b* makes *a* refer to the same object as *b*). In C++, copy semantics are used for both built-in and user-defined types. Pointer semantics for user-defined types can be implemented by overloading the assignment operator.

The beneficial effects of dealing with objects only through pointers, such as minimal recompilation after changes to the class declaration, can be achieved in C++ for specific classes by *not* allocating static, automatic, or member objects of those classes and avoiding the use of inline for their functions. Tools such as compilers and programs calculating minimal recompilation must be alert to these possibilities.

10

Derived Classes

This chapter explains *inheritance*. A class can be *derived* from another class, which is then called a *base* class of the derived class. A class may be derived from one or more classes. The derived class inherits the properties of its base classes, including its data members and member functions. In addition, the derived class can override *virtual* functions of its bases and declare additional data members, functions, and so on. Access to class members is checked for ambiguity.

Sharing among the (base) classes that make up a class can be expressed using *virtual base classes*. Classes can be declared *abstract* to ensure that they are used only as base classes.

The final reference manual section of this chapter (§10.4) is a summary of the C++ scope rules.

The commentary sections at the end of this chapter discuss the run-time mechanisms necessary to implement inheritance.

10   Derived Classes

A list of base classes may be specified in a class declaration using the notation:

> *base-spec:*
> > : *base-list*

> *base-list:*
> > *base-specifier*
> > *base-list* , *base-specifier*

> *base-specifier:*
>> *complete-class-name*
>> virtual *access-specifier_{opt}* *complete-class-name*
>> *access-specifier* virtual_{opt} *complete-class-name*

> *access-specifier:*
>> private
>> protected
>> public

The *class-name* in a *base-specifier* must denote a previously declared class (§9), which is called a base class for the class being declared.

> ■ Note that a class that has been named but not yet declared cannot be used as a base class (just as it cannot be used to declare variables − other than static members − until it has itself been declared).

> ```
> class X;
> class Y : public X { // error: X undeclared
>     X a;             // error: X undeclared
>     static X b;      // ok: 'static X' is not a definition
> };
> ```

> □

A class is said to be derived from its base classes. For the meaning of *access-specifier* see §11. Unless redefined in the derived class, members of a base class can be referred to as if they were members of the derived class. The base class members are said to be *inherited* by the derived class. The scope resolution operator :: (§5.1) may be used to refer to a base member explicitly. This allows access to a name that has been redefined in the derived class. A derived class can itself serve as a base class subject to access control; see §11.2. A pointer to a derived class may be implicitly converted to a pointer to an accessible unambiguous base class (§4.6). A reference to a derived class may be implicitly converted to a reference to an accessible unambiguous base class (§4.7).
For example,

```
class base {
public:
    int a, b;
};


class derived : public base {
public:
    int b, c;
};
```

```
void f()
{
    derived d;
    d.a = 1;
    d.base::b = 2;
    d.b = 3;
    d.c = 4;
    base* bp = &d;   // standard conversion:
                     // derived* to base*
}
```

assigns to the four members of d and makes bp point to d.

■ The terms *base class* and *derived class* were chosen in preference to the alternatives *superclass* and *subclass* because of confusion experienced by Simula users
about which was which. Similar problems have been observed among Object Pascal
users. Part of the confusion stems from the observations that a superclass contains a
subset of the attributes of its subclasses and that a superclass can be represented as a
sub-object of an object representing its subclass. This is one of C++'s few deliberate
departures from Simula's terminology. □

A class is called a *direct base* if it is mentioned in the *base-list* and an *indirect
base* if it is not a direct base but is a base class of one of the classes mentioned in
the *base-list*.

Note that in the *class-name* :: *name* notation, *name* may be a name of a
member of an indirect base class; the notation simply specifies a class in which to
start looking for *name*. For example,

```
class A { public: void f(); };
class B : public A { };
class C : public B { public: void f(); };

void C::f()
{
    f();      // Call C's f()
    A::f();  // call A's f()
    B::f();  // call A's f()
}
```

Here, A::f() is called twice since it is the only f() in B.

Initialization of objects representing base classes can be specified in constructors; see §12.6.2.

10.1 Multiple Base Classes

A class may be derived from any number of base classes. For example,

```
class A { /* ... */ };
class B { /* ... */ };
class C { /* ... */ };
class D : public A, public B, public C { /* ... */ };
```

The use of more than one direct base class is often called multiple inheritance.

The order of derivation is not significant except possibly for default initialization by constructor (§12.1), for cleanup (§12.4), and for storage layout (§5.4, §9.2, §11.1). The order in which storage is allocated for base classes is implementation dependent.

A class may not be specified as a direct base class of a derived class more than once but it may be an indirect base class more than once.

```
class B { /* ... */ };
class D : public B, public B { /* ... */ };   // illegal

class L { /* ... */ };
class A : public L { /* ... */ };
class B : public L { /* ... */ };
class C : public A, public B { /* ... */ };    // legal
```

Here, an object of class C will have two sub-objects of class L.

■ A derived class and its base classes can be represented by a directed acyclic graph (DAG) where an arrow means ''derived from.'' A DAG of classes is often referred to as a ''class lattice.'' It is often easier to understand complicated class lattices by drawing them. For example,

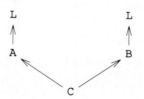

Note that L is replicated. This diagram really shows the relationship between the sub-objects of an object of class C. The importance of this will become apparent by comparison with the example below. We draw derived classes below their bases to match the order in which their declarations are seen by a compiler and in which they appear in a printout of the program.

Note also that such class DAGs are simply representations of classes used to ease understanding of the classes in a system and their relationships. Typically, an implementation does not supply a run-time structure that exactly matches the DAGs; that is, one cannot simply assume that for each arrow in the DAG there is a corresponding pointer in the representation of an object. On the contrary, typically such arrows represent information available to the programmer and the compiler, but not in the final object code. See §10.1c through §10.10c for an explanation of how one might handle the run-time aspects of inheritance. □

■ The reason that a given class may not appear more than once in a list of base classes is that every reference to it or its members would be ambiguous. For example,

```
class B { public: int b; };
class D : public B, public B { };      // error

void f(D* p)
{
    p->b = 7; // ambiguous
}
```

This problem does not arise when a class appears twice as an indirect base. An object of class `C` above has two `L` objects: `A::L` and `B::L`, which might be laid out in memory like this:

```
┌─────────────────────────┐
│                         │
│   L part (of A)         │
│   - - - - - - - - - -   │
│       A part            │
│                         │
├─────────────────────────┤
│                         │
│   L part (of B)         │
│   - - - - - - - - - -   │
│       B part            │
│                         │
├─────────────────────────┤
│                         │
│       C part            │
│                         │
└─────────────────────────┘
```

If these declarations come from an implementation of lists requiring each element to contain a link, and if `L` is a link class, then a `C` object can be on a list of `A`s and also on a list of `B`s.

Now suppose class `L` has a member `next`. How could a function `C::f()` refer to `L::next`? Obviously,

```
void C::f() { next = 0; }      // error
```

is ambiguous; is `A::next` to be set, or `B::next`, or both? Explicit qualification must be used, for example,

```
void C::f() { A::next = B::next; }
```

Because there are two `L` objects in a `C` object, casting (either implicit or explicit) between a pointer to an `L` and a pointer to a `C` is ambiguous, and therefore disallowed.

```
C* pc = new C;
L* pl = pc;          // error: ambiguous
pl = (L*) pc;        // error: still ambiguous
```

The following casts are unambiguous and may be used:

```
pl = (L*) (A*)pc;    // cast to the L in C's A
pc = (C*) (A*)pl;    // cast to the C containing A's L
```

Now consider a function expecting an *L* argument.

```
extern f(L*);
```

Because an *A* is also an *L*, *f ()* can be called with an *A* object, as follows:

```
A a;
f(&a);       // f will use A's L
```

On the other hand, because a *C* contains two *L* objects, *f ()* cannot be passed a *C*.
Casting the *C* object to an *A* before the call will disambiguate.

```
C c;
f(&c);               // error: ambiguous
f((A*) &c);          // f will use the L in C's A
```

□

The keyword `virtual` may be added to a base class specifier. A single sub-object of the virtual base class is shared by every base class that specified the base class to be virtual. For example,

```
class V { /* ... */ };
class A : virtual public V { /* ... */ };
class B : virtual public V { /* ... */ };
class C : public A, public B { /* ... */ };
```

Here class C has only one sub-object of class V.

■ Or graphically (in contrast to the *C*, *A*, *B*, *L* example above),

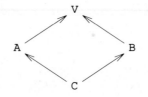

One important aspect of multiple inheritance as compared to single inheritance is that classes within a class lattice can share information without pushing that information towards the single root of an inheritance tree. With multiple inheritance in general and virtual base classes in particular it is possible for what we'll call "sibling classes," like *A* and *B* in the example above, to share information without affecting other classes in an inheritance lattice. This counteracts the tendency observed in single inheritance systems (such as C++ before the introduction of multiple inheritance) for information to drift toward the top of the tree. In effect, the root node of a single inheritance tree acts as a global name space for all classes in an inheritance tree and can suffer from a phenomenon observed in languages without inheritance, which is that all interesting information ends up being global.

A virtual base class provides a local point for sharing information, thus improving locality of reference and data hiding beyond what can be achieved without such classes. A virtual base class provides a statically typed interface to the information shared by its derived classes. Since a virtual base class is a perfectly ordinary C++ class, all the features of the language are available for expressing this sharing. In particular, virtual functions can be defined for a virtual base class; see §10.10c. □

A class may have both virtual and nonvirtual base classes of a given type.

```
class B { /* ... */ };
class X : virtual public B { /* ... */ };
class Y : virtual public B { /* ... */ };
class Z : public B { /* ... */ };
class AA : public X, public Y, public Z { /* ... */ };
```

Here class AA has two sub-objects of class B: Z's B and the virtual B shared by X and Y.

■ Or graphically,

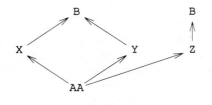

□

■ Because one wants to avoid undesired multiple calls of a function in a virtual class, programming using virtual bases can be more difficult than programming using nonvirtual bases. The example below shows one style for programming with virtual bases.

Let each class provide a protected function, _f(), doing the part of an operation f() that specifically relates to the class, and a public function f() calling _f() and the _f()s for its base classes.

```
class W {
protected:
    void _f() { /* code for what W needs to do */ }
    // ...
public:
    void f() { _f(); }
    // ...
};
```

```
class A : public virtual W {
protected:
    void _f() { /* code for what A needs to do */ }
    // ...
public:
    void f() { _f(); W::_f(); }
    // ...
};

class B : public virtual W  {
protected:
    void _f() { /* code for what B needs to do */ }
    // ...
public:
    void f() { _f(); W::_f(); }
    // ...
};

class C : public A, public B, public virtual W {
protected:
    void _f() { /* code for what C needs to do */ }
    // ...
public:
    void f() { _f(); A::_f(); B::_f(); W::_f(); }
    // ...
};
```

Additional support for programming using multiple inheritance, such as the method combination schemes in some Lisp dialects, was considered. None of the alternatives considered, however, seemed simple, general, and efficient enough to justify the complexity they would add to C++. In particular, it was not obvious how to combine the C++ strong static type checking with a scheme flexible enough to support directly the "mix-in" style of programming used in some Lisp dialects. □

10.1.1 Ambiguities

Access to base class members must be unambiguous. Access to a base class member is ambiguous if the expression used refers to more than one function, object, type, or enumerator. The check for ambiguity takes place before access control (§11). For example,

```
class A {
public:
    int a;
    int (*b)();
    int f();
    int f(int);
    int g();
};
```

```
class B {
    int a;
    int b();
public:
    int f();
    int g;
    int h();
    int h(int);
};

class C : public A, public B {};

void g(C* pc)
{
    pc->a = 1;   // error: ambiguous: A::a or B::a
    pc->b();     // error: ambiguous: A::b or B::b
    pc->f();     // error: ambiguous: A::f or B::f
    pc->f(1);    // error: ambiguous: A::f or B::f
    pc->g();     // error: ambiguous: A::g or B::g
    pc->g = 1;   // error: ambiguous: A::g or B::g
    pc->h();     // ok
    pc->h(1);    // ok
}
```

If the name of an overloaded function is unambiguously found overloading resolution also takes place before access control.

■ Note that reaching the *same* object or enumerator doesn't imply an ambiguity.

```
class A {
public:
    static a;
    enum { e };
};

class B : public A { };
class C : public A { };

class D : public B, public C { };

void g(D* pd)
{
    pd->a = 1;       // ok, 'a' is static
    int i = pd->e;   // ok, 'e' is an enumerator
}
```

□

Ambiguities can be resolved by qualifying a name with its class name. For example,

```
class A {
public:
    int f();
};

class B {
public:
    int f();
};

class C : public A, public B {
    int f() { return A::f() + B::f(); }
};
```

When virtual base classes are used, a single function, object, type, or enumerator may be reached through more than one path through the directed acyclic graph of base classes. This is not an ambiguity. The identical use with nonvirtual base classes is an ambiguity; in that case more than one sub-object is involved. For example,

```
class V { public: int v; };
class A { public: int a; };
class B : public A, public virtual V {};
class C : public A, public virtual V {};

class D : public B, public C { public: void f(); };

void D::f()
{
    v++;        // ok: only one 'v' in 'D'
    a++;        // error, ambiguous: two 'a's in 'D'
}
```

■ Or graphically, listing member names within braces,

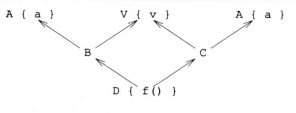

□

When virtual base classes are used, more than one function, object, or enumerator may be reached through paths through the directed acyclic graph of base classes. This is an ambiguity unless one of the names found *dominates* the others. The identical use with nonvirtual base classes is an ambiguity; in that case more than one sub-object is involved.

A name `B::f` *dominates* a name `A::f` if its class `B` has `A` as a base. If a name dominates another no ambiguity exists between the two; the dominant name is used when there is a choice. For example,

```
class V { public: int f(); int x; };
class B : public virtual V { public: int f(); int x; };
class C : public virtual V { };

class D : public B, public C { void g(); };

void D::g()
{
    x++;        // ok: B::x dominates V::x
    f();        // ok: B::f() dominates V::f()
}
```

■ Or graphically,

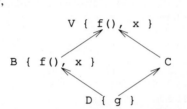

Note that dominance applies to names and not just to functions.

The dominance rule is necessary for virtual functions − since it *is* the rule for which function should be invoked for a virtual call − and experience showed it applying nicely to nonvirtual functions as well. Early use of a compiler that did not apply the dominance rule to nonvirtual functions led to programmer errors and contorted programs.

For virtual functions, the dominance rule is what guarantees that the same function is called independently of the static type of the pointer, reference, or name of the object for which it is called.

Note that in the following example *A2::f()* dominates *A1::f()* in both calls:

```
struct A1 { int f(); };
struct A2 : virtual A1 { int f(); };
struct A3 : A2 { };
struct A4 : A3 , virtual A1 { };

void f(A2* pa2, A4* pa4)
{
    pa2->f();    // call A2::f()
    pa4->f();    // call A2::f()
}
```

One might imagine that *A1::f()* was considered ''closer to'' *A4* and chosen for the call *pa4->f()* since *A1* is a direct base of *A4* and *A2* isn't. This is not the case. Consider

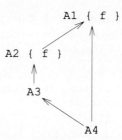

Examining the DAG shows that $A2::f$ dominates $A1::f$ and would have been called had $A1::f$ been virtual.

See §10.8c for a key example where dominance is essential. □

An explicit or implicit conversion from a pointer or reference to a derived class to a pointer or reference to one of its base classes must unambiguously refer to the same object representing the base class. For example,

```
class V { };
class A { };
class B : public A, public virtual V { };
class C : public A, public virtual V { };
class D : public B, public C { };

void g()
{
    D d;
    B* pb = &d;
    A* pa = &d;   // error, ambiguous: C's A or B's A ?
    V* pv = &d;   // fine: only one V sub-object
}
```

■ Or graphically,

```
     A               V               A
      ↖           ↗     ↖          ↗
        B                   C
         ↖               ↗
              D
```

Ambiguous uses of derived class members are detected at compile time. Only the *use* of a name in an ambiguous way is an error, however; combining classes that contain members with the same name in an inheritance scheme is not an error. Checking for ambiguity is done before access control or type checking (§10.1.1). Thus, an ambiguity exists when base class members have the same name, even if only one is accessible from the derived class. For example,

```
class A { public: int i; };
class B { private: char* i; };
class C : public A, public B { /* ... */ };     // OK


C* cptr=new C;
int j=cptr->i;          // error: A::i or B::i ?
```

Such ambiguities can be resolved using the `: :` operator, as follows:

```
int j=cptr->A::i;       // int i in the A part of C
```

A similar ambiguity arises if both *A* and *B* have a function `f ()`.

```
class A { public: void f(); };
class B { public: int f(); };
class C : public A, public B { /* ... */ };     // OK


C* cptr=new C;


void g1 ()
{
    C* cptr=new C;

    cptr->A::f();       // unambiguous: the f() in C's A
    cptr->B::f();       // unambiguous: the f() in C's B
}
```

One can also get an unambiguous call by restricting the context.

```
A* aptr = cptr;     // implicit conversion of C* to A*
aptr->f();          // unambiguous: calls A::f()
void g2 ()
{
    C* cptr = new C;
    A* aptr = cptr;     // implicit conversion of C* to A*
    aptr->f();          // unambiguous: calls A::f()
}
```

A major reason for virtual functions is to ensure that the same function is called for an object independently of the type of the expression used to access the object.

Where possible, one should resolve such ambiguous calls by providing a function in the derived class. For example,

```
class C : public A, public B {
public:
    int f() { A::f(); return B::f(); }
    // ...
};


void g3 ()
{
    C* cptr=new C;
    cptr->f();      // calls C::f
}
```

□

10.2 Virtual Functions

If a class base contains a virtual (§7.1.2) function vf, and a class derived
derived from it also contains a function vf of the same type, then a call of vf for
an object of class derived invokes derived::vf (even if the access is through
a pointer or reference to base). The derived class function is said to *override* the
base class function. If the function types (§8.2.5) are different, however, the functions are considered different and the virtual mechanism is not invoked (see
also §13.1). It is an error for a derived class function to differ from a base class'
virtual function in the return type only. For example,

```
struct base {
    virtual void vf1();
    virtual void vf2();
    virtual void vf3();
    void f();
};

class derived : public base {
public:
    void vf1();
    void vf2(int);        // hides base::vf2()
    char vf3();   // error: differs in return type only
    void f();
};

void g()
{
    derived d;
    base* bp = &d;    // standard conversion:
                      // derived* to base*
    bp->vf1();        // calls derived::vf1
    bp->vf2();        // calls base::vf2
    bp->f();          // calls base::f
}
```

The calls invoke derived::vf1, base::vf2, and base::f, respectively, for
the class derived object named d. That is, the interpretation of the call of a virtual function depends on the type of the object for which it is called, whereas the
interpretation of a call of a nonvirtual member function depends only on the type of
the pointer or reference denoting that object. For example, bp->vf1() calls
derived::vf1() because bp points to an object of class derived in which
derived::vf1() has overridden the virtual function base::vf1().

■ This is the property that makes derived classes and virtual functions the key to the
design of many C++ programs. A base class defines an interface for which a variety
of implementations are provided by derived classes. A pointer to an object of a
class can be passed into a context where the interface defined by one of its base
classes is known but where the derived class is unknown. The virtual function

mechanism ensures that the object is still manipulated by the functions defined for it (and not just by the functions defined for the base class). Only functions specified in the interface provided by the base class will be called and only if the actual arguments match the formal arguments required.

The use of derived classes and virtual functions is often called *object-oriented programming*. Furthermore, the ability to call a variety of functions using exactly the same interface – as is provided by virtual functions – is sometimes called *polymorphism*.

A virtual function call is usually implemented as an indirect function call through a per class table of functions generated by the compiler; see §10.7c and §10.8c. This ensures reasonable efficiency for such calls. □

The `virtual` specifier implies membership, so a `virtual` function cannot be a global (nonmember) (§7.1.2) function. Nor can a virtual function be a `static` member, since a virtual function call relies on a specific object for determining which function to invoke. A virtual function can be declared a `friend` in another class. An overriding function is itself considered virtual. The `virtual` specifier may be used for an overriding function in the derived class, but such use is redundant. A virtual function in a base class must be defined or declared pure (§10.3).

■ This ensures that undefined functions can be detected at link time so that a run-time check for undefined functions at each virtual function call is avoided. □

A virtual function that has been defined in a base class need not be defined in a derived class. If it is not, the function defined for the base class is used in all calls.

■ When the exact type of an object is known at compile time, the virtual function call mechanism need not be used. Instead, an ordinary member function call can be used. In the example above, *d.vf1()* can be evaluated without resort to a virtual function call because *d* is an object of type *derived,* so *derived::vf1* can be called directly. When a virtual function is called through a pointer or a reference, the actual type of the object is not necessarily known, so the virtual call mechanism must be used. A compiler with enough knowledge of control flow, however, can eliminate virtual function calls even in some of these cases, such as the calls through *bp* in the example above.

A direct call is a few memory references more efficient than a virtual function call (see §10.7c, §10.8c, §10.10c), but the real advantage of direct calls is for inline functions where the difference in run-time overhead can be significant. Inline virtual functions make perfect sense and are quite frequently used. Naturally, inlining is used only where the inline function is applied to an object of known type. As ever, it is wise to remember that overuse of inlining is self-defeating (see §7.1.2). □

Explicit qualification with the scope operator (§5.1) suppresses the virtual call mechanism. For example,

```
class B { public: virtual void f(); };
class D : public B { public: void f(); };

void D::f() { /* ... */ B::f(); }
```

Here, the call of f in D really does call B::f and not D::f.

■ An unqualified call

```
void D::f() { /* ... */ f(); }
```

would result in a recursive call of D::f.

Explicit qualification in user code is error prone and should be avoided wherever possible. For example,

```
void g()
{
    B* p = new D;
    p->B::f();  // call B::f(), sloppy code
}
```

Such use of explicit qualification scatters explicit knowledge of the details of the class declaration over the source code in a way that complicates code maintenance. As a rule of thumb, explicit qualification should be used only to access base class members from a member of a derived class.

Consider

```
class X {
public:
    virtual void f(int);
    virtual int g();
};

class Y : public X {
public:
    void f(short);  // hides base::f()
    short g();      // error: differs in return type only
};
```

Here, the likely intent was for the functions in class *Y* to override the functions in class *X*. This will not happen, though, because the types do not match exactly. The mismatch of return types for g() is simply an error and will be reported by the compiler. The argument type case is more subtle since the user might be trying to do some form of overloading; a warning can be issued in most such cases. □

■ C++ requires an exact type match between a virtual function in a base class and a function overriding it in a derived class. Why couldn't the function be overridden by a function with a slightly different type? For example, why not allow this?

```
class B {
    // ...
public:
    virtual void f(B*);
};
```

```
class D : public B {
    // ...
    void f(D*); // hides B::f(B*);
                // does not overide B::f(B*)
                // a warning would be appropriate
    int m;
};
```

After all, any $D*$ also points to a B, and often that really would be useful.

The reason is that if this were allowed a pointer to a base class could be implicitly converted to a pointer to its derived class, which could have unfortunate consequences (see §10.4c). Consider

```
void g(B* p1, B* p2)
{
    p1->f(p2);  // virtual call of f()
}


void h()
{
    g(new D, new B);
}
```

This would cause $D::f$ to be invoked with a pointer to a B as its second argument, which would make $D::f()$ refer past the end of the B object when accessing members of D.

```
void D::f(D* p)
{
    p->m = 7;
}
```

Consequently, an exact match on the types of all arguments is required when overriding a virtual function.

Then how about allowing a function returning a pointer to a base class to be overridden by a function returning a pointer to a derived class?

```
class B {
    // ...
public:
    virtual B* f();
};

class D : public B {
    // ...
public:
    D* f();  // error, but let's for a moment suppose
             // we can do it
};
```

That is safe because every D object contains a B object representing its base and would allow people to write code like this:

```
void h(D* p)
{
    D* p2 = p->f();
}
```

instead of

```
void h(D* p)
{
    D* p2 = (D*) p->f();
}
```

Allowing this, however, would imply a complication of the function call/return mechanism because a *B** and a *D** to the same object may not have the same absolute value. In particular, they will typically not have the same absolute value where *B* is a second or subsequent base of *D*. □

■ There is a way that implicit conversions of a pointer to a derived class to a pointer to a base type can cause a run-time error.

```
B* index(B* p, int i)
{
    return &p[i];
}
```

This innocent-looking code can be made to return a pointer to something that isn't a *B* even without having *i* out of range:

```
D v[10];

void bomb()
{
    B* p = index(v,2);
}
```

Here, the array name *v* is converted to a *D**, which is then converted to a *B**. Since `sizeof(B)<sizeof(D)`, given the declarations above, the offset calculation done by `index()` is all wrong, and the pointer returned most likely points into the middle of some *D* object.

As mentioned elsewhere (§8.2.4), the C array concept is weak and beyond repair. The way to avoid this problem is to use a proper array object type such as the one presented in §14.2. □

■ C++ does not contain a language-supported mechanism allowing a program to ask the question "of what class is this object *really* an object?" given only a pointer to a base class. There are two reasons for this.

First, such a mechanism would require every object − or at least every object of a user-defined type − to contain information identifying its type. This requirement would compromise object layout compatibility with languages such as C and Fortran, which is too high a price to pay; see also §9.1.

Second, providing a simple, convenient, and efficient way of asking that question would enable a style of programming that relies on switching on a type field rather than using virtual functions. The observation that in Simula programs this style has lead to messy, non-modular code strongly influenced the decision not to include such a facility in C++.

On the other hand, the absence of such a facility renders some programming tasks − such as object input/output and dynamic linking − notably harder because the user is forced to provide a facility for object type identification explicitly. For example,

```
class mybase {
        // ...
public:
        static int rep;
        virtual int* mytype();
        // ...
};

int* mybase::mytype() { return &rep; }

class myderived1 : public mybase {
        // ...
public:
        static int rep;
        int* mytype();
        // ...
};

int* myderived1::mytype() { return &rep; }
```

Given these definitions, a user can write

```
void f(mybase* p)
{
        if (p->mytype() == &myderived1::rep) {
                // ...
        }
}
```

Writing such code is tedious and repetitive − and therefore open to mechanization. Naturally, programmers are tempted to store other useful information in the *rep* object. Further, different people invent different schemes for object type identification. The last point is the most troublesome since it creates a barrier to the sharing of programs.

It has been repeatedly observed that a solution to the problem would be to define a standard class for containing ''useful information about a class'' and have compilers allocate one object of that class for each class used in a program. The compiler could then provide an operation that, when applied to an object, returned a pointer to the ''descriptor object'' for the class much as the virtual function *mytype()* above returned a pointer to an *int*. A class with no virtual functions would maintain object layout compatibility with other languages, and the type identification operator could return a value based on the class's static type. Only classes with virtual functions would allow the types of their objects to be identified at run-time given a pointer to a base class.

The key problem in the design of such a scheme is to decide what ''useful information'' class descriptor objects should contain and what the interface for accessing that information should be provided by a standard class descriptor class. □

10.3 Abstract Classes

The abstract class mechanism supports the notion of a general concept, such as a shape, of which only more concrete variants, such as circle and square, can actually be used. An abstract class can also be used to define an interface for which derived classes provide a variety of implementations.

An *abstract class* is a class that can be used only as a base class of some other class; no objects of an abstract class may be created except as objects representing a base class of a class derived from it. A class is abstract if it has at least one *pure virtual function*. A virtual function is specified *pure* by using a *pure-specifier* (§9.2) in the function declaration in the class declaration. A pure virtual function need be defined only if explicitly called with the *qualified-name* syntax (§5.1). For example,

```
class point { /* ... */ };
class shape {              // abstract class
    point center;
    // ...
public:
    point where() { return center; }
    void move(point p) { center=p; draw(); }
    virtual void rotate(int) = 0;  // pure virtual
    virtual void draw() = 0;       // pure virtual
    // ...
};
```

An abstract class may not be used as an argument type, as a function return type, or as the type of an explicit conversion. Pointers and references to an abstract class may be declared. For example,

```
shape x;            // error: object of abstract class
shape* p;           // ok
shape f();          // error
void g(shape);      // error
shape& h(shape&);   // ok
```

Pure virtual functions are inherited as pure virtual functions. For example,

```
class ab_circle : public shape {
    int radius;
public:
    void rotate(int) {}
    // ab_circle::draw() is a pure virtual
};
```

Since shape::draw() is a pure virtual function ab_circle::draw() is a pure virtual by default. The alternative declaration,

```
class circle : public shape {
    int radius;
public:
    void rotate(int) {}
    void draw(); // must be defined somewhere
};
```

would make class `circle` nonabstract and a definition of `circle::draw()` must be provided somewhere.

■ Originally, it was required that pure virtual functions be either defined in a derived class or redeclared to be pure. Experience showed that programmers needed a pure virtual function as a pure virtual function in a derived class more often than they wanted to define it in the derived class. In other words, a common use of an abstract class turned out to be as a base class for yet another abstract class.

Inheriting a pure virtual as a pure virtual is a safe default behavior. □

Member functions can be called from a constructor of an abstract class; the effect of calling a pure virtual function directly or indirectly for the object being created from such a constructor is undefined.

■ A likely result of (indirectly) calling a pure virtual function for a partly constructed object is a core dump. A compiler can warn against some, but not all, such calls. For example,

```
class X {
    virtual f() = 0;
    X(X* p) {
        f();     // error: pure virtual called
        p->f(); // probably OK
    };
};
```

A compiler can easily detect the first call of $X::f()$. The second call of $X::f()$ will be OK whenever the argument p points to an already created object of a class derived from class X.

Note that a pure virtual can be defined. It can be called using explicit qualification only, as follows:

```
class A {
    virtual void f() = 0;
    A() {
        A::f(); // ok
    }
};

void A::f()      // defined somewhere
{
    // ...
}
```

The reason this makes technical sense is that the explicit call $A::f()$ avoids use of the virtual call mechanism (§10.2) that cannot be used for a pure virtual function from within the constructor. If $A::f()$ calls a pure virtual function for its object then it in turn will encounter a disaster just as the constructor would have. A constructor for an abstract class will be called (only) in the process of creating an object of a derived class. Such constructors can be useful and occasionally need to call member functions. □

10.4 Summary of Scope Rules

The scope rules for C++ programs can now be summarized. These rules apply uniformly for all names (including *typedef-names* (§7.1.3) and *class-names* (§9.1)) wherever the grammar allows such names in the context discussed by a particular rule. This section discusses lexical scope only; see §3.3 for an explanation of linkage issues. The notion of point of declaration is discussed in (§3.2).

Any use of a name must be unambiguous (up to overloading) in its scope (§10.1.1). Only if the name is found to be unambiguous in its scope are access rules considered (§11). Only if no access control errors are found is the type of the object, function, or enumerator named considered.

A name used outside any function and class or prefixed by the unary scope operator :: (and *not* qualified by the binary :: operator or the -> or . operators) must be the name of a global object, function, enumerator, or type.

A name specified after X::, after obj., where obj is an X or a reference to X, or after ptr->, where ptr is a pointer to X must be the name of a member of class X or be a member of a base class of X. In addition, ptr in ptr-> may be an object of a class Y that has operator->() declared so ptr->operator->() eventually resolves to a pointer to X (§13.4.6).

A name that is not qualified in any of the ways described above and that is used in a function that is not a class member must be declared in the block in which it occurs or in an enclosing block or be a global name. The declaration of a local name hides declarations of the same name in enclosing blocks and global names. In particular, no overloading occurs of names in different scopes (§13.4).

A name that is not qualified in any of the ways described above and that is used in a function that is a nonstatic member of class X must be declared in the block in which it occurs or in an enclosing block, be a member of class X or a base class of class X, or be a global name. The declaration of a local name hides declarations of the same name in enclosing blocks, members of the function's class, and global names. The declaration of a member name hides declarations of the same name in base classes and global names.

A name that is not qualified in one of the ways described above and is used in a static member function of a class X must be declared in the block in which it occurs, in an enclosing block, be a static member of class X, or a base class of class X, or be a global name.

A function argument name in a function definition (§8.3) is in the scope of the outermost block of the function (in particular, it is a local name). A function argument name in a function declaration (§8.2.5) that is not a function definition is in a local scope that disappears immediately after the function declaration. A default argument is in the scope determined by the point of declaration (§3.2) of its formal argument, but may not access local variables or nonstatic class members; it is evaluated at each point of call (§8.2.6).

> ■ The scope of arguments in a function declaration that is not also a function defini-
> tion is useful only for catching errors. For example,
>
> ```
> extern int f(
>     int a,
>     int b = a  // error: local variable in argument list
> );
> ```
>
> See §8.2.5. □

A *ctor-initializer* (§12.6.2) is evaluated in the scope of the outermost block of the constructor it is specified for. In particular, it can refer to the constructor's argument names.

> ■ Note however, that the base class and member names are looked up in the scope
> of the class itself.
>
> ```
> class X {
>     int a;
> public:
>     X(int);
> };
>
> X::X(int a) :a(a) {}     // perverse, but legal
> ```
>
> □

Commentary

The rest of this chapter discusses techniques for implementing inheritance. The emphasis is on the run-time mechanisms provided by the compiler.

10.1c Single Inheritance

An object of a class is typically represented by a contiguous region of memory. Consider a simple class *A* declared as follows:

```
class A {
public:
    int a;
    void f(int i);
};
```

An object of class *A* will look like this:

```
┌─────────────────────────┐
│         int a;          │
└─────────────────────────┘
```

No information is stored in an *A* except the integer *a* specified by the user; in particular, no information about the member function *f ( )* is stored in the object.

Objects of derived classes are composed by concatenating the members of the base classes and of the derived class itself. Given these declarations,

```
class A {
    int a;
    void f(int);
};
```

```
class B : public A {
    int b;
    void g(int);
};
```

```
class C : public B {
    int c;
    void h(int);
};
```

an implementation of an object of class *C* may look like this:

```
┌─────────────────────────┐
│         int a;          │
│         int b;          │
│         int c;          │
└─────────────────────────┘
```

This is the normal layout used by most implementations, but because C++ does not guarantee the order in which storage is allocated for derived classes, a *C* object could plausibly be laid out as follows:

```
int c;
int b;
int a;
```

A more complicated representation of a class stores, for each class declared, a table of offsets of class members; a pointer to a class object includes a pointer to the offset table and a pointer to an instance of a class object. So given the class declarations above and a pointer

```
C* cptr=new C;
```

the layout in memory would look like this:

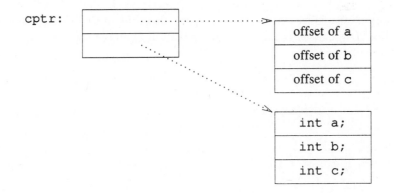

This scheme can benefit projects developing or maintaining large applications. If a class member's entry in the offset table is guaranteed not to change as long as that member exists and its type is not changed, code that accesses the member through the class offset table need not be recompiled, even though other members have been added to or deleted from the class declaration. Thus recompilation and relinking can be faster than when the normal class layout is used. The disadvantage is that because every access to a class object involves indirection, the generated code will be both larger and slower.

For the rest of this chapter, we will consider only the normal layout of class objects.

10.2c Multiple Inheritance

Given two classes

```
class A { /* ... */ af(int); };
class B { /* ... */ bf(int); };
```

a third can be declared using both as base classes, as follows:

```
class C : public A, public B { /* ... */ };
```

An object of class C can be laid out as a contiguous object like this:

```
+-------------------+
|                   |
|     A part        |
|                   |
+-------------------+
|                   |
|     B part        |
|                   |
+-------------------+
|                   |
|     C part        |
|                   |
+-------------------+
```

As with single inheritance, there is no guarantee about the order in which storage is allocated for base classes (§10.1), so alternatively a C object might be laid out as follows:

```
+-------------------+
|                   |
|     B part        |
|                   |
+-------------------+
|                   |
|     C part        |
|                   |
+-------------------+
|                   |
|     A part        |
|                   |
+-------------------+
```

Accessing a member of class A, B, or C is handled exactly as in single inheritance: the compiler knows the location in the object of each member and generates the appropriate code (without indirection or other unnecessary overhead).

If the object is laid out with class A first, followed by B and then C, calling a member function of A or C is the same as calling a member function with single inheritance. Calling a member function of B given a pointer to a C object is slightly more complicated. Consider

```
C* pc = new C;
pc->bf(2);   // assume C has no other member called bf
```

Naturally, `B::bf()` expects a pointer to a B object as its *this* pointer. To get a pointer to the B part of the containing C object, the offset of a B in a C, a compile-time constant we'll call "*delta(B)*," must be added to *pc*. The compiler transforms the call to the equivalent of

```
((B*)((char*)pc+delta(B)))->bf(2);
```

The relationship of *pc* and the *this* pointer passed to *B::bf* are shown below.

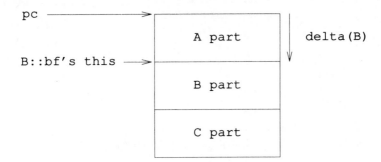

10.3c Multiple Inheritance and Casting

With multiple inheritance, casting may change the value of a pointer. Given the declarations

```
class A { /* ... */ };
class B { /* ... */ };
class C : public A , public B { /* ... */ };

C* pc = new C;
B* pb;
```

casting *pc* to a *B**, either implicitly or explicitly, as in either of the following:

```
pb = pc;
pb = (B*) pc;
```

must be translated by the compiler to the equivalent of

```
pb = (B*) ((char*)pc+delta(B));
```

Here, the offset of the *B* part in a *C* object, *delta(B)*, is added to *pc* (just as when the *this* pointer is computed for a member function of *B* given a pointer to a *C* object, which is an implicit cast). Similarly, casting *pb* to a pointer to a *C* (which must be explicit − see §10.4c). For example,

```
pc = (C*) pb;
```

is translated to

```
pc = (C*) ((char*)pb-delta(B));
```

Thus casting yields a pointer referring to the appropriate part of the object. In this example, *pc* will point to a *C* object, and *pb* will point to the *B* part of the same *C* object, as shown below.

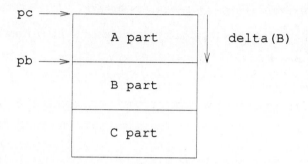

Comparison of pointers is treated similarly. The expression

> *(pc == pb)*

is interpreted as

> *((B*) pc == pb)*

(It is *not* treated as *pc==(C*)pb* since there is a standard conversion from a derived class to its base, but not a standard conversion from a base class to its derived class; see §10.4c.) The generated code for the comparison will be equivalent to

> *((B*)((char*)pc+delta(B)) == pb)*

Casting a value to a pointer to a base class and then to some other type may not yield the same result as casting directly to the second type. That is, for some class *B* and a pointer *p* to a class *C* derived from *B*, *(char*)(B*)p != (char*)p.*

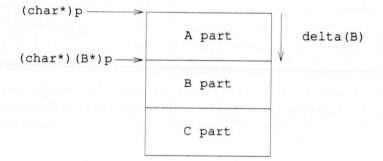

When *B* is a base class of *C* and *p* is a *C**, however, the following relationships are guaranteed:

> *(C*)p == p*
> *(B*)p == p*
> *(B*)p == (C*)p*

There is precedent in both C and C++ for the casting operation to produce one value given another, and not simply to reinterpret a bit pattern. For example, *(float)(int) 1.2* is not equal to *1.2*. C implementations for machines on which pointers to character have a different representation from pointers to other data provides another example. On such machines casting to and from character pointers often involves producing a value with a bit pattern that differs from that of the original pointer.

This is not the whole story, however. Consider a pointer with the value zero.

```
C* pc = 0;
B* pb = 0;
if (pb == 0) { /* do something */ }
pb = pc;
if (pb == 0) { /* do something */ }
```

According to the discussion above, the assignment of *pc* to *pb* will be interpreted as

```
pb = (B*)((char*)pc+delta(B));
```

and the second comparison will fail because *pb* will have the value *(B*) ((char*)0+delta(B))*. In casting, therefore, an implementation must treat a pointer with the value zero as a special case. To handle the assignment

```
pb = pc;
```

correctly, the code generated must do the equivalent of

```
pb = (pc==0) ? 0 : (B*) ((char*)pc+delta(B));
```

10.4c Multiple Inheritance and Implicit Conversion

A pointer to a derived class may be implicitly converted to a pointer to a base class, but a pointer to a base class may not be implicitly converted to point to a derived class (§10). To see why this must be so, consider the following (explicit conversions are used here to illustrate):

```
class A { /* ... */ };
class B { /* ... */ };
class C : public A, public B { /* ... */ };

C* pc = new C;
B* pb = (B*)pc;      // OK; pb points to B part of C
```

The result looks like this:

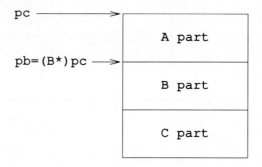

Because an object of a derived class always contains a sub-object of its base class, the conversion of a pointer to the derived class to point to the base class object within the derived class object to which it points is legal. Any given object of a class that is a base class for another class, however, is not necessarily part of an object of that derived class. The following code, were it legal, would lead to trouble:

```
B* pb = new B;
C* pc = (C*)pb;     // error: where does pc point?
```

The result looks like this:

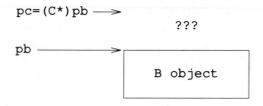

Any use of *pc* will most likely produce a runtime error. Few implementations check for bad casts like this, but it would be legal for a compiler to report such an error.

Because a pointer to a derived class can be implicitly converted to a pointer to its base class, the use of a pointer to a derived class and a pointer to a base class for that derived class in the same expression is legal.

```
struct A {};
struct B : A {};
struct C : A {};

void f(int i, A* pa, B* pb, C* pc)
{

    i ? pa : pb;        // ok
    i ? pb : pa;        // ok
    i ? pb : pc;        // error
}
```

An effect of there being no implicit conversion from a base class to its derived class is that the use in a single expression of pointers to two classes independently derived from a common base class will be an error (unless an explicit conversion function has been supplied). Here, *pb* and *pc* are pointers to two different types; their use in the same expression is a type mismatch.

10.5c Virtual Base Classes

Suppose we have an inheritance hierarchy similar to the *A*, *B*, *C*, *L* example in §10.1, except that only one object of the base class *L* is required in a *C* object. Then *L* could be declared a virtual base class, as follows:

```
class L { /* ... */ };
class A : public virtual L { /* ... */ };
class B : public virtual L { /* ... */ };
class C : public A, public B { /* ... */ };
```

Each *A* object or *B* object will contain an *L*, but only one object of class *L* will exist in a *C* object. Clearly the object representing the virtual base class *L* cannot be in the same position relative to both *A* and *B* in all objects. Therefore a pointer to *L* must be stored in all objects of classes that have *L* as a virtual base. An implementation of *A*, *B*, and *C* objects will look something like this:

```
A* aptr = new A;
B* bptr = new B;
C* cptr = new C;
```

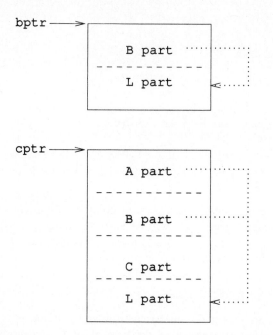

The virtualness of *L* in *A*, *B*, and *C* is a property of the derivation, and not a property of *L* itself.

Except that it results in a unique object in its derived classes, a virtual base class behaves the same way a nonvirtual base class does. Every virtual base of a given class type in an inheritance structure refers to the same object.

A class may be both an ordinary and a virtual base in the same inheritance structure. Given these declarations,

```
class L { /* ... */ };
class A : public virtual L { /* ... */ };
class B : public virtual L { /* ... */ };
class C : public A, public B { /* ... */ };
class D : public L { /* ... */ };
class E : public D, public C { /* ... */ };
```

an *E* object will contain two *L* objects, one virtual and one nonvirtual. An implementation of an *E* object will look something like this:

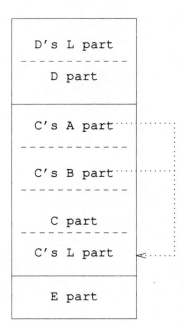

10.6c Virtual Base Classes and Casting

One can cast from a derived class to a virtual base class. The generated code will use the pointer to the virtual base stored in the derived class (shown in the diagrams in §10.5c above).

Casting from a virtual base class to a derived class is disallowed to avoid requiring an implementation to maintain pointers to enclosing objects.

10.7c Single Inheritance and Virtual Functions

Virtual functions can be implemented with a table of pointers to virtual functions, the *vtbl*. With single inheritance, a class's *vtbl* will point to the appropriate functions, and every object of that class will contain a pointer to the *vtbl*.

Given the following declarations:

```
class A {
public:
    int a;
    virtual void f(int);
    virtual void g(int);
    virtual void h(int);
};
```

```
class B : public A {
public:
     int b;
     void g(int);
};

class C : public B {
public:
     int c;
     void h(int);
};
```

a class *C* object will look something like this:

```
┌─────────────────┐
│   int a;        │          vtbl:
│      vptr    ········>  ┌─────────────┐
│   int b;        │       │   &A::f     │
│   int c;        │       │   &B::g     │
└─────────────────┘       │   &C::h     │
                          └─────────────┘
```

A call to a virtual function is transformed by the compiler into an indirect call. For example,

```
C* pc=new C;
pc->g(2);
```

becomes something like

```
(*(pc->vptr[1])) (pc,2);
```

Implementing virtual functions with multiple inheritance will require multiple *vtbls* (§10.8c), but notice that for a class derived through a single inheritance chain, there will be a single instance of each virtual function to which any call will resolve, whether the function is called through a pointer to an object of the derived class or through a pointer to any of its base classes. Thus there is a single set of functions associated with a derived class, which can be stored in a single *vtbl*.

10.8c Multiple Inheritance and Virtual Functions

With multiple inheritance, implementing virtual functions is slightly more complicated. Consider the following declarations:

```
class A {
public:
    virtual void f();
};
```

```
class B {
public:
    virtual void f();
    virtual void g();
};

class C : public A , public B {
public:
    void f();
};
```

Because class C is derived from class A and from class B, the following calls will all invoke C::f():

```
pa->f();
pb->f();
pc->f();
```

On entry to C::f, the *this* pointer must point to the beginning of the C object, and not to the B part (this discussion assumes that a class object is laid out in memory as shown above (§10.2c); note that the A part coincides with the beginning of a C object). It cannot always be known at compile time, however, that the B pointed to by pb is part of a C, so the offset of a B object within a C object, delta (B), is not a constant at compile time. Consequently delta (B) must be stored where it can be found at run time. Because the offset is used only for calling a virtual function, the logical place to store it is in the virtual function table.

A plausible implementation for a vtbl entry would be

```
struct vtbl_entry {
    void (*fct) ();
    int delta;
};
```

Using an *int* as the type of the offset will limit the size of an object, but on most machines an *int* will be large enough to hold the offset for any reasonably sized object. A third member may be added to a vtbl entry to support pointers to members using the same layout for both vtbl entries and pointers to members for uniformity; see §8.1.2c.

The *this* pointer to be passed to a virtual function can be computed by subtracting the offset of the object for which the virtual function was defined from the offset of the object used to invoke the function, then subtracting this difference from the pointer used in the call (for a more complicated example, see §10.10c). Here, the value of delta (B) will be needed to find the beginning of an object containing a B, in this case a C, given a pointer to a B. The generated code will subtract the value of delta (B) from the value of the pointer, so the negative of the offset, -delta (B), is stored. An object of class C, then, will look something like this:

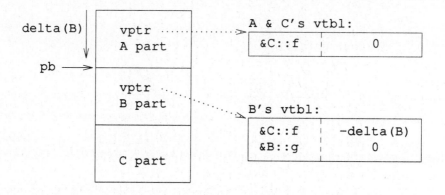

The *vtbl* for *B* in *C* is different from the *vtbl* of a separately allocated *B*. Each combination of base class and derived class has its own *vtbl*. In general, an object of a derived class needs a *vtbl* for each base class plus one for the derived class except that a derived class can share a *vtbl* with its first base class. Thus in the example above only two *vtbls* are used for an object of type *C* (one for an *A* in a *C* shared with the table for a *C* object, plus one for a *B* object in a *C*).

The call

```
pb->f();
```

in the example above invokes *C::f*, having been transformed by the compiler to something like this:

```
register vtbl_entry* vt = &pb->vtbl[index(f)];
(*vt->fct)((B*)((char*)pb+vt->delta));
```

An alternative implementation avoids storing the delta for the *this* pointer in the virtual function table. Instead, a pointer to code to be executed is stored. When no adjustment to *this* is needed, the pointer in the *vtbl* points to the instance of the virtual function to be executed; when *this* must be adjusted, the pointer in the *vtbl* points to code that adjusts the pointer then executes the appropriate instance of the virtual function. The class *C*, declared above, would be represented in this scheme as follows:

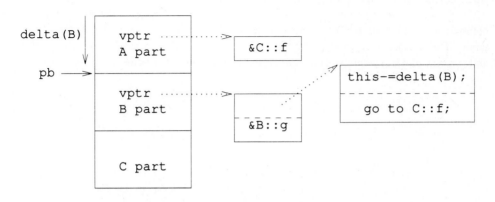

This scheme allows more compact virtual function tables and potentially faster calls to virtual functions. The drawback of such a scheme is that it is less portable.

The code that adjusts the *this* pointer is usually called a *thunk*. This name goes back at least as far as the early implementations of Algol60, where such small pieces of code were used to implement call-by-name.

10.8.1c Virtual Function Tables

In some C++ implementations, the code for a virtual function table is duplicated in the object file produced for each C++ source file that declares or includes declarations of the class containing the virtual functions.

Consider a header file containing the following:

```
class A {
public:
    virtual void f();
};

class B {
public:
    virtual void f();
    virtual void g();
};

class C: public A, public B {
public:
    void f();
};
```

Now suppose that these declarations are included in multiple C++ source files. Each time a naive compiler processes these declarations, even if it knows the declarations came from a header file, it will not know whether the virtual function tables have already been generated in a separate compilation. Therefore, it must

generate the tables. Because most linkers will report an error if an identifier is
defined more than once, virtual function tables must have unique names. Unique
names can be created by including the name of the source file in the name of a
table. The declarations above, when included in the files *windows.c*, *debug.c*,
and *interface.c*, might yield tables named as follows (name encoding is discussed in §7.2.1c):

```
_____vtbl__1A__windows_c
_____vtbl__1B__windows_c
_____vtbl__1A__debug_c
_____vtbl__1B__debug_c
_____vtbl__1A__interface_c
_____vtbl__1B__interface_c
```

(There are no tables for *C* objects because *C* shares *A*'s virtual function table.)

The obvious drawback of this implementation is that the tables generated for
each translation unit after the first duplicate the contents of the tables generated for
the first translation unit. For a program with many virtual functions declared in
many translation units, this duplication may significantly increase the size of the
generated code.

Smarter compilers eliminate most of this duplication, producing more compact
code, by identifying a unique translation unit for which a given *vtbl* will be generated. One reasonable heuristic used is to select the translation unit containing the
definition of the (lexically) first noninline virtual member function (if there is one)
as the translation unit for which a class's *vtbl* will be laid down (obviously, the
file name will not be included in the *vtbl* name). Under this scheme, duplicate
vtbl's will be generated for classes having no nonvirtual member functions,

10.9c Instantiation of Virtual Functions

Because constructors for base classes are called before the constructor for the
derived class, an object of a derived class and its environment, including its virtual
function table (§10.7c and §10.8c), is built from the bottom up. Thus a virtual
function defined in a derived class cannot be invoked for an object of that class
until the object has been constructed. Consider the following example:

```
class A {
public:
    virtual void f() { printf("A::f() called"); }
    A() { }
};
```

```
class B : public A {
public:
    B() { f(); }            // call virtual f()
    void g() { f(); }    // call virtual f()
};

class C : public B {
public:
    void f() { printf("C::f() called"); }
    C() { }
};

main()
{
    C c;          // will produce "A::f() called"
    c.g() ;       // will produce "C::f() called"
}
```

When *B::B()* is executing, the *C* part of the object being constructed exists only as raw storage and cannot be accessed through a virtual function. The available *f()* is *A::f()*. The first point at which *C::f()* can be called as *f()* is the first statement in the constructor *C::C()*.

10.10c Virtual Base Classes with Virtual Functions

Building the tables for virtual function calls gets more complicated when virtual base classes are used. Consider the following declarations:

```
class W {
public:
    virtual void f();
    virtual void g();
    virtual void h();
    virtual void k();
    // ...
};

class MW : public virtual W {
public:
    void g();
    // ...
};

class BW : public virtual W {
public:
    void f();
    // ...
};
```

```
class BMW : public BW , public MW, public virtual W {
public:
    void h();
    // ...
};
```

The inheritance relationship for this example can be shown in a directed acyclic graph (arrows point from derived classes to their base classes) as follows:

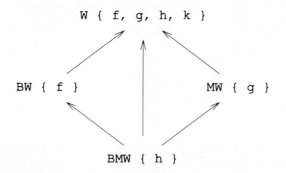

W { f, g, h, k }

BW { f }   MW { g }

BMW { h }

The member functions for *BMW* can be used like this:

```
void g(BMW* pbmw)
{
    pbmw->f();   // invokes BW::f()
    pbmw->g();   // invokes MW::g()
    pbmw->h();   // invokes BMW::h()
}
```

Now consider the following invocation of the virtual function $f()$:

```
void h(BMW* pbmw)
{
    MW* pmw = pbmw;

    pmw->f();     // invokes BW::f()!
}
```

A call to a virtual function through one path in an inheritance structure may result in the invocation of a function redefined on another path. This is an elegant way for a base class to act as a means of communication between sibling classes, such as *BW* and *MW* above. Suppose class *W* represents windows, class *BW* represents windows with borders, class *MW* represents windows with associated menus, and class *BMW* represents windows with associated menus and borders.

Sometimes a menu needs to know where the inside of its containing window is so that it can determine where it may be displayed. Now suppose the virtual function $f()$ returns the boundaries of the inside of a window. The menu will need the instance of $f()$ provided by *BW*, the border class, not the instance provided by

W, the window class — or else the menu could be displayed so that it overwrote part of the border. In some window systems that is undesirable.

If the base class *W* had a virtual function *f()* that was redefined in both *MW* and *BW* but not in *BMW*, an ambiguity would exist. A compiler can detect such ambiguities when it builds a derived class's table of virtual functions. To avoid ambiguous function definitions, all redefinitions of a virtual function from a virtual base class must occur on a single path through the inheritance structure.

The layout of a *BMW* object and its *vtbl*s might look like this:

```
                              BW & BMW's vtbl:
                          ┌─────────────────────────────────────────┐
┌──────────────────┐      │ &BW::f  ┊              0                 │
│     vptr         │····· │ &MW::g  ┊          delta(BW)             │
│   BW part        │      │ &BMW::h ┊              0                 │
│                  │      │ &W::k   ┊          delta(W)              │
├──────────────────┤      └─────────────────────────────────────────┘
│                  │      MW's vtbl:
│     vptr         │····· ┌─────────────────────────────────────────┐
│   MW part        │      │ &BW::f  ┊          -delta(MW)            │
│                  │      │ &MW::g  ┊              0                 │
├──────────────────┤      │ &BMW::h ┊          -delta(MW)           │
│                  │      │ &W::k   ┊     delta(W)-delta(MW)         │
│   BMW part       │      └─────────────────────────────────────────┘
│                  │      W's vtbl:
├──────────────────┤      ┌─────────────────────────────────────────┐
│                  │      │ &BW::f  ┊           -delta(W)            │
│     vptr         │····· │ &MW::g  ┊     delta(MW)-delta(W)         │
│   W part         │      │ &BMW::h ┊           -delta(W)           │
│                  │      │ &W::k   ┊               0                │
└──────────────────┘      └─────────────────────────────────────────┘
```

A virtual function must be passed a *this* pointer to an object of the class for which the function was defined. Thus, an offset will be stored with each function pointer in a *vtbl*. When an object is laid out in memory as shown above, the offset stored with the virtual function pointer can be computed by subtracting the offset of the class for which the *vtbl* was constructed from the offset of the class supplying the function. Here is an example:

```
void callvirt(W* pw)
{
    pw->f();
}
```

```
main ()
{
    callvirt (new BMW);
}
```

In *main*, *callvirt ()* is called with a pointer to a *BMW*, which must be converted to a *W* pointer because *callvirt* expects a *W** argument. So when
callvirt calls *f ()* (through a *BMW* pointer converted to a *W* pointer), *W*'s *vtbl*
will be used; *W*'s *vtbl* indicates that *BW::f ()* is the instance of the virtual function *f ()* to be invoked. To pass *BW::f ()* a *this* pointer to a *BW*, the pointer
pw will have to be cast back to a *BMW* pointer (by subtracting the offset of *W*) and
then converted to a *BW* pointer (by adding the offset of *BW* in a *BMW* object). The
value of the offset of a *BW* in a *BMW* object minus the offset of a *W* in a *BMW* is the
offset stored with the entry for *BW::f ()* in *W*'s *vtbl*.

10.11c Renaming

Merging two class hierarchies by using them as bases classes for a common derived
class can cause a practical problem where the same name is used in both hierarchies, but where it refers to different operations in the different hierarchies. For
example,

```
class Lottery {
    // ...
    virtual int draw();
};


class GraphicalObject {
    // ...
    virtual void draw();
};


class LotterySimulation
    : public Lottery ,
    public GraphicalObject {
    // ...
};
```

In *LotterySimulation* we would like to override both *Lottery::draw ()*
and *GraphicalObject::draw ()*, but with two distinct functions, since
draw () has completely different meanings in the two base classes. We would
also like *LotterySimulation* to have distinct, unambiguous names for the
inherited functions *Lottery::draw ()* and *GraphicalObject::draw ()*.

The semantics of this concept are simple, and the implementation is trivial; the
problem seems to be to find a suitable syntax. The following has been suggested:

```
class LotterySimulation
    : public Lottery ,
    public GraphicalObject {
    // ...
    virtual int l_draw() = Lottery::draw;
    virtual void go_draw() = GraphicalObject::draw;
};
```

This would extend the pure virtual syntax in a natural manner.

However, it was noted by Doug McIlroy that this problem does have a solution within C++. Renaming can be achieved through the introduction of an extra class for each class with a virtual function that needs to be overridden by a function with a different name plus a forwarding function for each such function. For example:

```
class LLottery : public Lottery {
    virtual int l_draw() = 0;
    int draw() // overrides Lottery::draw
        { return l_draw(); }
};
```

```
class GGraphicalObject : public GraphicalObject {
    virtual int go_draw() = 0;
    void draw() // overrides GraphicalObject::draw
        { go_draw(); }
};
```

```
class LotterySimulation
    : public LLottery ,
    public GGraphicalObject {
    // ...
    int l_draw();
    void go_draw();
};
```

Consequently, a language extension to express renaming is not *necessary* and is only worthwhile if the need to resolve such name clashes proves common.

11

Member Access Control

This chapter explains mechanisms for control of access to class members. Access control is based on the use of the keywords `public`, `private`, and `protected` to control access to individual members of a class and on the use of `private` and `public` specifiers to control whether a derived class is considered a subtype of a base class or not. The `friend` mechanism provides a way of granting individual functions and classes access to members of a class.

Access control applies uniformly to function members, data members, member constants, and nested types.

11   Member Access Control

A member of a class can be

> `private`; that is, its name can be used only by member functions and friends of the class in which it is declared.

> `protected`; that is, its name can be used only by member functions and friends of the class in which it is declared and by member functions and friends of classes derived from this class (see §11.5).

> `public`; that is, its name can be used by any function.

■ The C++ access control mechanisms provide protection against accident − *not* against fraud. Any programming language that supports access to raw memory will leave data open to deliberate tampering in ways that violate the explicit type rules specified for a given data item. For example, a pointer to a *foo* can be explicitly converted to a pointer to a *bar*, after which any guarantees provided by the type system for objects of type *foo* can be violated. Furthermore, a programming environment that lets a programmer update any part of a program will leave data open to arbitrary access. For example, the definition of class *foo* can be edited to make its representation public, after which arbitrary operations can be applied to the representation of a *foo*, again violating any guarantees provided by the type system for objects of type *foo*.

These possibilities are considered problems of the management of programming and of programming environments and *not* language problems.

Another point to note is that it is access to members that is controlled, *not* their visibility. For example,

```
int i;

class X {
private:
    int i;
};

class Y : public X {
    void f() { i++; }   // error: X::i is private
};
```

Here, the *i* incremented is *X::i*, and the access is an error because *X::i* is private. Had *i* been invisible instead of simply inaccessible, the global *i* would have been updated.

The reason access control rather than visibility control was chosen was to ensure that changes in access status would not quietly change the meaning of a program. It was felt that better error messages and fewer obscure errors would result from this approach. On the other hand, this decision clearly makes more work for programmers using multiple inheritance by increasing the frequency of name clashes that must be manually resolved. □

■ Note that access control is applied uniformly to all names. For example,

```
class X {
private:
    enum E1 { a1, b1 };
    int i1;
    void f1();
public:
    enum E2 { a2, b2 };
    int i2;
    void f2();
};

void h(X* p)
{
    X::E2 e2 = X::a2;    // ok: E2 is public
    int x2 = X::a2;      // ok: a2 is public
    p->i2 = 2;           // ok: i2 is public
    p->f2();             // ok: f2 is public
```

```
    X::E1 e1 = X::a1;      // error: E1 is private
    int x1 = X::a1;        // error: a1 is private
    p->i1 = 1;             // error: i1 is private
    p->f1();               // error: f1 is private
}
```

□

Members of a class declared with the keyword class are private by default. Members of a class declared with the keywords struct or union are public by default. For example,

```
class X {
    int a;  // X::a is private by default
};

struct S {
    int a;  // S::a is public by default
};
```

11.1 Access Specifiers

Member declarations may be labeled by an *access-specifier* (§10):

   access-specifier : *member-list*$_{opt}$

An *access-specifier* specifies the access rules for members following it until the end of the class or until another *access-specifier* is encountered. For example,

```
class X {
    int a;  // X::a is private by default: 'class' used
public:
    int b;  // X::b is public
    int c;  // X::c is public
};
```

Any number of access specifiers is allowed and no particular order is required. For example,

```
struct S {
    int a;  // S::a is public by default: 'struct' used
protected:
    int b;  // S::b is protected
private:
    int c;  // S::c is private
public:
    int d;  // S::d is public
};
```

The order of allocation of data members with separate *access-specifier* labels is implementation dependent (§9.2).

■ For example, the members of this class

```
class X {
     int a,b,c;
protected:
     int d,e,f;
public:
     int g,h,i;
private:
     int j,k,l;
};
```

might be allocated in the order they appear

```
struct X1 {
     int a,b,c;
     int d,e,f;
     int g,h,i;
     int j,k,l;
};
```

Another reasonable layout would be

```
struct X2 {
     int g,h,i;   // public members
     int d,e,f;   // protected members
     int a,b,c;   // private members
     int j,k,l;   // private members
};
```

Placing the public members first and the private members last has the advantage for implementations that pursue a strategy of minimal recompilation after a change to a program. If a user changes the private data for a class but leaves its public interface unchanged then previously compiled code that uses only public data need not be recompiled. Typically, it makes more sense simply not to use public data. Protected data, however, is not uncommon.

The requirement (§9.2) that members not separated by access specifier labels be allocated in the order in which they are declared provides compatibility with existing C code. □

11.2 Access Specifiers for Base Classes

If a class is declared to be a base class (§10) for another class using the public access specifier, the public members of the base class are public members of the derived class and protected members of the base class are protected members of the derived class. If a class is declared to be a base class for another class using the private access specifier, the public and protected members of the base class are private members of the derived class. Private members of a base class remain inaccessible even to derived classes unless friend declarations within the base class declaration are used to grant access explicitly.

In the absence of an *access-specifier* for a base class, public is assumed when the derived class is declared struct and private is assumed when the class is declared `class`. For example,

```
class B { /* ... */ };
class D1 : private B { /* ... */ };
class D2 : public B { /* ... */ };
class D3 : B { /* ... */ };       // 'B' private by default
struct D4 : public B { /* ... */ };
struct D5 : private B { /* ... */ };
struct D6 : B { /* ... */ };      // 'B' public by default
```

Here B is a public base of D2, D4, and D6, and a private base of D1, D3, and D5.

■ In the absence of an access specifier, a base class of a class declared with the keyword `class` is private; in the absence of a *virtual* specifier, a base class is nonvirtual. Explicitly using the keyword *private* is recommended for declaring private base classes because the compiler messages caused by accidental use of private base classes can be most confusing. For example, novices often don't know about access specifiers and get confused by this:

```
class X { public: f(); };
class Y : X { };            // no access specifier
                            // private by default

void g(Y* p)
{
    p->f();        // error
}
```

Even experts can get caught. A compiler can be most helpful by issuing a warning for the missing access specifier.

Having *private* as the default was chosen to reflect the general view that things that are not explicitly declared public are private. Defining a default access specifier was probably a mistake.

An access specifier or *virtual* specifier applies only to the base class immediately following it. Thus, for example,

```
class D : public virtual A, B, C { /* ... */ };
```

declares *D* to have a public virtual base *A*, and private nonvirtual bases *B* and *C*. ☐

Specifying a base class *private* does not affect access to static members of the base class. If, however, an object or a pointer requiring conversion is used to select the static member the usual rules for pointer conversions apply.

■ This can cause an attempt to use a static member of a private base class to fail just as an attempt to use a nonstatic member would.

```
class B {
public:
    static void f();
    void g();
};
```

```
class D : private B { };

class DD : public D {
    void h();
};

void DD::h()
{
    B::f();          // ok
    D::f();          // error: cannot convert 'this' to a B*
    this->f();       // error: cannot convert 'this' to a B*
    this->B::f();    // error: cannot convert 'this' to a B*
    f();             // error: cannot convert 'this' to a B*
    g();             // error: cannot convert 'this' to a B*
}
```

Had the call of $B::f()$ in $DD::h()$ not been allowed, we would have the absurdity of a member function having less access than a global function.

```
void k()
{
    B::f();          // ok
}
```

☐

Members and friends of a class X can implicitly convert an X* to a pointer to a private immediate base class of X.

■ For example,

```
class B { };
class D : private B {
public:
    friend B* f(D* p) { return p; }
    B* mem() { return this; }
};

B* g(D* p)
{
    return p;    // error: B is a private base of D
}
```

☐

11.3 Access Declarations

The access to a member of a base class in a derived class can be adjusted by mentioning its *qualified-name* in the `public` or `protected` part of a derived class declaration. Such mention is called an *access declaration*.
    For example,

```
class B {
    int a;
public:
    int b, c;
    int bf();
};

class D : private B {
    int d;
public:
    B::c;   // adjust access to 'B::c'
    int e;
    int df();
};

int ef(D&);
```

The external function `ef` can use only the names `c`, `e`, and `df`. Being a member of D, the function `df` can use the names `b`, `c`, `bf`, `d`, `e`, and `df`, but not `a`. Being a member of B, the function `bf` can use the members `a`, `b`, `c`, and `bf`.

■ Note that no type can be specified when adjusting the access of the name. For example,

```
class B { /* ... */ };
class D : private B {
    int d;
public:
    int B::c;   // error:qualifier in member declaration
                // or type in access declaration
};
```

□

An access declaration may not be used to restrict access to a member that is accessible in the base class, nor may it be used to enable access to a member that is not accessible in the base class. For example,

```
class B {
public:
    int a;
private:
    int b;
protected:
    int c;
};
```

```
class D : private B {
public:
    B::a;    // make 'a' a public member of D
    B::b;    // error: attempt to grant access
             // can't make 'b' a public member of D
protected:
    B::c;    // make 'c' a protected member of D
    B::a;    // error: attempt to reduce access
             // can't make 'a' a protected member of D
};
```

■ Allowing the writer of the derived class to increase access would enable a programmer to violate the guarantee that only the members and friends listed in the
class declaration can access the private members.

Allowing downward adjustments of accessibility of base class members in
derived classes would give a more convenient notation when one wants to provide
all but a few of the public members of a base class as public members of the derived
class. It would also complicate the rules, however, for what is a public base class.

Suppose, for the moment, that C++ did allow this declaration:

```
class DD : public B {
private:
    B::a;        // error
};
```

Now, even though *DD* is publicly derived from *B*, it would not have *B* as a public
base class. The reason is that the access to members of *B* through a pointer to a *DD*
object differs from the access to the members of *B* through a pointer to a *B* object.
In particular, the standard conversion of a *DD** to a *B** would grant a user access to
B::a even though it had been explicitly declared *private* for a *DD*. Consequently, *B* could not be considered a public base class of *DD*. Any functionality or
expressive power that might be added to the language by allowing downward adjustments of accessibility would not offset users' confusion about what constituted a
public base class and the added complication in the definition and implementation of
the language. □

An access declaration for the name of an overloaded function adjusts the access to
all functions of that name in the base class. For example,

```
class X {
public:
    f();
    f(int);
};
```

```
class Y : private X {
public:
    X::f;    // makes X::f() and X::f(int) public in Y
};
```

■ These rules imply that it is not possible to adjust access to overloaded functions that do not have the same access.

```
class X {
private:
    f(int);
public:
    f();
};

class Y : private X {
public:
    X::f;        // error
};
```

□

The access to a base class member cannot be adjusted in a derived class that also defines a member of that name. For example,

```
class X {
public:
    void f();
};

class Y : private X {
public:
    void f(int);
    X::f;  // error: two declarations of f
};
```

■ One could imagine a powerful language extension that allowed the previous example by letting an adjustment of access act as a way of overloading functions so that the declaration of Y would have been equivalent to

```
class Y : private X {
public:
    void f(int);
    void f() { X::f(); }
};
```

This would have implications, however, for type checking. In the previous example $X::f()$ is a member of X and is applied to an object through an $X*$ pointer. When a pointer of type $Y*$ is used to call $X::f$ the pointer suffers a standard conversion. Had the access adjustment been considered to redefine f in the scope of Y this would not have been the case. It is possible to construct examples using overloaded operators where this change in interpretation would be significant. □

11.4 Friends

A friend of a class is a function that is not a member of the class but is permitted
to use the private and protected member names from the class. The name of a
friend is not in the scope of the class, and the friend is not called with the member
access operators (§5.2.4) unless it is a member of another class. The following
example illustrates the differences between members and friends:

```
class X {
      int a;
      friend void friend_set(X*, int);
public:
      void member_set(int);
};

void friend_set(X* p, int i) { p->a = i; }
void X::member_set(int i) { a = i; }

void f()
{
      X obj;
      friend_set(&obj,10);
      obj.member_set(10);
}
```

■ Note that a friend is as much a part of the interface of a class as a member is.
Since a friend declaration has to appear in the declaration of the class of which it is
a friend, no violation of the protection mechanisms is implied. Friendship, like all
other access, is granted by the class − *not* unilaterally grabbed by the friend.

The friend mechanism is important in two ways. First, a function can be a
friend of two classes. For example,

```
class Vector;

class Matrix {
      friend Vector operator+(const Matrix&, const Vector&);
};

class Vector {
      friend Vector operator+(const Matrix&, const Vector&);
};
```

This can lead to increased efficiency by letting a friend function bypass unsuitable
access functions provided to general users. Alternatively, the use of friends can lead
to cleaner interfaces by avoiding complicating the interfaces of both classes with
member functions specifically designed to serve what would otherwise have been a
global function with no special access to the representation of the classes.

Second, a friend function allows user-defined conversions to be used for its first
argument, where member functions do not. This allows programmers to express the
notion that an lvalue is required by an operation by making that operation a member

and, conversely, to express the notion that an lvalue is not required by making that operation a friend. For example,

```
class complex {
    // ...
    complex operator+=(complex);
    friend complex operator+(complex, complex);
};
```

Here the member `complex::operator+=` requires a complex lvalue as its first argument, so `1+=z` is an error when `z` is a complex number. On the other hand, the friend `operator+(complex, complex)` will accept any value that is a complex number or can be converted into one, so `1+z` is ok.

In addition, some programmers prefer the usual function call notation supported by friend functions to the member call notation required for member functions. Often such preferences have a rational bias. Consider a matrix inversion routine; there are two choices.

```
m.invert();     // one preference
invert(m);      // another preference
```

We would expect `m.invert()` to invert `m` and `invert(m)` to leave `m` unchanged and return a new matrix that is the inverse of `m` so the usage would be

```
m.invert();          // one preference
m2 = invert(m);      // another preference
```

Note that a virtual function must be a member. □

When a `friend` declaration refers to an overloaded name or operator, only the function specified by the argument types becomes a friend.

■ One could imagine declaring all functions called `f` friends by a single declaration, but doing so would be a bit indiscriminate. It would enable a user to grab access to a class simply by declaring a function `f` with a hitherto unused argument type. □

A member function of a class X can be a friend of a class Y. For example,

```
class Y {
    friend char* X::foo(int);
    // ...
};
```

All the functions of a class X can be made friends of a class Y by a single declaration using an *elaborated-type-specifier* (§9.1):

```
class Y {
    friend class X;
    // ...
};
```

■ Note that only an *elaborated-type-specifier* and not a complete class declaration is allowed in a friend declaration, so this is an error:

```
class Y {
    friend class X { int a; };    // error
    // ...
};
```

□

■ Another use of friends is to provide access to the representation of a class to functions that cannot be member functions because they will be called from another
language. For example,

```
class T;

extern "C" void interface_function(T*);

class T {
        // ...
        friend void interface_function(T*);
};
```

Naturally, the same effect could be had by defining interface functions to call
member functions, but that could lead to the doubling of the number of functions
needed and to a doubling of the function call overhead. □

Declaring a class to be a friend also implies that private and protected names from
the class granting friendship can be used in the class receiving it. For example,

```
class X {
    enum { a=100 };
    friend class Y;
};

class Y {
    int v[X::a];  // ok, Y is a friend of X
};

class Z {
    int v[X::a];  // error: X::a is private
};
```

If a class or a function mentioned as a friend has not been declared its name is
entered in the same scope as the name of the class containing the friend declaration
(§9.1).

■ This implies that a friend declaration may be the first mention of a class or a function name. There is no way, however, of declaring a member function earlier than
its class.

```
class Y; // forward declaration of the name 'Y'

class X {
    friend void Y::f();   // error: Y undefined
    void g();
};

class Y {
    friend void X::g();   // ok: X defined
    void f();
};
```

The only way of specifying mutual friendship between two classes is to declare all of the second class a friend of the first. For example,

```
class XX {
    friend class YY;      // all of YY,
                          // including YY:f(), is a friend
    void g();
};

class YY {
    friend void XX::g(); // ok: XX defined
    void f();
};
```

☐

A function first declared in a friend declaration is equivalent to an `extern` declaration (§3.3, §7.1.1).

■ This implies

```
static void f() { /* ... */ }

class X {
    friend g();       // implies: extern g();
};

class Y {
    friend void f();      // ok: f() still has internal linkage
};

static g() { /* ... */ }    // error: inconsistent linkage
```

Odd maybe, but it follows directly from the linkage rules (§7.1.1), which were the strictest ANSI C compatible rules we could find. ☐

A `friend` function defined in a class declaration is `inline` and the rewriting rule specified for member functions (§9.3.2) is applied. A `friend` function defined in a class is in the (lexical) scope of the class in which it is defined. A friend function defined outside the class is not.

■ For example,

```
typedef char* T;

class X {
    typedef int T;
    friend T f(T) { /* ... */ }   // int f(int)
    friend T h(T);                // int h(int)
};

void h(T) { /* ... */ }           // void h(char*)
```

Here, the function called *h ()* declared as a friend of class *X* is not the function called *h ()* defined outside *X*; their types differ. □

Friend declarations are not affected by *access-specifiers* (§9.2). Friendship is neither inherited nor transitive. For example,

```
class A {
    friend class B;
    int a;
};

class B {
    friend class C;
};

class C   {
    void f(A* p)
    {
        p->a++;  // error: C is not a friend of A
                 // despite being a friend of a friend
    }
};

class D : public B   {
    void f(A* p)
    {
        p->a++;  // error: D is not a friend of A
                 // despite being derived from a friend
    }
};
```

■ The rule against inheriting friendship is sometimes not appreciated; that is, it occasionally gets in the way of a user. Consider, however, the effect of allowing friendship to be inherited. That would make it possible for a user to grab access. Or − using a more imaginative vocabulary − this would become possible:

```
class ReallySecure {
friend class TrustedUser;
    // ...
};

class TrustedUser {
    //...
};

class Spy : public TrustedUser {
    // aha!
};
```

The mechanism for allowing a user to grab access (to an explicitly defined interface) is *protected* members. □

11.5 Protected Member Access

A friend or a member function of a derived class can access a protected static member of a base class. A friend or a member function of a derived class can access a protected nonstatic member of one of its base classes only through a pointer to, reference to, or object of the derived class (or any class derived from that class). For example,

```
class B {
protected:
    int i;
};

class D1 : public B {
};

class D2 : public B {
    friend void fr(B*,D1*,D2*);
    void mem(B*,D1*);
};

void fr(B* pb, D1* p1, D2* p2)
{
    pb->i = 1;  // illegal
    p1->i = 2;  // illegal
    p2->i = 3;  // ok (access through a D2)
}
```

```
void D2::mem(B* pb, D1* p1)
{
    pb->i = 1;   // illegal
    p1->i = 2;   // illegal
    i = 3;       // ok (access through 'this')
}

void g(B* pb, D1* p1, D2* p2)
{
    pb->i = 1;   // illegal
    p1->i = 2;   // illegal
    p2->i = 3;   // illegal
}
```

■ The access specifiers *private* and *public* provide a way to distinguish uses of the members of a class by the implementer of the class from uses by others, whom we might call "the general public." This mechanism serves the traditional notions of data abstraction well. A derived class, however, constitutes a different kind of user of a class, and the notions of object-oriented programming relying on derived classes are not well served by the simple public/private scheme.

Without the *protected* mechanism, the programmer of a class that is intended to be used as a base class must often make data public or provide unsafe interface functions to serve the needs of the programmers of derived classes. In effect, what would have been the *protected* interface gets exposed to the general public for which it most likely is unsuited. An equally unacceptable alternative is to force implementers of derived classes – that is, often, the programmers providing the implementations for the interface specified by the base class – to use only the restricted interface intended for the general public. The sharp private/public distinction doesn't adequately reflect the reality of programming with class hierarchies.

Conversely, had only *protected* been supported, it would have been impossible for the programmer of a class to protect data because anyone could come along and grab access by deriving a class. This would preclude enforcing meaningful interfaces and maintaining the level of data abstraction that allows changing the underlying representation of an object. Often, such a change would not be practical because too many users had granted themselves access and thus become critically dependent on implementation details that would better have been left hidden.

One way of understanding *protected* is as a mechanism for the writer of a class to give other programmers the right to grant themselves access to a specific subset of the representation and operations. □

■ Consider allowing a derived class to access protected members of any object with the type of one of its base classes. That is, relax the restriction that access to a protected member must be through a pointer to, reference to, or object of the derived class. This would allow a class to access the base class part of an unrelated class (as if it were its own) without the use of an explicit cast. This would be the only place where the language allowed that.

There are examples where the restriction appears to provide protection against accidents. For example, suppose I am running a bank, and I have many different kinds of accounts. I would like to have a base class, *Account*, that has information common to all kinds of accounts, including the account balance, so a friend of *Account* can walk the list of all *Accounts* and tell me the financial position of my bank at any time. Each kind of *Account*, however, has its own rules for updating the balance (for example, what rate of interest is paid, when it is compounded, what types of deposits are accepted, special penalties for early withdrawals, and so on), so the derived classes which are all the different kinds of accounts contain the code for updating the balance. The member functions of *checking_accounts*, however, should not be able to access the balance in an *AutoLoan_account*. The restriction prevents that.

The example that caused the restriction to be introduced was a logically equivalent example involving device drivers. A driver for one kind of device accidentally updated the information relating to another kind of device, and the system mysteriously crashed. The accidentally updated information was stored in a common base class and accessed through a pointer to that base class and not the appropriate derived type. Naturally, the use of a virtual function for performing the update would have avoided the problem. □

11.6 Access to Virtual Functions

The access rules (§11) for a virtual function are determined by its declaration and are not affected by the rules for a function that later overrides it. For example,

```
class B {
public:
    virtual f();
};

class D : public B {
private:
    f();
};

void f()
{
    D d;
    B* pb = &d;
    D* pd = &d;

    pb->f();   // ok: B::f() is public,
               // D::f() is invoked
    pd->f();   // error: D::f() is private
}
```

Access is checked at the call point using the type of the expression used to denote the object for which the member function is called (B* in the example above). The access of the member function in the class in which it was defined (D in the example above) is in general not known.

■ Private virtual functions provide a way for the implementation of a base class to rely on derived classes without the functions involved being exposed to the general users of the base class. Whether the derived class chooses to expose the functions to its users is not a concern for the base class writer. □

11.7 Multiple Access

If a name can be reached by several paths through a multiple inheritance graph, the access is that of the path that gives most access. For example,

```
class W { public: void f(); };
class A : private virtual W { };
class B : public virtual W { };
class C : public A, public B {
    void f() { W::f(); }  // ok
};
```

Since `W::f()` is available to `C::f()` along the public path through B, access is legal.

■ The alternative, granting the least access to the derived class, was considered, but rejected as an inconvenience providing at most the illusion of protection. If a member of a class is accessible through any path, it is, in fact, accessible; making the user go through contortions to get to it in some but not all cases seemed pointless and self-defeating. □

Commentary

11.1c General Ideas

What protection is needed depends critically on what needs to be protected and from whom. In other words, there is a wide variety of needs that depend critically on the applications being written and the philosophy of the programmers involved in the project.

C++ does not attempt to provide the most detailed control of protection or to provide every conceivable mechanism for expressing every conceivable protection need. Doing that would imply a complexity far greater than what is provided, which already gives an uncommon degree of expressiveness.

A few basic principles pervade the system:

[1] Protection is provided by compile-time mechanisms, against accident, not against fraud or explicit violation.

[2] Access is granted by a class, not unilaterally taken.

[3] Access control is done for *names* and does not depend on the type of what is named.

[4] The unit of protection is the class, not the individual object.

[5] Access is controlled, not visibility.

The last two points are explained below.

11.2c Per Class Protection

The class is the unit of protection in C++. This implies that class members and friends have access to all objects of their class for which they have a pointer, a reference, or a name. For example,

```
class list {
    list* next;
public:
    int on(list*);
};

int list::on(list* p)
{
    list* q = this;
    for(;;) {
        if (p == q) return 1;
        if (q == 0) return 0;
        q = q->next;
    }
}
```

The chasing of the private `list::next` pointer is accepted because `list::on()` has access to every object of class *next* it can somehow name.

This can be contrasted to the approach where a member function has access only to the object for which it was invoked and must go through the public interface to access all other objects of its class. Following such a discipline we would have written something like this:

```
int list::on(list* p)
{
    if (p == this) return 1;
    if (p == 0) return 0;
    return next->on(p);
}
```

Doing things that way provides a finer grain of control and protection at the cost of run-time. C++ gives the programmer the choice of programming style, but unfortunately it does not provide any support for enforcing per object protection.

Another important aspect of the C++ protection system is that it applies uniformly to all names. There are no special rules for data member names, function member names, type names, or any other names.

11.3c Access Control

As mentioned (§11), C++ provides access control, not visibility control; that is, the object, function, or whatever referred to in an expression is determined without regard to the access specification, then type checking is done, and only if no error was found is access control applied. The intent is to minimize the effect of changes of access control and to enable a reader to understand a program without having to consider access control declarations. Making a name public or private will not quietly change the meaning of a program from one legal interpretation to another.

It was noticed that people often change access status of functions during program development and that access control specifiers often went unnoticed by people reading programs. Thus it was concluded that visibility control would imply errors and confusion avoided by access control. For example,

```
class X {
    int aa;
public:
    void g(int);
    void g(double);
};


class Y : public X {
    // ...
    void f();
};


void Y::f()
{
    g(1);        // call g(int);
}
```

Making `X::g(int)` private will not quietly change the meaning of the call to a call of `X::g(double)`. Had visibility control − rather than access control − been used, a quiet change of meaning would have been the result of that change.

As far as confusion is concerned, the opposite − access control implies confusion avoided by visibility control − is also true. In such cases, however, the problem is detected by the compiler and easily bypassed by the programmer. For example,

```
int aa;
void g(int);
```

```
class X {
    int aa;
    void g(int);
public:
    void g(double);
};

class Y : public X {
    // ...
    void f();
};

void Y::f()
{
    aa++;          // error: X::aa private
    g(1);          // error: X::g private
}
```

Here, both the use of `aa` and the call of `g()` are resolved to *X*'s private members. If the intent was to use the global names, the program is easily changed to achieve that.

```
void Y::f()
{
    ::aa++;
    ::g(1);
}
```

Had the intent been to use the public function `X::g(double)`, that too could easily be achieved.

```
void Y::f()
{
    g(1.0);
}
```

Here is another example:

```
class A {
private:
    dump();
    // ...
};

class B {
    // ...
public:
    dump();
    // ...
};
```

```
class C: public A, public B {
    void f()
    {
        dump(); // error: ambiguous
    }
};
```

Again, it is not obvious what the intent of the programmer was. Consequently, the safest course is to rely on access control, not visibility control, and flag the ambiguity. The ambiguity can be easily resolved by the user.

```
class C: public A, public B {
    void f() { B::dump(); }
};
```

Special Member Functions

Some member functions have special meaning in the sense that they affect the way a compiler treats objects of their class; that is, they affect the semantics even when they are not explicitly used.

This chapter describes *constructors*, *destructors*, and *conversions*, and the free store management operators, `new` and `delete`. Constructors initialize class objects. Destructors are invoked when class objects are destroyed; they are useful for cleaning up. A conversion function specifies a conversion between a class object and another type.

Copying of class objects and the use of temporaries are also covered in this chapter.

12   Special Member Functions

Some member functions are special in that they affect the way objects of a class are created, copied, and destroyed, and how values may be converted to values of other types. Often such special functions are called implicitly.

These member functions obey the usual access rules (§11). For example, declaring a constructor `protected` ensures that only derived classes and friends can create objects using it.

■ A discussion of the use of access control for special member functions can be found in §12.2c. □

12.1 Constructors

A member function with the same name as its class is called a constructor; it is used to construct values of its class type. If a class has a constructor, each object of that class will be initialized before any use is made of the object; see §12.6.

■ A constructor is called whenever an object of a class with a constructor is created. An object can be created in any of the following ways:
  − as a global variable,
  − as a local variable,
  − through explicit use of operator *new*,
  − through explicit call of a constructor, or
  − as a temporary object.
  It can also be allocated as part of another object (allocated in one of the ways above)
  − as a data member of class or
  − as an object representing a base class.
  In each case the job of the constructor is to create the basic structure of the object; that is, to initialize any virtual function tables, to construct the objects representing base classes (if any), to construct the objects representing nonstatic data members (if any), to lay down information that allows finding objects representing virtual bases (if any), and to execute the code specified in the body of the constructor (if any). For explicit uses of operator *new*, it may also be the job of the constructor to call an *operator new ()* function to allocate memory.

  In other words, a constructor turns raw memory into an object for which the rules of the type system hold. This process is undone by a destructor: After a destructor has been called, the memory that once was an object is again just bits. The most obvious example of the difference between raw memory and a properly constructed object is that virtual functions will work only after construction and before destruction of an object; special rules apply during construction and destruction (§10.9c, §12.7).

  The type system makes it hard, but not impossible, to use an object before it is completely constructed. Use of a partially constructed object is undefined since it would violate any explicit or implicit invariants assumed about objects of the class.
  □

A constructor can be invoked for a `const` or `volatile` object. A constructor may not be declared `const` or `volatile` (§9.3.1). A constructor may not be `virtual`. A constructor may not be `static`.

■ In principle, *everything* that is needed to create an object is known to the programmer at the point where an object is created. There is no object until after it has been created. The virtual mechanism exists to allow operations to be done on an object in the absence of knowledge of the exact type of the object.

  Sometimes one would like to create an object of a class that one does *not* know. All that one knows is that it should be "just like something else." People have been discussing various techniques for doing this under the label "virtual constructors." C++ does not have "virtual constructors" but it does support some simple techniques for handling such cases. For example, an object of a class with some kind of "clone" operation can be passed along and used.

```
class X {
public:
    // ...
    virtual X* clone(); // create a copy of me
                        // (state copied)
    virtual X* newX();  // make a default version
                        // of my class (state not copied)
};

X* X::clone()    // default implementation
{
    return new X(*this);         // use copy constructor
}

X* X::newX()     // default implementation
{
    return new X();      // use default constructor
}

void f(X* p)
{
    X* p1 = p->clone();
    X* p2 = p->newX();
}
```

Here $f()$ is making objects of a type about which the only thing known is that it is an X or a class derived from X.

An alternative technique is to make a function that creates objects of a class X and pass along pointers to such functions. Such a function is described below in this section. The recipient of the function will now not need to know the exact type of the object that function creates. □

Constructors are not inherited. Default constructors and copy constructors, however, are generated (by the compiler) where needed (§12.8). Generated constructors are `public`.

■ Consider what might happen if constructors were inherited.

```
class B {
public:
    int a;
    B();
    B(int);
    B(B&);
};

class D : public B {
public:
    int b;
};
```

```
f()      // note: illegal, a ''what if'' example
{
    B b;
    D d1;        // only B part initialized
    D d2 = b;    // only B part of d2 initialized
    D d3 = d1;   // only B part of d3 initialized
                 // this is NOT a copy
                 // of derived objects!
    d3 = 1;      // assignment to B part of D
}
```

Worst would be the initialization of *d3*. Here, inheriting the constructor from the base class would quietly change the meaning of copying. The ability to assign an integer to a *D* would often be surprising.

In fact, constructors *D::D()* and *D::D(const D&)* are generated, but the example still fails because there is no way of creating a *D* from an integer.

Like constructors – and for the same reasons – assignment operators are generated instead of being inherited. □

A *default constructor* for a class X is a constructor of class X that can be called without an argument.

■ A default constructor is typically of the form *X::X()*, but a constructor that can be called with no arguments because it has default arguments, X::X(int=0), for example, is also a default constructor. Allowing constructors with default arguments, such as X::X(int=0), is a recent extension. The restriction was considered worthwhile because it allowed an array of objects to be initialized by a standard function taking a pointer to function argument specifying what initialization needed to be done for each element in the array. Allowing default initializers forces the compiler to be a little bit clever about that. □

A default constructor will be generated for a class X only if no constructor has been declared for class X.

A *copy constructor* for a class X is a constructor that can be called to copy an object of class X; that is, one that can be called with a single argument of type X. For example, X::X(const X&) and X::X(X&,int=0) are copy constructors. A copy constructor is generated only if no copy constructor is declared.

A copy constructor for a class X may not take an argument of type X. For example, X::X(X) is illegal.

■ The reason for this restriction is that passing an argument is defined as applying the appropriate constructor to construct the object used by the function given the actual argument. For example, had we been able to declare *X(X)*,

```
X a;
extern f(X);    // note: illegal, a ''what if'' example

void g()
{
    f(a);       // means f(X(a))
                // which in turn means f(X(X(a)))
                // which in turn means f(X(X(X(a))))
                // ...
}
```

The restriction avoids the infinite recursion and any clever language rules that would have to be introduced to avoid it had $X::X(X)$ been legal. Control of copying objects of class X is exercised by the declaration of a copy constructor that usually has the form $X::X(const\ X\&)$. □

Constructors for array elements are called in order of increasing addresses (§8.2.4).

If a class has base classes or member objects with constructors, their constructors are called before the constructor for the derived class. The constructors for base classes are called first. See §12.6.2 for an explanation of how arguments can be specified for such constructors and how the order of constructor calls is determined.

An object of a class with a constructor cannot be a member of a union.

■ It would not have been possible to guarantee that the constructor was called for a union member with a constructor. For example, a union might have members of several classes each with their own constructors. For the same reason, objects of classes with destructors (§12.4) or user-defined assignments (§13.4.3) may not be union members. □

No return type (not even `void`) can be specified for a constructor. A `return` statement in the body of a constructor may not specify a return value. It is not possible to take the address of a constructor.

■ No explicit return value is needed because a constructor is defined to construct an object, and any value a function implementing a constructor may return is an implementation detail and invisible to the user (except when looking at generated code, say, with a debugger).

The reason one cannot take the address of a constructor is that constructors have semantics that are closely tied to the semantics of memory allocation in all its varieties, and consequently the implementer (compiler writer) should not be constrained to implement constructors exactly like ordinary functions. Had it been possible to take the address of a constructor, the resulting pointer could be passed into a context where it was not known to be a pointer to a constructor, so it would have to obey all the usual rules and implementation-dependent details of other pointers to member functions. This would constrain the implementation of either pointers to members or constructors or − even worse − expose details of the implementation of constructors to users. The effect would eventually be to force those implementation details to be either incompatibilities among implementations or part of the language definition.

Note also that an explicit call of a constructor does not mean the same as the use of the same syntax for an ordinary member function; see the example at the end of this section. A constructor differs from all other nonstatic member functions in that it is *not* called for an object of its class even though it has a `this` pointer; it is called for a chunk of raw memory and must turn that into an object of its class.

Now if the functionality of a pointer to a constructor really is needed, it can be obtained by indirection, as follows:

```
class X {
public:
    X();
};

void f()           // not this way:
{
    X& (X::* p)() = &X::X;   // error: cannot take
                             // address of constructor
    // ...
}

X* makeX(void* p = 0)
{
    if (p)
        return new(p) X();   // place object at 'p'
    else
        return new X();
}

void g()           // this way!
{
    X* (*p)(void*) = &makeX;
    // ...
}
```

The definition of `makeX()` assumes a suitable overloading of `operator new()`. For example,

```
// explicit placement operator:

void* operator new(size_t, void* p) { return p; }
```

□

A constructor can be used explicitly to create new objects of its type, using the syntax

   class-name (*expression-list$_{opt}$*)

For example,

```
complex zz = complex(1,2.3);
cprint( complex(7.8,1.2) );
```

An object created in this way is unnamed (unless the constructor was used as an initializer for a named variable as for `zz` above), with its lifetime limited to the expression in which it is created; see §12.2.

Member functions may be called from within a constructor; see §12.7.

    ■ Calling a constructor from within a constructor is allowed, but often what it does isn't what the user expected.

```
class C {           // warning: bad code!
    // ...
public:
    C(int i) { /* common initialization */ }
    C() { C(0); }
    C(char* p) { C(0); /* do stuff with 'p' */ }
    // ...
};
```

Such code is sometimes written by programmers who want to factor out the common parts of a set of constructors. The snag is that the explicit calls of `C(0)` each create a temporary object of class `C` and initialize that. Such calls have no effect on the object the calling constructor was invoked to initialize. The way to factor out initialization code is to have an explicit initialization function that is not a constructor.

```
class C {
    // ...
    void init(int i) { /* common initialization */ }
public:
    C(int i) { init(i); }
    C() { init(0); }
    C(char* p) { init(0); /* do stuff with 'p' */ }
    // ...
};
```

It is often wise to make such initialization functions private.

    Making such initialization functions `virtual` would have no effect since it is not possible to refer to the yet unconstructed derived class parts of an object from the constructor of a base class (§10.9c, §12.7). □

12.2 Temporary Objects

In some circumstances it may be necessary or convenient for the compiler to generate a temporary object. Such introduction of temporaries is implementation dependent. When a compiler introduces a temporary object of a class that has a constructor it must ensure that a constructor is called for the temporary object. Similarly, the destructor must be called for a temporary object of a class where a destructor is declared.

    ■ The implementation's use of temporaries can be observed, therefore, through side effects produced by constructors and destructors. □

For example,

```
class X {
    // ...
public:
    // ...
    X(int);
    X(X&);
    ~X();
};

X f(X);

void g()
{
    X a(1);
    X b = f(X(2));
    a = f(a);
}
```

Here, one might use a temporary in which to construct X(2) before passing it to f() by X(X&); alternatively, X(2) might be constructed in the space used to hold the argument for the first call of f(). Also, a temporary might be used to hold the result of f(X(2)) before copying it to b by X(X&); alternatively, f()'s result might be constructed in b. On the other hand, for many functions f(), the expression a=f(a) requires a temporary for either the argument a or the result of f(a) to avoid undesired aliasing of a.

The compiler must ensure that a temporary object is destroyed. The exact point of destruction is implementation dependent. There are only two things that can be done with a temporary: fetch its value (implicitly copying it) to use in some other expression, or bind a reference to it. If the value of a temporary is fetched, that temporary is then dead and can be destroyed immediately. If a reference is bound to a temporary, the temporary must not be destroyed until the reference is. This destruction must take place before exit from the scope in which the temporary is created.

■ The only perfectly safe rule for the destruction of temporaries would be to require them not to be destroyed until the last reference to them disappeared. Since this is not done − to avoid the overheads involved in the mechanisms needed to ensure that − a temporary may sometimes be destroyed earlier than a user would like. Consider

```
class String {
    char *ptr;
    // initialize with concatenated string:
    String(const String &s1, const String &s2);
```

```
public:
    String(const char *s) { /* set ptr */ }
    String(const String &s) { /* set ptr */ }
    ~String() { delete ptr; }
    operator char*() { return ptr; }
    String operator+(const String &s)
        { return String(*this, s); }
};

void foo(const char *s) { /* do something */ }

main()
{
    String x("foo");
    String y("bar");
    foo(x + y); // not guaranteed to work
}
```

Note, in particular, that the conversion operator passes a pointer to the representation of the *String* out of the class. The rule for destruction of temporaries allows this implementation:

```
put x+y in temp1
convert temp1 to char* and put the result in temp2
destroy temp1
foo(temp2)
```

so the example may not work as apparently expected. It has been suggested that temporaries should be guaranteed to persist until the end of the expression in which they are created. That would ensure that the example above worked. Then, however, the use of explicit variables could cause problems.

```
main()
{
    String x("foo");
    String y("bar");
    const char* p = x + y;
    foo(p);      // still not guaranteed to work
}
```

So how about guaranteeing that temporaries persist until the end of the block in which they are created? That is still not good enough.

```
main()
{
    String x("foo");
    String y("bar");
    const char* p;
    {
        p = x + y;
    }
    foo(p);      // still not guaranteed to work
}
```

Then how about guaranteeing that temporaries persist until the end of the function in which they are created? That is still not good enough.

```
const char* f()
{
    String x("foo");
    String y("bar");
    return x + y; // still not guaranteed to work
}
```

So, as stated above, the problem is that a pointer to a temporary object (or to part of a temporary object) was passed out of the context in which the compiler knew it existed. The only perfect solution for this is garbage collection. Many occurrences, however, can be completely analyzed at compile time. A compiler can often warn users about potential portability problems of such examples. For example, a thorough compiler with access to all source code in a program could detect the return of a pointer to (part of) an object from a function and warn when such a function is applied to a temporary. The function `String::operator char*()` and the conversions of `x+y` to a `char*` above are examples of this. In particular, since `String::operator char*()` is inline, its definition is available. Thus, enough information for issuing a warning (or delaying destruction) is available even in the presence of separate compilation. □

Another form of temporaries is discussed in §8.4.3.

■ A further discussion of temporaries and the possibilities for their elimination can be found in (§12.1c). □

12.3 Conversions

Type conversions of class objects can be specified by constructors and by conversion functions.

Such conversions, often called *user-defined conversions*, are used implicitly in addition to standard conversions (§4). For example, a function expecting an argument of type X can be called not only with an argument of type X but also with an argument of type T where a conversion from T to X exists. User-defined conversions are used similarly for conversion of initializers (§8.4), function arguments (§5.2.2, §8.2.5), function return values (§6.6.3, §8.2.5), expression operands (§5), expressions controlling iteration and selection statements (§6.4, §6.5), and explicit type conversions (§5.2.3, §5.4).

User-defined conversions are applied only where they are unambiguous (§10.1.1, §12.3.2). Conversions obey the access control rules (§11). As ever access control is applied after ambiguity resolution (§10.4).

■ Examples of how to use access control for special member functions in general and conversions in particular can be found in §12.2c. □

See §13.2 for a discussion of the use of conversions in function calls as well as examples below.

12.3.1 Conversion by Constructor

A constructor accepting a single argument specifies a conversion from its argument
type to the type of its class. For example,

```
class X {
    // ...
public:
    X(int);
    X(const char*, int = 0);
};


void f(X arg) {
    X a = 1;            // a = X(1)
    X b = "Jessie";     // b = X("Jessie",0)
    a = 2;              // a = X(2)
    f(3);               // f(X(3))
}
```

When no constructor for class X accepts the given type, no attempt is made to find
other constructors or conversion functions to convert the assigned value into a type
acceptable to a constructor for class X. For example,

```
class X { /* ... */ X(int); };
class Y { /* ... */ Y(X); };
Y a = 1;                    // illegal: Y(X(1)) not tried
```

■ A constant of a class type cannot appear in a program in the same sense that 1.2
and $12e3$ appear as constants of type *double*. A constant of an appropriate basic
type, however, can be used where a constant of a class type is expected if a constructor taking a single argument exists to provide an interpretation. Furthermore, if
the class has a constructor simple enough to substitute inline, it is reasonable to use
a constructor invocation as a constant. For example,

```
class complex {
    double re,im;
public:
    complex(double r, double i = 0) { re=r; im=i; }
    // ...
};


complex z1 = complex(1.2);
complex z2 = 3;


z1 = complex(3.5,7)+2.7*z2;
```

Note that the last example here requires overloaded operators + and * (see
§13.3).

A constructor taking a single argument need not be called explicitly. This occasionally leads to unintended implicit uses of conversions. For example,

```
class Vector {
    // ...
public:
    Vector(int s); // make vector with 's' elements
    // ...
};

void f()
{
    Vector v(10);         // intended use
    // ...
    v = 10;       // unintended use
}
```

Here, *v=10* is taken to mean convert *10* to a vector and assign, *v=Vector(10)*. Strangely enough, such errors do not appear to be a genuine problem.

When the programmer wants to be absolutely certain that no unintentional implicit conversion happens, a constructor taking a single argument can be avoided in favor of an explicitly named function.

```
class Vector {
private:
    // ...
    Vector(int s); // make vector with 's' elements
public:
    static Vector make(int s) { return Vector(s); }
    // ...
};

void f()
{
    Vector v = Vector::make(10);
    // ...
    v = 10;                       // error: private constructor
    v = Vector::make(10);   // ok
}
```

□

12.3.2 Conversion Functions

A member function of a class X with a name of the form

> *conversion-function-name:*
>   operator *conversion-type-name*

> *conversion-type-name:*
>   *type-specifier-list ptr-operator$_{opt}$*

specifies a conversion from X to the type specified by the *conversion-type-name*. Such member functions are called conversion functions. Classes, enumerations, and *typedef-name*s may not be declared in the *type-specifier-list*.

■ Conversion functions can do two things that cannot be specified by constructors:
  1. Define a conversion from a class to a basic type,
  2. Define a conversion from one class to another without modifying the declaration for the other class.

□

Neither argument types nor return type may be specified.

■ For example,

```
class X {
    int* operator int*();       // error
    operator void*(int);        // error
    operator char*();           // ok
};
```

□

Here is an example:

```
class X {
    // ...
public:
    operator int();
};

void f(X a)
{
    int i = int(a);
    i = (int)a;
    i = a;
}
```

In all three cases the value assigned will be converted by `X::operator int()`. User-defined conversions are not restricted to use in assignments and initializations. For example,

```
void g(X a, X b)
{
    int i = (a) ? 1+a : 0;
    int j = (a&&b) ? a+b : i;
    if (a) { // ...
    }
}
```

Conversion operators are inherited.

■ For example,

```
struct S {
    operator int();
};

struct SS : public S { };

void f()
{
    SS a;
    int i = a;   // i = a.S::operator int()
}
```

□

Conversion functions can be virtual.

■ For example,

```
#include <iostream.h>

class X {
public:
    virtual operator const char*() { return "X"; }
};

class Y : public X {
    operator const char*() { return "Y"; }
};

void main()
{
    X* p = new Y;
    cout << *p << '\n'; // prints "Y"
}
```

□

At most one user-defined conversion (constructor or conversion function) is implicitly applied to a single value. For example,

```
class X {
    // ...
public:
    operator int();
};

class Y {
    // ...
public:
    operator X();
};
```

```
Y a;
int b = a;     // illegal:
               // a.operator X().operator int() not tried
int c = X(a); // ok: a.operator X().operator int()
```

User-defined conversions are used implicitly only if they are unambiguous.

■ Ambiguities can arise both from multiple choices of user-defined conversions and from multiple choices between user-defined and built-in conversions. Consider, for example,

```
class Boolean {
    int b;
public:
    Boolean operator+(Boolean);
    Boolean(int i) { b = i!=0; }
    operator int() { return b; }
};

Boolean bool(1);
```

Given this, an expression like *(bool+1)* would be ambiguous because it could be interpreted as either

```
(bool.operator int() + 1)
```

or

```
(bool.operator + (Boolean(1)))
```

The user can avoid the ambiguity by explicitly writing the expression intended. □

■ Defining a conversion by both a constructor and a conversion function can lead to ambiguities. For example,

```
class B;

class A {
public:
    // ...
    A(B&);
};

class B {
public:
    // ...
    operator A();
};

B b;
A a = b;            // error: A(b) or b.operator A() ?
```

□

A conversion function in a derived class does not hide a conversion function in a base class unless the two functions convert to the same type. For example,

```
class X {
public:
    // ...
    operator int();
};

class Y : public X {
public:
    // ...
    operator void*();
};

void f(Y& a)
{
    if (a) {      // error: ambiguous
        // ...
    }
}
```

■ That is, conversions to different types are considered functions with different names, *not* as overloaded versions of a function of the same name.

This rule has the desirable property of allowing the maximum number of potential ambiguities to be caught. □

■ Note that since conversion functions do not take arguments, they cannot be overloaded. □

12.4 Destructors

A member function of class `cl` named `~cl` is called a destructor; it is used to destroy values of type `cl` immediately before the object containing them is destroyed.

■ Another way of looking at a destructor is as an operation that reverses the effect of a constructor: A destructor turns an object into raw memory. □

A destructor takes no arguments, and no return type can be specified for it (not even `void`). It is not possible to take the address of a destructor.

■ As with constructors (§12.1), this restriction is imposed to allow the compiler writer the freedom to implement destructors in ways that are different from ordinary member functions. In particular, one popular technique for implementing destructors involves a hidden argument specifying whether memory in which the object is allocated should be deallocated by the destructor and whether destructors should be called for virtual base classes.

If the equivalent to the address of a destructor is needed, wrap an explicit call to the destructor in a function, preferably a virtual member function for safety, and pass the pointer to that function instead; see §12.1. □

A destructor can be invoked for a const or volatile object. A destructor may not be declared const or volatile (§9.3.1). A destructor may not be static.

Destructors are not inherited. If a base or a member has a destructor and no destructor is declared for its derived class a default destructor is generated. This generated destructor calls the destructors for bases and members of the derived class. Generated destructors are public.

The body of a destructor is executed before the destructors for member objects. Destructors for nonstatic member objects are executed before the destructors for base classes. Destructors for nonvirtual base classes are executed before destructors for virtual base classes. Destructors for nonvirtual base classes are executed in reverse order of their declaration in the derived class. Destructors for virtual base classes are executed in the reverse order of their appearance in a depth-first left-to-right traversal of the directed acyclic graph of base classes; "left-to-right" is the order of appearance of the base class names in the declaration of the derived class.

■ Look at the diagram in §12.6.2 illustrating construction order. The order of destruction is the reverse of the order of construction. □

■ Note that all calls of member and base destructors are implicit; the programmer need not − and should not try to − write any code to make this happen. See §12.6.2 for a further discussion of declaration order. □

Destructors for elements of an array are called in reverse order of their construction.

A destructor may be virtual.

■ It is often a good idea to declare a destructor virtual. If a destructor is not virtual one can get caught in this mess:

```
class B {
    // ...
public:
    B();
    ~B();
};

class D : public B {
    // ...
public:
    D();
    ~D();
};

void f()
{
    B* p = new D();   // create a D
    delete p;         // delete a B
}
```

Since *B*'s destructor was not virtual, the delete statement calls *B::~B()* and not

$D::~D()$ as was presumably needed for correct operation. Declaring $B::~B()$
virtual solves the problem.

```
class B {
    // ...
    B();
    virtual ~B();
};
```

Note that if a class has a destructor, all its derived classes are guaranteed to have
destructors.

So why are destructors not virtual by default? The reason is that an object with
a virtual function needs some form of data that allows it to determine which version
of a virtual function to call. Typically, that is a pointer to a table of virtual functions, a *vptr* (see §10.7c, §10.8c). Sometimes it is undesirable to add such data.
This overhead can be critical when many small objects are involved and even worse
when it increases the size of something that would fit in a register into something
that cannot. In both cases, a *point* defined as two 16-bit integers can be an example; with a *vptr* added, such a point would have a 64-bit representation. Even
worse, adding a *vptr* makes a storage layout that is distinctively C++, which is
unacceptable for data structures that have to be shared with code written in other
languages. For example, the class describing an I/O layout for a machine with
memory mapped I/O, an array of complex numbers to be given to a Fortran library,
or a C operating system data structure must not be modified quietly by a C++ compiler for the convenience of the programmer.

As a rule of thumb, declare a virtual destructor in every base class that has a virtual function. □

Member functions may be called from within a destructor; see §12.7.

An object of a class with a destructor cannot be a member of a union.

Destructors are invoked implicitly (1) when an `auto` (§3.5) or temporary
(§12.2, §8.4.3) object goes out of scope, (2) for constructed static (§3.5) objects at
program termination (§3.4), (3) through use of the `delete` operator (§5.3.4) for
objects allocated by the `new` operator (§5.3.3), and (4) explicitly called. When
invoked by the `delete` operator, memory is freed by the destructor for the most
derived class (§12.6.2) of the object using an `operator delete()` (§5.3.4). For
example,

```
class X {
    // ...
public:
    X(int);
    ~X();
};


void g(X*);
```

```
void f()            // common use:
{
    X* p = new X(111);  // allocate and initialize
    g(p);
    delete p;           // cleanup and deallocate
}
```

Explicit calls of destructors are rarely needed. One use of such calls is for objects placed at specific addresses using a new operator. Such use of explicit placement and destruction of objects can be necessary to cope with dedicated hardware resources and for writing memory management facilities. For example,

```
void* operator new(size_t, void* p) { return p; }

void f(X* p);

static char buf[sizeof(X)];

void g()            // rare, specialized use:
{
    X* p = new(buf) X(222);  // use buf[]
                             // and initialize
    f(p);
    p->X::~X();              // cleanup
}
```

■ An explicit call of a destructor must use -> or . explicitly. An attempt to rely on implicit use of the *this* pointer would lead to confusion between the use of the ~ as part of the name of the destructor and using the unary ~ operator (§5.3).

```
class X {
    // ...
public:
    X();
    virtual ~X();
    X& operator~();
    void f();
    // ...
};

void X::f()
{
    X aa = X();     // construct an X
    ~aa;            // apply complement operator to 'aa'
    aa.~X();        // destroy 'aa'
    this->~X();     // destroy '*this'
    ~X();           // create an X and complement it
}
```

Explicitly calling destructors should be limited to the rare cases when it genuinely is needed. □

■ As usual, explicit qualification of a function name in a call suppresses the virtual function call mechanism. For example,

```
class XX : public X {
        // ...
public:
        ~XX();    // note that X::~X was virtual
};

void g()
{
        XX a;
        extern gg(X&);
        h(a);
}

void h(X& a)
{
        a.X::~X();    // static call
        a.~X();       // virtual call
}
```

The call *h(a)* in *g()* will cause the second destructor call in *h()* to invoke *XX*'s destructor. □

The notation for explicit call of a destructor may be used for any simple type name. For example,

```
int* p;
// ...
p->int::~int();
```

Using the notation for a type that does not have a destructor has no effect. Allowing this enables people to write code without having to know if a destructor exists for a given type.

12.5 Free Store

When an object is created with the new operator, an operator new() function is (implicitly) used to obtain the store needed (§5.3.3).

If operator new() cannot allocate storage it will return 0.

■ The programmer can affect the behavior of the default *operator new()* by calling a function

```
extern void (*set_new_handler (void(*)()))();
```

declared in the standard header <new.h>. If *operator new()* cannot find storage to return, it calls a function – often referred to as the "new-handler" – determined by the last call of the function *set_new_handler()*. A call of *set_new_handler()* returns the old new-handler and makes its argument the new-handler. A zero argument indicates to *set_new_handler()* that no new-handler should be used; that is also the default setting. If there is a new-handler, *operator new()* will call it and make another attempt to allocate memory. Here is a simple example of a *set_new_handler()*:

```
typedef void (*PFVV)();

extern PFVV _new_handler = 0;

extern PFVV set_new_handler(PFVV handler)
{
    PFVV rr = _new_handler;
    _new_handler = handler;
    return rr;
}
```

Here is an example of a simple *operator new()*:

```
#include <stdlib.h>

extern void* _last_allocation;

extern void* operator new(size_t size)
{
    void* p;

    while ( (p=malloc(size))==0 ) {
        if(_new_handler)
            (*_new_handler)();
        else
            return 0;
    }
    return _last_allocation=p;
}
```

☐

An X::operator new() for a class X is a static member (even if not explicitly declared static). Its first argument must be of type size_t, an implementation-dependent integral type defined in the standard header <stddef.h>; it must return void*. For example,

```
class X {
    // ...
    void* operator new(size_t);
    void* operator new(size_t, Arena*);
};
```

■ The reason that *X::operator new()* and *X::operator delete()* must be static members is that they are called before the constructor and after the destructor, respectively. In other words they do *not* operate on an object of class *X*; rather, they allocate the memory in which a constructor will create an object of class *X* and on some memory in which a destructor just destroyed an object of class *X*, respectively. Giving them a *this* pointer (that is, allowing them to be nonstatic) would simply give these functions data and functions that could not be used with even the most minimal degree of safety.

The degree of separation between allocation and initialization (and between deallocation and cleanup) that this implies makes for cleaner programs. □

See §5.3.3 for the rules for selecting an `operator new()`.

■ Note that the usual scope, access, and overloading rules apply to calls of *operator new()*. The following, for example, is an error:

```
class X {
private:
    void* operator new(size_t);
public:
    X();
};

X* p = new X;    // error X::operator new() is private
```

Consider also,

```
class Y {
    // ...
public:
    void *operator new (size_t size, int flag);
};

Y* p1 = new Y;      // error: tries to call
                    // Y::operator new(size_t)
Y* p2 = new(7) Y;   // ok:
                    // calls Y::operator new(size_t,int)
```

The reason is that the declaration of *Y::operator new()* has hidden the global *operator new()*.

A more subtle version of this error may occur when a constructor is defined.

```
class Y {
    // ...
public:
    void *operator new (size_t s, int flag);
    Y() {}         // may be error
};
```

Here, an implementation is allowed to place a call of *operator new()* in the body of the constructor to implement the constructor semantics (see §12.1). If it does so, it will call an *operator new()* with a single argument, but *Y::operator new()* requires two.

In either case, the solution is to provide a *Y::operator new()* that accepts a single argument. For example,

```
class Y {
    // ...
public:
    void *operator new (size_t s)
        { return ::operator new(s); }
    void *operator new (size_t s, int flag);
};
```

Naturally, if a call to an *operator new()* is embedded in a constructor by the implementation, it will be used only for invocations of *new* for which it is appropriate. □

An X::operator delete() for a class X is a static member (even if not explicitly declared static) and must have its first argument of type void*; a second argument of type size_t may be added. It cannot return a value; its return type must be void. For example,

```
class X {
    // ...
    void operator delete(void*);
};

class Y {
    // ...
    void operator delete(void*, size_t);
};
```

Only one operator delete() may be declared for a single class; thus operator delete() cannot be overloaded. The global operator delete() takes a single argument of type void*.

If the two argument style is used, operator delete() will be called with a second argument indicating the size of the object being deleted. The size passed is determined by the destructor (if any) or by the (static) type of the pointer being deleted; that is, it will be correct either if the type of the pointer argument to the delete operator is the exact type of the object (and not, for example, just the type of base class) or if the type is that of a base class with a virtual destructor.

■ Note that if the base class has a destructor, then a destructor will exist for all classes derived from it. If the user doesn't declare one, a default version is generated. Since the size of an object of the class is known where a destructor is defined, the information necessary for getting the size right is always available for a class with a virtual destructor. □

The global operator new() and operator delete() are used for arrays of class objects (§5.3.3, §5.3.4).

Since X::operator new() and X::operator delete() are static they cannot be virtual.

■ They are inherited, though. □

A destructor finds the `operator delete()` to use for freeing store using the usual scope rules. For example,

```
struct B {
    virtual ~B();
    void* operator new(size_t);
    void operator delete(void*);
};


struct D : B {
    ~D();
    void* operator new(size_t);
    void operator delete(void*);
};


void f()
{
    B* p = new D;
    delete p;
}
```

Here, storage for the object of class D is allocated by `D::operator new()` and, thanks to the virtual destructor, deallocated by `D::operator delete()`.

12.6 Initialization

An object of a class with no constructors, no private or protected members, no virtual functions, and no base classes can be initialized using an initializer list; see §8.4.1. An object of a class with a constructor must either be initialized or have a default constructor (§12.1). The default constructor is used for objects that are not explicitly initialized.

12.6.1 Explicit Initialization

Objects of classes with constructors (§12.1) can be initialized with a parenthesized expression list. This list is taken as the argument list for a call of a constructor doing the initialization. Alternatively a single value is specified as the initializer using the = operator. This value is used as the argument to a copy constructor. Typically, that call of a copy constructor can be eliminated. For example,

```
class complex {
    // ...
public:
    complex();
    complex(double);
    complex(double,double);
    // ...
};

complex sqrt(complex,complex);
```

■ Note that since class *complex* has constructors it is considered to have a public copy constructor with the default implementation even though no copy constructor is explicitly declared (§12.1). □

```
complex a(1);              // initialize by a call of
                           // complex(double)
complex b = a;             // initialize by a copy of 'a'
complex c = complex(1,2);  // construct complex(1,2)
                           // using complex(double,double)
                           // copy it into 'c'
complex d = sqrt(b,c);     // call sqrt(complex,complex)
                           // and copy the result into 'd'
complex e;                 // initialize by a call of
                           // complex()
complex f = 3;             // construct complex(3) using
                           // complex(double)
                           // copy it into 'f'
```

■ For each of these, a compiler will be able to construct the complex value directly in the variable created (see §12.1, §12.8), but only for *a* and *e* is the compiler required to do so; in the other cases a temporary object may be used (§12.2). Note, however, that access control is applied for the copy constructor (§11), so had *complex(const complex&)* been private only the declarations of *a* and *e* would have been legal. □

Overloading of the assignment operator = has no effect on initialization.

■ Specifying initialization using = as normal expression evaluation followed by a copy operation (that is usually optimized away) has three effects:
- The set of values acceptable for initialization and assignment will be identical except where the user specifically defines constructors and/or assignment operators to ensure they are not.
- Access control is applied for the copy constructor (just as it is for assignment).
- The use of a temporary *and* its possible elimination are explicitly allowed, giving implementers a degree of freedom that is sometimes needed.

Note that initialization and assignment are generally very different operations. Initialization occurs wherever an object is created. That is,

- when a variable is defined with an explicit initial value,
- when a variable is defined without an explicit initial value but the variable is of a class with a default constructor,
- when a function returns a value,
- when an argument is passed,
- when an explicit or implicit conversion in an expression results in the creation of an object with a constructor,
- when an object is created with the *new* operator with an explicit initial value,
- when an object is created with the *new* operator without an explicit initial value but the object is of a class with a default constructor, and
- when a constructor is used explicitly in an expression.

Assignment occurs when an assignment operator is used in an expression. An assignment operation will always invoke a predefined, user-defined, or default assignment operator. The left operand of an assignment is always a previously constructed object, whereas an object being initialized never is. Assignment operations typically rely on being invoked only for fully constructed objects.

Initialization of a declared variable (or constant) takes a variety of syntactic forms.

```
T x(a);
T x = a;
T x = T(a);
T x = (T)a;
```

These are most often equivalent, but there are distinctions that are of interest mostly to compiler writers. We will ignore built-in types and consider only classes. Consider

```
struct T {
    T(int);        // conversion: int -> T
    T(const T&);
};

struct S {
    operator T();          // conversion: S -> T
};


S a;

T x1 = a;
T x2(a);
T x3 = T(a);
T x4 = (T)(a);
```

All these initializations are legal, but not for the same reasons. Where the explicit = is used, the meaning is "construct the value specified in a temporary object, and then copy it to the variable being initialized using the copy constructor." A good compiler notices that there is no need to introduce the temporary and eliminates it. For

```
T x2(a);
```

a constructor (which happens to be the copy constructor) is called directly for *x2*. Constructing the copy constructor's argument using the conversion function, however, may require a temporary.

Had no copy constructor been declared for *T*, all would have happened exactly as before because a copy constructor would have been generated. Again, a good compiler would eliminate the use of the generated copy constructor.

Had *T*'s copy constructor been private, a difference could have been detected.

```
class T {
    T(const T&);
public:
    T(int);
};

T x5(1);          // ok
T x6 = T(1);      // error: T::T(const T&) is private
```

In both cases, $T::T(int)$ is called to create the *T*. In the latter case, however, the copy constructor is needed to initialize *x6*, and since we assumed it to be private, the initialization fails. The temporary can be eliminated (§12.1c), but the semantics are not affected.

Except for access control issues and the possible use of temporaries, the forms

```
T x(a);
```

```
T x = T(a);
```

```
T x = (T)a;
```

are always equivalent. The forms

```
T x = a;
```

and

```
T x = T(a);
```

differ in that the latter is considered a direct call of a conversion function or a constructor, whereas an implicit user-defined conversion is involved in the former. Since at most one user-defined conversion is implicitly applied to a value in a single expression (§13.2) this can lead to differences. For example,

```
class Vector {
public:
    Vector(int);
};

class Bignum {
public:
    operator int();
};
```

```
void f()
{
    Bignum b;
    // ...
    Vector v1(b);           // ok
    Vector v2 = Vector(b);  // ok
    Vector v3 = b;          // error: max one implicit
                            // user-defined conversion
}
```

Access control is applied to user-defined conversions just as it is to all other functions (§11). Similarly, ambiguity control is applied to initialization involving user-
defined conversions just as it is to all other function calls (§10.1.1). For example,

```
struct X {
};

struct T {
    T(int);
    T(X);
};

struct S {
    operator int();
    operator X();
};

S a;

T x = T(a);   // error: ambiguous
              // T(a.operator int()) or T(a.operator X())
```

An example of each form of class object initialization follows:

```
T x = a;      // make a T from 'a', then copy it to 'x'
              // max 1 implicit user-defined conversion

T x = T(a);   // make a T from 'a', then copy it to 'x'
              // max 1 implicit user-defined conversion
              // plus the explicit conversion to T

T x = (T)a;   // identical to T x = T(a);

T x(a);       // call a constructor for T,
              // maybe the copy constructor
```

☐

The initialization that occurs in argument passing and function return is
equivalent to the form

```
T x = a;
```

The initialization that occurs in new expressions (§5.3.3) and in base and member
initializers (§12.6.2) is equivalent to the form

```
T x(a);
```

■ For built-in types, the only differences are between forms that are explicit casts and forms that are not. For example,

```
typedef int* T;

T x1 = 1;        // error: cannot initialize int* with int
T x2(1);         // error: cannot initialize int* with int
T x3 = T(1);     // ok: explicit cast to int*
T x4 = (T)1;     // ok: explicit cast to int*
```

□

Arrays of objects of a class with constructors use constructors in initialization (§12.1) just like individual objects. If there are fewer initializers in the list than elements in the array, the default constructor (§12.1) is used. If there is no default constructor the *initializer-list* must be complete. For example,

```
complex cc = { 1, 2 }; // error; use constructor
complex v[6] = { 1,complex(1,2),complex(),2 };
```

Here, `v[0]` and `v[3]` are initialized with `complex::complex(double)`, `v[1]` is initialized with `complex::complex(double,double)`, and `v[2]`, `v[4]`, and `v[5]` are initialized with `complex::complex()`.

■ In other words, given a default constructor that initializes a complex number to `(0,0)`, the initializations above are equivalent to this more explicit variant:

```
complex v[6] = {
    complex(1,0),
    complex(1,2),
    complex(0,0),
    complex(2,0),
    complex(0,0),
    complex(0,0)
};
```

□

An object of class M can be a member of a class X only if (1) M does not have a constructor, or (2) M has a default constructor, or (3) X has a constructor and if every constructor of class X specifies a *ctor-initializer* (§12.6.2) for that member. In case 2 the default constructor is called when the aggregate is created. If a member of an aggregate has a destructor, then that destructor is called when the aggregate is destroyed.

Constructors for nonlocal static objects are called in the order they occur in a file; destructors are called in reverse order. See also §3.4, §6.7, §9.4.

■ A static array member can be initialized in a definition outside the class declaration, as in this example:

```
struct Table1 {
    static const int powers[8];
    static int values[4];
};
const int Table1::powers[8] = {2,4,8,16,32,64,128,256};
int Table1::values[4] = {0,0,0,0};
```

A nonstatic array member that is not *const* can be initialized in each object of the class type with supplied or default argument values in a constructor, as follows:

```
struct Table2 {
    int tbl[2];

    Table2(int tbl0=255, int tbl1=256) {
        tbl[0]=tbl0;
        tbl[1]=tbl1;
    };
};
```

There is, however, no member initialization syntax for nonstatic *const* arrays. For example,

```
struct Table4 {
    const int tbl[2];

    Table4() : tbl(99,100) {};          // syntax error
    Table4() : tbl{99,100} {};          // syntax error
    Table4() : tbl({99,100}) {};        // syntax error
};
```

A nonstatic member that is not an array, whether *const* or not, can be initialized through a member initialization list, as follows:

```
struct Table3 {
    int (*tbl)[];
    const int max;
    int size;

    Table3() : max(64), size(16) {};
};
```

☐

12.6.2 Initializing Bases and Members

Initializers for immediate base classes and for members not inherited from a base class may be specified in the definition of a constructor. This is most useful for class objects, constants, and references where the semantics of initialization and assignment differ.

■ Disallowing the initialization of indirect bases and of inherited members prevents multiple initializations of a single base or member.

```
class X {
public:
    int& x;
    X();
    X(int& r) : x(r) { /* ... */ }
    ~X();
};

class B : public X {
public:
    int b;
    B(int i) : X(i), b(i) { /* ... */ }
};

class D: public B {
    int d;
    int d2;
public:
    D() : B(2),
          b(3), // error: 'b' is inherited
          X(d), // error: 'X' is an indirect class
          x(d2) // error: 'x' is inherited
        { /* ... */ }
};
```

□

A *ctor-initializer* has the form

> *ctor-initializer:*
> 　　: *mem-initializer-list*

> *mem-initializer-list:*
> 　　*mem-initializer*
> 　　*mem-initializer* , *mem-initializer-list*

> *mem-initializer:*
> 　　*complete-class-name* (*expression-list*$_{opt}$)
> 　　*identifier* (*expression-list*$_{opt}$)

■ See §18.3 for the old ":(*expression-list*)" form of base class initializers. □

The argument list is used to initialize the named nonstatic member or base class object. This is the only way to initialize nonstatic `const` and reference members. For example,

```
struct B1 { B1(int); /* ... */ };
struct B2 { B2(int); /* ... */ };

struct D : B1, B2 {
    D(int);
    B1 b;
    const c;
};


D::D(int a)  : B2(a+1), B1(a+2), c(a+3), b(a+4)
{ /* ... */ }

D d(10);
```

First, the base classes are initialized in declaration order (independent of the order of *mem-initializers*), then the members are initialized in declaration order (independent of the order of *mem-initializers*), then the body of D::D() is executed (§12.1). The declaration order is used to ensure that sub-objects and members are destroyed in the reverse order of initialization.

Virtual base classes constitute a special case. Virtual bases are constructed before any nonvirtual bases and in the order they appear on a depth-first left-to-right traversal of the directed acyclic graph of base classes; ''left-to-right'' is the order of appearance of the base class names in the declaration of the derived class.

■ Consider

```
class A { /* ... */ };
class B { /* ... */ };

class C : public virtual A, public virtual B { /* ... */ };
class D : public virtual B, public virtual A { /* ... */ };

class E : public C, public D { /* ... */ };
```

The usual way of drawing the sub-objects simply obscures the order of initialization of virtual base objects by not representing the order of declaration of A and B in C and D adequately.

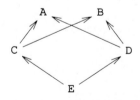

Drawing each occurrence of a virtual base separately even though there is only one A and one B in an E helps.

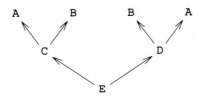

The order of construction is

```
C's A
C's B
C
(D's B already done, ignore)
(D's A already done, ignore)
D
E
```

□

A *complete object* is an object that is not a sub-object representing a base class. Its class is said to be the *most derived* class for the object. All sub-objects for virtual base classes are initialized by the constructor of the most derived class. If a constructor of the most derived class does not specify a *mem-initializer* for a virtual base class then that virtual base class must have a default constructor or no constructors. Any *mem-initializer*s for virtual classes specified in a constructor for a class that is not the class of the complete object are ignored. For example,

```
class V {
public:
    V();
    V(int);
    // ...
};

class A : public virtual V {
public:
    A();
    A(int);
    // ...
};

class B : public virtual V {
public:
    B();
    B(int);
    // ...
};
```

```
class C : public A, public B, private virtual V {
public:
    C();
    C(int);
    // ...
};
```

```
A::A(int i) : V(i) { /* ... */ }
B::B(int i) { /* ... */ }
C::C(int i) { /* ... */ }
```

```
V v(1); // use V(int)
A a(2); // use V(int)
B b(3); // use V()
C c(4); // use V()
```

A *mem-initializer* is evaluated in the scope of the constructor in which it appears. For example,

```
class X {
    int a;
public:
    const int& r;
    X(): r(a) {}
};
```

initializes X::r to refer to X::a for each object of class X.

12.7 Constructors and Destructors

Member functions may be called in constructors and destructors. This implies that virtual functions may be called (directly or indirectly). The function called will be the one defined in the constructor's (or destructor's) own class or its bases, but *not* any function overriding it in a derived class. This ensures that unconstructed objects will not be accessed during construction or destruction. For example,

```
class X {
public:
    virtual void f();
    X() { f(); }    // calls X::f()
    ~X() { f(); }    // calls X::f()
};
```

```
class Y : public X {
    int& r;
public:
    void f()
    {
        r++;   // disaster if 'r' is uninitialized
    }
    Y(int& rr) :r(rr) {}
};
```

The effect of calling a pure virtual function directly or indirectly for the object being constructed from a constructor, except using explicit qualification, is undefined (§10.3).

12.8 Copying Class Objects

A class object can be copied in two ways, by assignment (§5.17) and by initialization (§12.1, §8.4) including function argument passing (§5.2.2) and function value return (§6.6.3). Conceptually, for a class X these two operations are implemented by an assignment operator and a copy constructor (§12.1).

> ■ In practice, a good compiler can generate bitwise copies for most class objects since they have the bitwise copy semantics; no assignment function must be generated unless the user takes its address. □

The programmer may define one or both of these. If not defined by the programmer, they will be defined as memberwise assignment and memberwise initialization of the members of X, respectively.

If all bases and members of a class X have copy constructors accepting const arguments, the generated copy constructor for X will take a single argument of type const X&, as follows:

```
X::X(const X&)
```

Otherwise it will take a single argument of type X&:

```
X::X(X&)
```

and initialization by copying of const X objects will not be possible.

Similarly, if all bases and members of a class X have assignment operators accepting const arguments, the generated assignment operator for X will take a single argument of type const X&, as follows:

```
X& X::operator=(const X&)
```

Otherwise it will take a single argument of type X&:

```
X& X::operator=(X&)
```

and assignment by copying of const X objects will not be possible. The default assignment operator will return a reference to the object for which is invoked.

Objects representing virtual base classes will be initialized only once by a generated copy constructor. Objects representing virtual base classes will be assigned only once by a generated assignment operator.

> ■ This can be achieved only by a consistent strategy for all constructors and assignment operators. For example, every constructor of a class with a virtual base could be given a hidden argument indicating whether the virtual base has already been constructed. Such consistency is not easily achieved for, say, user-defined assignment operators. □

Memberwise assignment and memberwise initialization implies that if a class X has a member of a class M, M's assignment operator and M's copy constructor are used to implement assignment and initialization of the member, respectively. If a class has a `const` member, a reference member, or a member or a base of a class with a private `operator=()`, the default assignment operation cannot be generated. Similarly, if a member or a base of a class M has a private copy constructor then the default copy constructor cannot be generated.

The default assignment and copy constructor will be declared, but they will not be defined (that is, a function body generated) unless needed. That is, `X::operator=()` will be generated only if no assignment operation is explicitly declared and an object of class X is assigned an object of class X or an object of a class derived from X or if the address of `X::operator=` is taken. Initialization is handled similarly.

If implicitly declared, the assignment and the copy constructor will be public members and the assignment operator for a class X will be defined to return a reference of type X& referring to the object assigned to.

If a class X has any `X::operator=()` that takes an argument of class X, the default assignment will not be generated. If a class has any copy constructor defined, the default copy constructor will not be generated. For example,

```
class X {
    // ...
public:
    X(int);
    X(const X&, int = 1);
};

X a(1);             // calls X(int);
X b(a,0);           // calls X(const X&,int);
X c = b;            // calls X(const X&,int);
```

■ Consider also,

```
class Y {
public:
    Y& operator=(int);
    Y(int);
};

void f()
{
    Y a = 1;
    Y b = a;     // ok
    a = b;       // ok
}
```

In other words, unless explicitly declared *private*, copy operations are available for class objects. □

Assignment of class X objects is defined in terms of X::operator=(const X&). This implies (§12.3) that objects of a derived class can be assigned to objects of a public base class. For example,

```
class X {
public:
    int b;
};

class Y : public X {
public:
    int c;
};

void f()
{
    X x1;
    Y y1;

    x1 = y1;     // ok
    y1 = x1;     // error
}
```

Here y1.b is assigned to x1.b and y1.c is not copied.

■ Quietly slicing an object in two and using only part of it in the assignment seems dangerous. The possibility of doing this, however, follows directly from the type rules of the language. Disallowing it involves arguing against the rule that ''an object of a derived class can be used wherever an object of a base class can be used,'' which would be hard to justify.

Consider protecting the programmer against the slicing assignment operation above. A major variant of the problem would remain even if the compiler made *x1=y1* an error.

```
void f()
{
        X x1;
        Y y1;
        X* px = &y1;
        x1 = *px;          // y1 is sliced!
}
```

Any serious attempt to protect the user against slicing copy operations would involve a prohibition against assignments and initializations involving pointers and references. This does not seem sensible and would constitute a major incompatibility with C. □

Copying one object into another using the default copy constructor or the default assignment operator does not change the structure of either object. For example,

```
struct s {
    virtual f();
    // ...
};

struct ss : public s {
    f();
    // ...
};

void f()
{
    s a;
    ss b;
    a = b;         // really a.s::operator=(b)
    b = a;         // error
    a.f();         // calls s::f
    b.f();         // calls ss::f
    (s&)b = a;     // assign to b's s part
                   // really ((s&)b).s::operator=(a)
    b.f();         // still calls ss::f
}
```

The call a.f() will invoke s::f() (as is suitable for an object of class s (§10.2)) and the call b.f() will call ss::f() (as is suitable for an object of class ss).

■ Note that an object of a class X with a constructor is still acceptable as an argument to a function that uses the ellipsis rather than a specific argument declaration (§8.2.5). For example,

```
class X {
    // ...
    X(const X&);
};

int f(int ...);

void g(X aa)
{
    f(1,aa);   // aa's contents copied without
               // the use of the constructor!
}
```

What happens is that the representation of *aa* is passed. What is transmitted is *not* an object of class *X*; should the constructors and destructors of *X,* or any other functions, maintain a use count or a list of objects of class *X*, then that accounting is not affected by an *X* used as an argument for the ellipsis.

Clearly this mechanism breaks the type system. It provides a way of obtaining a copy of the representation of an object. This can be useful for low-level applications. Note that the receiver (that is, the definition of the function with an ellipsis argument) does not receive an object of class *X*, and if one is needed, one will have to be made – using proper construction – based on the information passed.

Such copying is clearly implementation dependent for all but the simplest classes. If a class has virtual functions or virtual base classes the representation passed will contain "housekeeping" information about which no general assumptions can be made. □

Commentary

This commentary section discusses how to eliminate temporary objects, tells how to use access control with the special member functions, and gives a table summarizing the built-in properties of special member functions.

12.1c Temporary Elimination

The introduction of temporary objects is often necessary, especially when handling expressions involving overloaded operators. Such temporaries, with the calls of constructors, destructors, and copy operations they imply, can be expensive. The question is, "how aggressive can a compiler be in optimizing these temporaries away?" Or stated the other way, "when can a compiler avoid introducing such temporaries?"

The fundamental rule is that the introduction of a temporary object and the calls of its constructor/destructor pair may be eliminated if the only way the user can detect its elimination or introduction is by observing side effects generated by the constructor or destructor calls (§12.1, §12.4). These techniques were first discussed for C++ in Bjarne Stroustrup: *Operator Overloading for C++*, Proc. IFIP WG2.4 Conference on System Implementation Languages, September 1984.

12.1.1c Function Return Values

Consider a class *Matrix* with an addition operator and only the default assignment operator.

```
class Matrix {
    // ...
    friend Matrix operator+(const Matrix&, const Matrix&);
};
```

When this *operator+* is used

```
m1 = m2 + m3;    // m1, m2, and m3 are of type Matrix
```

a temporary is generated to hold the result of *m2+m3*, and this temporary is then assigned to *m1*.

Consider first the explicit assignment itself. The assignment can be eliminated only by constructing the result of *m2+m3* directly in *m1*. This can be done only if the overwriting of the old value of *m1* was equivalent to creating a new *Matrix* object and copying that into *m1*. This would occur only if *Matrix* assignment preserved the default semantics and the matrices *m1*, *m2*, and *m3* have nonoverlapping representations. For example, eliminating the assignment when *m1* and *m2* are the same object could lead to trouble unless it was known that the code in the addition operator worked correctly given such aliasing. A compiler typically does not have enough information to perform such optimizations. On the other hand, for initializations such as

```
Matrix m1 = m2 + m3;
```

it is trivial to avoid using an extra temporary object for the result of the addition.

One way of doing this is to compile functions returning an object of class *Matrix* into a function with the address of an object in which to construct the return object as an extra argument. Thus, the function

```
Matrix operator+(const Matrix&, const Matrix&);
```

can be compiled into the equivalent of a function with three pointer arguments.

```
void matrix_add(
    Matrix* __result,    /* added by compiler */
    Matrix* arg1,
    Matrix* arg2
);
```

so the initialization

```
Matrix m1 = m2 + m3;
```

generates code like this:

```
matrix_add(&m1,&m2,&m3);
```

whereas the assignment

```
m1 = m2 + m3;
```

must protect against aliasing and generates code like

```
struct Matrix temp;      /* no implicit initialization */
matrix_add(&temp,&m2,&m3);
m1 = temp;
```

It is usually a good idea to define operations such as `+=` and `*=` for arithmetic classes. Their use completely bypasses the introduction of temporaries since they by definition operate on a specific object, and aliasing is easy to manage in the code of the operations. For example,

```
Matrix& Matrix::operator+=(const Matrix& a)
{
    // add a to *this
    return *this;
}
```

Now consider the definition of the addition operation. It would typically look like this:

```
Matrix operator+(const Matrix& a1, const Matrix& a2)
{
    Matrix sum;
    // add a1 and a2 and place result in sum
    return sum;
}
```

Here a straightforward implementation will initialize *sum* to some default value and fill it with the correct return value. Then the `return` statement will copy *sum* into a temporary using `Matrix(const Matrix&)`.

A smarter implementation will note that the local variable *sum* is redundant and eliminate it by using the object pointed to by `result` instead. In other words, the generated code will look something like this:

```
void matrix_add(
    Matrix* __result,    /* added by compiler */
    Matrix* arg1,
    Matrix* arg2
)
{
    // construct *__result
    // add a1 and a2 and place result in *__result
    return;
}
```

Note that the result object still needs to be constructed before it can be filled. The construction of objects such as matrices can be inexpensive, but isn't always. Writing the definition of *operator+()* slightly differently eliminates the apparently redundant construction of *sum* to a default value.

```
Matrix operator+(const Matrix& a1, const Matrix& a2)
{
    Matrix sum = a1;
    sum += a2;
    return sum;
}
```

This allows the compiler to generate close to optimal code.

```
void matrix_add(
    Matrix* __result,    /* added by compiler */
    Matrix* arg1,
    Matrix* arg2
)
{

    // construct *__result as a copy of a1
    // add a2 to *__result
    return;
}
```

For less clever implementations, better code is often generated when the return expression is a constructor call. For example, an overloaded *operator+* (§13 and §13.4) for class *complex* might be defined to add two *complex* values without use of an explicit temporary variable.

```
complex operator +(complex a1, complex a2)
{
    return complex(a1.re+a2.re, a1.im+a2.im);
}
```

Code like this might be generated:

```
void complex_add(complex* __result, complex a1, complex a2)
{
    __result->re = a1.re + a2.re;
    __result->im = a1.im + a2.im;
}
```

Inlining would complete the optimization of `complex` addition.

12.1.2c Inline Functions

Where a function call is implemented as a subroutine call, some amount of copying
is necessary to pass arguments and return values. When inlining is used such
copies can be avoided where doing so does not involve side effects beyond the
calls of constructors, destructors, and copy operations. In essence, the local copies
of function arguments can be treated as temporary objects and sometimes eliminated. For example,

```
inline int putc(char x, FILE* p)
{
    return --p->_cnt>=0
        ? int(*p->_ptr++=unsigned(x))
        : _flsbuf(unsigned(x),p);
}


void f(char* buf, FILE* f)
{
    putc('a',f);
    putc(*buf++,f);
}
```

Since the first call of `putc` does not involve side effects on its arguments, a simple
expansion suffices, whereas the side effect on the first argument of the second call
requires the introduction of a temporary. The generated code might look something
like this:

```
void f(char* buf, FILE* f)
{
    // putc('a',f) :
    --f->_cnt>=0
        ? int(*f->_ptr++=unsigned('a'))
        : _flsbuf(unsigned('a'),f);

    // putc(*buf++,f) :
    char temp = *buf++;
    --f->_cnt>=0
        ? int(*f->_ptr++=unsigned(temp))
        : _flsbuf(unsigned(temp),f);
}
```

12.2c Access Control and Special Functions

Access control is applied to special member functions exactly as it is to other
member functions. This can be used to control the availability of the operations
implemented using the special member functions. For example, one could restrict
copying of objects of a class *X* to be done only by members and friends of class *X*
like this:

```
class X {
    // Objects of class X cannot be copied
    // except by members and friends of X
    void operator=(X&);
    X(X&);
    // ...
public:
    X(int);
    // ...
};

void f() {
    X a(1);
    X b = a;     // error: X::X(X&) private
    b = a;       // error: X::operator=(X&) private
}
```

Both explicit and implicit copy operations are affected by this, so even argument
passing and value return can be prevented for objects of a given class. For example,

```
X f(X a)
{
    return a;        // error: X::X(X&) private
}

void g()
{
    X a=0;
    f(a);     // error: X::X(X&) private
}
```

Constructors and destructors obey access rules exactly as other functions do.
They may be declared *private* or *protected*.

Declaring all a class's constructors private has the effect that only static
members of that class, friends of that class, or member functions, invoked through
existing objects of the class, may create objects of the class type; declaring a
class's constructors protected allows friends of the class and members and friends
of classes derived from that class to create objects of the class type. Thus, making
all a class's constructors private or protected will disallow static (global) allocation
of objects of the class and restrict the use of automatic (stack) objects to member

and friend functions. For example,

```
class X {
private:
    X();
public:
    void* operator new(size_t);
    X* makeX() { return new X; }
};


X a;    // illegal; constructor is private

void g(X* p) {
    X b;                        // illegal
    X* c = new X;               // illegal
    X* d = p->makeX();          // fine;
}
```

Restricting the access to a class's constructors has the effect of restricting use of
the *new* operator for objects of the class type, even if the *new* operator is declared
public, because *new* implicitly calls a constructor.

Interestingly, making a destructor private or protected also has the effect of
disallowing automatic and static allocation of objects of that class type because
such objects could never be destroyed. If a class's destructor is private, only
member and friend functions of that class may destroy objects; if the destructor is
protected, only member and friend functions of the class or of classes derived from
it may destroy objects. For example,

```
class X {
private:
    ~X();
public:
    void elim() { delete this; }
};


X a;    // illegal, destruction cannot be done

void g() {
    X b;                // illegal, destruction cannot
                        // be done
    X* p = new X;       // fine, but object might never
                        // go away
    delete p;           // error: g() is neither friend
                        // nor member
    p->elim();          // fine
}
```

Objects of a class for which access to the destructor is restricted can be allocated
on the free store, as in *g()* above, but *delete* cannot be called for such objects.

Restricting the access to a class's destructor restricts use of the *delete* operator on operands of the class type, even if the *delete* operator is declared *public*, because *delete* implicitly calls the destructor.

12.3c Summary of Member, Friend, and Special Functions

The table below summarizes the characteristics of constructors, destructors, conversion functions, operator functions, and other member and friend functions.

	inherited	can be virtual	can have return type	member or friend	generated by default
constructor	no	no	no	member	yes
destructor	no	yes	no	member	yes
conversion	yes	yes	no	member	no
=	no	yes	yes	member	yes
( )	yes	yes	yes	member	no
[ ]	yes	yes	yes	member	no
->	yes	yes	yes	member	no
op=	yes	yes	yes	either	no
new	yes	no	void*	static member	no
delete	yes	no	void	static member	no
other operator	yes	yes	yes	either	no
other member	yes	yes	yes	member	no
friend	no	no	yes	friend	no

13

Overloading

This chapter gives the syntax and semantics of operator and function overloading. Overloading allows multiple functions with the same name to be defined provided their argument lists differ sufficiently for calls to be resolved. By overloading operators, the programmer can redefine the meaning of most C++ operators (including function call (), subscripting [], assignment =, address-of &, and class member access ->) when at least one operand is a class object.

13 Overloading

When several different function declarations are specified for a single name in the same scope, that name is said to be overloaded. When that name is used, the correct function is selected by comparing the types of the actual arguments with the types of the formal arguments. For example,

```
double abs(double);
int abs(int);


abs(1);        // call abs(int);
abs(1.0);      // call abs(double);
```

Since for any type T, a T and a T& accept the same set of initializer values, functions with argument types differing only in this respect may not have the same name. For example,

```
int f(int i)
{
    // ...
}
```

```
int f(int& r)    // error: function types
                 // not sufficiently different
{
     // ...
}
```

Similarly, since for any type T, a T, a const T, and a volatile T accept the
same set of initializer values, functions with argument types differing only in this
respect may not have the same name. It is, however, possible to distinguish
between const T&, volatile T&, and plain T& so functions that differ only in
this respect may be defined.

■ Functions that differ only in these ways accept the same set of initializer *values*,
but they don't accept the same set of initializers. Consider

```
void f1(int);
void f2(int&);
void f3(const int&);

void g()
{
    f1(2.2);      // ok
    f2(2.2);      // error: temporary needed to
                  // initialize nonconst reference
    f3(2.2);      // ok (temporary used)
}
```

Here, the value *2.2* is an acceptable value for initializing an *int*. The floating
point constant *2.2* will be truncated to the integer value *2* (§4.4). Where a reference is used as the argument type, however, a temporary variable is needed to hold
that integer. Using such a temporary is acceptable only for *const* references
(§8.4.3).

As mentioned (§4.1), relying on implicit conversions from *double* to *int* is
poor style because they might – as in the example above – change the value. Compilers can help the programmer avoid surprises by warning about such conversions.

If a user really wants to call *f2()* with the value *2.2*, an explicit variable of
type *int* must be introduced.

```
void h()
{
        int a = int(2.2);
        f2(a);            // ok
}
```

□

Similarly, it is possible to distinguish between const T*, volatile T*, and
plain T* so functions that differ only in this respect may be defined.

Functions that differ only in the return type may not have the same name.

■ Consider

```
X operator+(const X&, const Y&);
Y operator+(const X&, const Y&);  // error: function types
                                  // differ only in return
                                  // type
void f(X a, Y b)
{
    X r1 = a+b;     // error: ambiguous
    Y r2 = a+b;     // error: ambiguous
}
```

Here, it is obvious to the human reader that *r1* should be initialized by a call of the first *operator+* and *r2* by a call of the second. In general, however, it is not that simple for humans or compilers to determine what the programmer really meant. Further, allowing overloading based on the return type would invalidate the desirable property that C++ expressions can be analyzed bottom up looking at only a single operator and its operands at a time. □

Member functions that differ only in that one is a static member and the other isn't may not have the same name (§9.4).

A typedef is not a separate type, but only a synonym for another type (§7.1.3). Therefore, functions that differ by typedef "types" only may not have the same name. For example,

```
typedef int Int;

void f(int i) { /* ... */ }
void f(Int i) { /* ... */ }  // error: redefinition of f
```

Enumerations, on the other hand, are distinct types and can be used to distinguish overloaded functions. For example,

```
enum E { a };

void f(int i) { /* ... */ }
void f(E i)   { /* ... */ }
```

Argument types that differ only in a pointer * versus an array [ ] are identical. Note that only the second and subsequent array dimensions are significant in argument types (§8.2.4).

```
f(char*);
f(char[]);       // same as f(char*);
f(char[7]);      // same as f(char*);
f(char[9]);      // same as f(char*);

g(char(*)[10]);
g(char[5][10]);  // same as g(char(*)[10]);
g(char[7][10]);  // same as g(char(*)[10]);
g(char(*)[20]);  // different from g(char(*)[10]);
```

■ Note that *char*, *unsigned char*, and *signed char* are distinct types, so six distinct functions are declared here:

```
h(char);
h(unsigned char);
h(signed char);

h(char*);
h(unsigned char*);
h(signed char*);
```

□

13.1 Declaration Matching

Two function declarations of the same name refer to the same function if they are in the same scope and have identical argument types (§13). A function member of a derived class is *not* in the same scope as a function member of the same name in a base class. For example,

```
class B {
public:
    int f(int);
};

class D : public B {
public:
    int f(char*);
};
```

Here D::f(char*) hides B::f(int) rather than overloading it.

```
void h(D* pd)
{
    pd->f(1);           // error:
                        // D::f(char*) hides B::f(int)
    pd->B::f(1);        // ok
    pd->f("Ben");       // ok, calls D::f
}
```

A locally declared function is not in the same scope as a function in file scope.

```
int f(char*);
void g()
{
    extern f(int);
    f("asdf");   // error: f(int) hides f(char*)
                 // so there is no f(char*) in this scope
}
```

■ One might consider ignoring scope issues when resolving overloaded functions; that is, consider every function that would be in scope had it not been hidden by a name in an enclosed scope. This, however, would lead to surprises when an unsuspected function was invoked by a call. For example,

```
class X1 {
public:
        void f(int);
};


// chain of derivations X(n) : X(n-1)

class X9 : public X8 {
public:
        void f(double);
};


void g(X9* p)
{
        p->f(2);            // X9::f() or X1::f()
}
```

Unless the programmer has an unusually deep understanding of the program, the assumption will be that `p->f(2)` calls `X9::f()` – and not `X1::f()` declared deep in the base class. Under the C++ rules, this is indeed the case.

Had the rules allowed `X1::f(int)` to be chosen as a better match, unintentional overloading of unrelated functions would be a distinct possibility. In general, protection against accidental overloading is not easy for a compiler to provide, but see §10.2 for a discussion of how it might be handled for virtual functions. Virtual functions – which are by definition meant to be defined, overridden, called at different levels of a class lattice, and so on – are the ones for which these problems most naturally occur. If the intent really were to call `X1::f()`, the declaration of `X9` can be modified to ensure that.

```
class X1 {
public:
        void f(int);
};


// chain of derivations X(n) : X(n-1)

class X9 : public X8 {
public:
        void f(double);
        void f(int i) { X8::f(i); }
};


void g(X9* p)
{
        p->f(2);            // calls X1::f(int) indirectly
}
```

□

■ Allowing overloading across scopes would be particularly dangerous for functions written to modify the total state of an object in some way. For example,

```
struct B {
        // ...
        void operator=(int i);
        B(int i);
};

struct D : B {
        // ...
};

void f()
{ .
        D x = 1;    // error (fortunately)
        // ...
        x = 2;      // error (fortunately)
}
```

Had that initialization and assignment been allowed, only the B part of x would have been initialized and assigned to. For most classes such a partial initialization and update would lead to nasty surprises. □

Different versions of an overloaded member function may be given different access rules. For example,

```
class buffer {
private:
    char* p;
    int size;

protected:
    buffer(int s, char* store) { size = s; p = store; }
    // ...

public:
    buffer(int s) { p = new char[size = s]; }
    // ...
};
```

13.2 Argument Matching

A call of a given function name chooses, from among all functions by that name that are in scope and for which a set of conversions exists so that the function could possibly be called, the function that best matches the actual arguments. The best-matching function is the intersection of sets of functions that best match on each argument. Unless this intersection has exactly one member, the call is illegal. The function thus selected must be a strictly better match for at least one argument than every other possible function (but not necessarily the same argument for each function). Otherwise, the call is illegal.

■ The details of what makes a "best-matching sequence" are described below as are details of how to consider arguments for overloaded operators and member functions. For now, consider an exact match better than any conversion and an *int* to *double* conversion better than any user-defined conversion. We can then examine the handling of multiple arguments in isolation.

The basic principle for handling overloaded function calls with more than one argument is to look at each argument separately. If one function provides a better than or equal match for every argument and provides a strictly better match than all other functions for at least one argument, then it is called; otherwise the call is an error.

Consider

```
class X { public: X(int); };
class Y {};

void f(X,int);
void f(X,double);
void f(Y,double);

void g() { f(1,1); }
```

First *f(Y, double)* is excluded because there is no conversion from *int* to *Y*.

Then the sets of best matches can be calculated for each argument, as follows:

```
set for 1st argument:    { f(X,int)  f(X,double) }
set for 2nd argument:    { f(X,int) }
```

where the conversion *int* to *X* defined by *X's* constructor is used in all three cases. The intersection of these two sets is *f(X, int)*, so the resolution of the call *f(1,1)* is *f(X(1),1)*. The identical conversions *X(1)* canceled themselves out so the function was selected on the basis of second argument.

As an example of an ambiguity, consider

```
struct X { X(int); };

void f(X,int);
void f(int,X);

void g() { f(1,1); }      // error: ambiguous
```

Here the sets of best matches are

```
set for 1st argument:    { f(int,X) }
set for 2nd argument:    { f(X,int) }
```

Since the intersection of these sets is empty the call *f(1, 1)* is ambiguous.

Note that if there are two types that can be converted into each other, all calls involving an argument of each will fail.

```
f(int,double);
f(double,int);

void g() { f(1,1); }    // error: ambiguous
```

The sets

```
set for 1st argument:    { f(int,double) }
set for 2nd argument:    { f(double,int) }
```

have an empty intersection, so the call $f(1,1)$ is ambiguous.

It follows that the binary operations for built-in types do not obey these ambiguity rules. For example,

```
1+1.0
```

would be ambiguous. The explicit rules in §4.5, however, resolve this to a floating point addition. The problem with the (C and C++) rules for conversion of arithmetic types is that a value of any arithmetic type can implicitly be converted into any other arithmetic type.

Up to this point we have not used the rule that the best-matching function must provide not only a match that is better than or equal to the matches of all other functions for each argument, but also must provide a match that is strictly better for at least one argument. Here is an example where that rule is necessary to avoid an anomaly:

```
struct A {};
struct B : A {};
struct C {};          // unrelated
struct D : B, C {};


void f(C*,C*);
void f(A*,B*);


D* pd;

void g()
{
        f(pd,pd);    // error: ambiguous
}
```

The best-match sets are

```
set for 1st argument:    { f(C*,C*) f(A*,B*) }
set for 2nd argument:    { f(C*,C*) f(A*,B*) }
```

The intersection has two members, so the call $f(pd,pd)$ is ambiguous. Now add a third function.

```
void f(C*,C*);
void f(A*,B*);
void f(B*,A*);

void gg()
{
        f(pd,pd);      // still ambiguous
}
```

A conversion of a $D*$ to a $B*$ is better than the conversion of $D*$ to $A*$, so we get the best-match sets:

```
set for 1st argument:   { f(C*,C*) f(B*,A*) }
set for 2nd argument:   { f(C*,C*) f(A*,B*) }
```

The intersection has only one member $f(C*,C*)$. The match for $f(C*,C*)$, however, is not strictly better than the alternatives for any argument so the call is ambiguous. Without the rule requiring that a function must be strictly better for at least one argument we would have been required to call $f(C*,C*)$. That would have implied that by adding a function declaration the programmer could resolve an ambiguity so that one of the original functions would have been called. That anomaly does not seem to be a desirable property. □

■ There used to be a rule stating that "a call needing only standard conversions is preferred over one requiring user-defined conversions." The origin of this rule was an attempt to speed up compilation by reducing the number of possibilities the compiler has to examine. It is unclear whether this was ever a significant improvement. That rule predated the intersection rule and resolved some examples that would otherwise have been ambiguities. For example,

```
struct complex { complex(double); };

void h(int,complex);
void h(double,double);

void hh()
{
    h(3,4);        // used to be ok: h(double(3),double(4))
                   // now ambiguous
}
```

Users considered the call above ambiguous, however, despite the opinions of the manual and the compiler, and were surprised by the resolution. Worse, by adding an argument requiring a user-defined conversion, such calls could become ambiguous.

```
void h(int,complex,complex = 0);
void h(double,double,complex = 0);
```

```
          void hh()
          {
              h(3,4);        // used to be ok: h(double(3),double(4))
                             // now ambiguous
              h(3,4,0);      // ambiguous
          }
```

☐

For purposes of argument matching, a function with n default arguments (§8.2.6) is considered to be $n+1$ functions with different numbers of arguments.

■ That is, for argument matching purposes

```
          int f(int a, int b = 0);
```

is equivalent to

```
          int f(int a, int b);
          inline int f(int a) { return f(a,0); }
```

This is, in fact, an elegant way of implementing default arguments. It implies that default arguments can cause ambiguities. For example,

```
          int f();
          int f(int i = 1);

          void g()
          {
              f(11);  // fine
              f();    // error: ambiguous: f() or f(1)
          }
```

☐

For purposes of argument matching, a nonstatic member function is considered to have an extra argument specifying the object for which it is called. This extra argument requires a match either by the object or pointer specified in the explicit member function call notation (§5.2.4) or by the first operand of an overloaded operator (§13.4). No temporaries will be introduced for this extra argument and no user-defined conversions will be applied to achieve a type match.

■ For example,

```
class X {
public:
    void f();
};

class Y {
public:
    operator X();
};

void g()
{
    Y a;
    a.f();        // error
}
```

The conversion is not tried, so the interpretation

```
(a.Y::operator X()).f();
```

is not used. □

Where a member of a class X is explicitly called for a pointer using the -> operator, this extra argument is assumed to have type const X* for const members, volatile X* for volatile members, and X* for others. Where the member function is explicitly called for an object using the . operator or the function is invoked for the first operand of an overloaded operator (§13.4), this extra argument is assumed to have type const X& for const members, volatile X& for volatile members, and X& for others. The first operand of ->* and .* is treated in the same way as the first operand of -> and ., respectively.

An ellipsis in a formal argument list (§8.2.5) is a match for an actual argument of any type.

For a given actual argument, no sequence of conversions will be considered that contains more than one user-defined conversion or that can be shortened by deleting one or more conversions into another sequence that leads to the type of the corresponding formal argument of any function in consideration. Such a sequence is called a *best-matching* sequence.

For example, int→float→double is a sequence of conversions from int to double, but it is not a best-matching sequence because it contains the shorter sequence int→double.

■ Consider also,

```
struct foo { operator char(); };

struct ostream {
    ostream& operator<<(char);
    ostream& operator<<(double);
};
```

```
        foo x;
        ostream cout;

        main()
        {
            cout << x;   // call ostream::operator<<(char)
        }
```

The sequence *foo→char* is shorter than *foo→char→double*, so
ostream::operator<<(char) is chosen. □

Except as mentioned below, the following *trivial conversions* involving a type T
do not affect which of two conversion sequences is better:

from:	to:
T	T&
T&	T
T[]	T*
T(args)	T(*)(args)
T	const T
T	volatile T
T*	const T*
T*	volatile T*

Sequences of trivial conversions that differ only in order are indistinguishable.
Note that functions with arguments of type T, const T, volatile T, T&,
const T&, and volatile T& accept exactly the same set of values. Where
necessary, const and volatile are used as tie-breakers as described in rule [1]
below.

A temporary variable is needed for a formal argument of type T& if the actual
argument is not an lvalue, has a type different from T, or is a volatile and T
isn't. This does not affect argument matching. It may, however, affect the legality
of the resulting match since a temporary may not be used to initialize a non-const
reference (§8.4.3).

Sequences of conversions are considered according to these rules:

[1] Exact match: Sequences of zero or more trivial conversions are better than
all other sequences. Of these, those that do not convert T* to const T*,
T* to volatile T*, T& to const T&, or T& to volatile T& are better
than those that do.

[2] Match with promotions: Of sequences not mentioned in [1], those that contain only integral promotions (§4.1), conversions from float to double,
and trivial conversions are better than all others.

[3] Match with standard conversions: Of sequences not mentioned in [2], those
with only standard (§4.1, §4.2, §4.3, §4.4, §4.5, §4.6, §4.7, §4.8) and trivial
conversions are better than all others. Of these, if B is publicly derived
directly or indirectly from A, converting a B* to A* is better than converting
to void* or const void*; further, if C is publicly derived directly or
indirectly from B, converting a C* to B* is better than converting to A* and

converting a `C&` to `B&` is better than converting to `A&`. The class hierarchy acts similarly as a selection mechanism for pointer to member conversions (§4.8).

[4] Match with user-defined conversions: Of sequences not mentioned in [3], those that involve only user-defined conversions (§12.3), standard (§4) and trivial conversions are better than all other sequences.

[5] Match with ellipsis: Sequences that involve matches with the ellipsis are worse than all others.

■ Why these rules? Wouldn't simpler rules do? Several issues are involved. The aim is to allow overloading to be used effectively and safely; that is, to allow as many reasonable distinctions between types as possible while still catching ambiguities. The degenerate case, that of having two functions taking unrelated arguments, leaves each function with exactly the same semantics as it had without overloading.

The effects of overloading are independent of the order of function declarations. Adding a new declaration should not affect existing calls in surprising ways, but it should be able to affect them in reasonable, predictable ways: consider adding a function declaration that provides an exact match for a call − to eliminate a conversion. Furthermore, the standard conversion and promotion rules (of C and C++) must be preserved when overloading is used − because the programmer does not necessarily know when overloading is happening.

Several rules exist to limit the number of ambiguities detected. The C rules allow all arithmetic types to be freely converted to each other. The distinctions among different types of conversion in rules [1], [2], and [3] prevent calls of functions involving arithmetic types from degenerating into a mess of unavoidable ambiguities. The rule limiting to one the number of acceptable user-defined conversions has a similar effect and also serves to avoid incomprehensible resolutions. Users can help with the resolution of a call by specifying explicit conversions.

The rules for overloading resolution have changed over time. The main motivation for the changes has been to eliminate order dependencies and to allow the detection of more ambiguities. The general philosophy is that any dependence of declaration order is undesirable because it can lead to subtle ambiguities. Different versions of an overloaded function can be included from different header files; the order of overloaded function declarations is generally neither known by users, nor under their control. Similarly, a user can explicitly resolve a call that is deemed ambiguous, but if a call has been resolved in an unexpected way, much time can be lost looking for a run-time error. Another change has been to allow sensitivity for more types, such as being able to distinguish *float* and *double* for programmers on machines supporting both single and double precision floating point arithmetic.

The following section presents a series of examples illustrating the rules above. First the five rules are illustrated in order, then examples of resolutions of calls with multiple arguments are presented, and finally examples involving default arguments and the ellipsis are shown. To ease reference the rules have been repeated. □

[1] Exact match: Sequences of zero or more trivial conversions are better than all other sequences. Of these, those that do not convert `T*` to `const T*`, `T*` to `volatile T*`, `T&` to `const T&`, or `T&` to `volatile T&` are better than those that do.

■ This is the rule that makes C++ overloading sensitive to the type distinctions ordinarily erased by the (C and C++) integral promotion rules (§4.1) and rules for promotion of floating types (§4.3).

Consider

```
void f(char);
void f(int);
void f(unsigned);
void f(long);

void g()
{
    f('c');     // call f(char)
    f(1u);      // call f(unsigned)
    f(1);       // call f(int)
    f(1L);      // call f(long)
}
```

Note that the type of the character constant `'c'` really is *char*.

Similarly,

```
void f(float);
void f(double);
void f(int);

void g()
{
    f(1.0);   // call f(double)
    f(1.0F);  // call f(float)
    f(1);     // call f(int)
}
```

It is possible to define functions that differ only in *const* in a pointer or reference.

```
void f(char*);
void f(const char*);
void f2(char*);
void f3(const char*);

void g(char* pc, const char* pcc)
{
    f(pc);      // call f(char*)
    f(pcc);     // call f(const char*)

    f2(pc);     // call f2(char*)
    f2(pcc);    // error: cannot initialize 'char*'
                // with 'const char*'

    f3(pc);     // call f3(const char*)
    f3(pcc);    // call f3(const char*)
}
```

In other words, ''constness'' acts as a tie-breaker where needed but does not affect argument matching otherwise. This is especially important for const objects and `const` member functions.

```
class X {
public:
    void f() const;
    void f();
    // ...
};

void g(const X& a, X b)
{
    a.f();      // calls X::f() const
    b.f();      // calls X::f()
}
```

The usual array-to-pointer conversion takes place.

```
void f(char*);
void g()
{
    char v[10];
    char* p = v;
    f(v);       // call f(char*)
    f(p);       // call f(char*)
}
```

□

[2] Match with promotions: Of sequences not mentioned in [1], those that contain only integral promotions (§4.1), conversions from `float` to `double`, and trivial conversions are better than all others.

■ This rule exists to allow promotions to be preferred over standard conversions. For example,

```
void f(int);
void f(double);

void g()
{
    short aa = 1;
    float ff = 1.0;

    f(aa);      // call f(int)
    f(ff);      // call f(double)
}
```

Without this rule, the calls would be ambiguous because a *short* can be converted to either an *int* or a *double*, and a *float* can be converted to either an *int* or a *double*.

The distinction between "exact match" and "match with promotions" can be used to distinguish between integer types and between floating types. For example, enumerators are of the type of their enumeration (§7.2) and can be used in overloaded function calls.

```
enum e { A, B } ee;
enum { A2, B2 };

void f(int);
void f(e);

void g()
{
    f(0);    // call f(int), 0 is an int
    f(A);    // call f(e)
    f(A+1);  // call f(int), A is promoted to int
             // before the addition
    f(ee);   // call f(e)
    f(A2);   // call f(int), A2 is promoted to int
}
```

Note that integral promotions (§4.1) are implementation dependent.

```
int f(int);
int f(unsigned);

void g(unsigned short us)
{
    int i = f(us);
}
```

Here `f(int)` is called if `sizeof(short)<sizeof(int)`; otherwise
`f(unsigned)` is called. This could lead to nasty surprises when a program is
ported to a new implementation, but the rule is necessary to avoid an incompatibility
with the ANSI C integral promotion rules (§4.1). □

[3] Match with standard conversions: Of sequences not mentioned in [2], those
with only standard (§4) and trivial conversions are better than all others. Of
these, if B is publicly derived directly or indirectly from A, converting a B*
to A* is better than converting to `void*` or `const void*`; further, if C is
publicly derived directly or indirectly from B, converting a C* to B* is
better than converting to A* and converting a C& to B& is better than converting to A&. The class hierarchy acts similarly as a selection mechanism
for pointer to member conversions (§4.8).

■ This rule ensures that ambiguities between standard conversions are caught and
that all standard conversions are considered equal. For example,

```
void f(char);
void f(float);

void g()
{
    f(1);    // ambiguous: f(char) or f(float)
    f(1L);   // ambiguous: f(char) or f(float)
}
```

There was serious discussion of preferring value-preserving conversions to potentially value-destroying conversions beyond the distinction between promotions and conversions. Attempting to elaborate the overloading resolution to make it more "natural" failed for several reasons: What is value-destroying depends critically on the actual value, which must *not* be considered in the overloading stage. Overloading resolution is based only on type. What is value-destroying depends critically on the implementation of the various data types. What is value-destroying on one machine may be safe on another. For example, the conversion of a *long* to a *float* may – or may not – be a value-destroying conversion. One implementation-dependent conversion rule was necessary to maintain ANSI C compatibility, but even that is probably one too many.

Another idea for improvement was to define a type lattice describing the acceptable conversions. Conversions between types that were close in the lattice would be better than conversions between types that were more distant. This was defeated by complexity, the implementation dependence of many C standard conversions, and the existence of several inherently value-destroying standard conversions (for example, *double* to *int* and *int* to *char*). Such conversions go the wrong way in any reasonable conversion lattice.

Note that the use of references does not change the set of values accepted compared to their corresponding object types.

```
void f(const char&);
void f(short);

void g()
{
    f('c');        // call f(const char&)

    const char ch = 'c';
    f(ch);         // call f(const char&)

    short s = 3;
    f(s);          // call f(short)

    f(3);          // error: ambiguous
                   // f(short) or f(const char&) ?
}
```

Here, a temporary variable is needed for the first call of *f()* because *'c'* is a literal (of type *char*). On the other hand, a temporary may not be used to initialize a non-*const* reference, so a call may be determined to be an error after the selection of a function.

```
void f(char&);
void f(short);

void g()
{
    f('c');        // error: call f(char&),
                   // requires temporary
}
```

Here, *f(char&)* is preferred to *f(short)* exactly as in the example above, but

since a temporary is required to hold *'c'* and the reference is not *const*, the call
is not accepted. This does *not* lead to an otherwise legal call of *f(short)*.

Note that *0* is of type *int* so it is an exact match for an *int* argument but a
match with standard conversions for arguments of types *short*, *double*, *char**,
and so on. For example,

```
void f(char);
void f(double);

void g()
{
    f('a');  // call f(char)
    f(0);    // error, ambiguous: f(char) or f(double)?
    f(1.0);  // call f(double)
}
```

Rule [3] implies that a value-preserving conversion − a promotion − is preferred
to a potentially value-destroying standard conversion. For example,

```
void f(char);
void f(int);

void g(short s)
{
    f(s);        // call f(int)
}
```

An inheritance hierarchy defines a preference order for the standard pointer and
reference conversions (§4.6, §4.7).

```
class A {};
class B : public A {};
class C : public B {};

void g(A*);
void g(B*);

C cc;

void f()
{
    g(&cc);      // call g(B*)
}
```

In a sense, void* is the root of such hierarchies.

```
void h(void*);
void h(A*);

void hh()
{
    h(&cc);  // call h(A*)
    h(0);    // error: ambiguous, h(void*) or h(A*)?
}
```

□

[4] Match with user-defined conversions: Of sequences not mentioned in [3], those that involve only user-defined conversions (§12.3), standard (§4) and trivial conversions are better than all other sequences.

■ Preferring a standard conversion to a user-defined conversion seems reasonable and is usually the right thing to do. In particular, it makes code that relies only on standard conversions (such as C code) immune to any added user-defined types. Preferring standard conversions to user-defined conversions occasionally masks ambiguities, though. In the following example, selecting the right choice is non-trivial:

```
class Real {     // high precision real numbers
    // ...
    Real(double);        // make a Real from a double
};

double sqrt(double);
Real sqrt(Real);

void g(long ll)
{
    double d = sqrt(ll);        // call sqrt(double)
}
```

The compiler cannot determine the precision with which the user wants the square root calculated. The language is defined to prefer the standard conversion of the *long ll* to a *double* over the user-defined conversion to a *Real*. In such cases some programmers would prefer an ambiguity error. □

[5] Match with ellipsis: Sequences that involve matches with the ellipsis are worse than all others.

■ If the ellipsis is used, all type information vanishes and type checking is broken. Consequently, this possibility is taken only if all else fails:

```
class Real {
    // ...
public:
    Real(double);
};

void f(int ...);
void f(int, Real);

void g()
{
    f(1,1);                // call f(int, Real)
    f(1,"Annemarie");   // f(int ...)
}
```

The ellipsis can also cause ambiguities.

```
        f(int);
        f(int ...);
        f(int, char* ...);

        void g()
        {
            f(1);                // error, ambiguous: f(int) or f(int ...)
            f(1,2);              // fine: f(int ...)
            f(1,"asdf");         // fine: f(int, char* ...)
            f(1,"asdf",2);       // fine: f(int, char* ...)
        }
```

□

User-defined conversions are selected based on the type of variable being initialized or assigned to.

```
        class Y {
            // ...
        public:
            operator int();
            operator double();
        };

        void f(Y y)
        {
            int i = y;      // call Y::operator int()
            double d;
            d = y;          // call Y::operator double()
            float f = y;    // error: ambiguous
        }
```

Standard conversions (§4) may be applied to the argument for a user-defined conversion, and to the result of a user-defined conversion.

```
        struct S {  S(long); operator int(); };

        void f(long), f(char*);
        void g(S), g(char*);
        void h(const S&), h(char*);

        void k(S& a)
        {
            f(a);      // f(long(a.operator int()))
            g(1);      // g(S(long(1)))
            h(1);      // h(S(long(1)))
        }
```

If user-defined coercions are needed for an argument, no account is taken of any standard coercions that might also be involved. For example,

```
class x {
public:
    x(int);
};

class y {
public:
    y(long);
};

void f(x);
void f(y);

void g()
{
    f(1);          // ambiguous
}
```

The call f(1) is ambiguous despite f(y(long(1))) needing one more standard conversion than f(x(1)).

No preference is given to conversion by constructor (§12.1) over conversion by conversion function (§12.3.2) or vice versa.

```
struct X {
    operator int();
};

struct Y {
    Y(X);
};

Y operator+(Y,Y);

void f(X a, X b)
{
    a+b;   // error, ambiguous:
           //     operator+(Y(a), Y(b)) or
           //     a.operator int() + b.operator int()
}
```

13.3 Address of Overloaded Function

A use of a function name without arguments selects, among all functions of that name that are in scope, the (only) function that exactly matches the target. The target may be

an object being initialized (§8.4)

the left side of an assignment (§5.17)

a formal argument of a function (§5.2.2)

a formal argument of a user-defined operator (§13.4)

a function return type (§8.2.5)

Note that if f() and g() are both overloaded functions, the cross product of possibilities must be considered to resolve f(&g), or the equivalent expression f(g).

For example,

```
int f(double);
int f(int);
int (*pfd)(double) = &f;
int (*pfi)(int) = &f;
int (*pfe)(...) = &f; // error: type mismatch
```

The last initialization is an error because no f() with type int(...) has been defined, and not because of any ambiguity.

Note also that there are no standard conversions (§4) of one pointer to function type into another (§4.6).

■ The reason no implicit conversions are performed for pointer to function types is that allowing a conversion loosens the requirements on the types of arguments (as in the last initialization above) and would *implicitly* violate the guarantee that a function will be called with arguments of the type it is declared to accept. A programmer can, however, *explicitly* request such a potentially dangerous conversion for a function that has not been overloaded.

```
int (*pfe)(...) = (int(*)(...))&g; // ok
```

Naturally, it then becomes the programmer's responsibility to ensure that *g()* is called with arguments of the right type, in this case a single *int*. The opposite conversion

```
int h(int ...);
int (*p)(int,int) = &h; // error: type mismatch
```

would be harmless in the sense that it increases the constraints on the arguments, but allowing it would not be worth the added complexity.

Allowing it would also have a detrimental effect in that it would constrain implementations to use fundamentally similar mechanisms to implement calls of functions for which the argument types are known and calls of varadic functions. This would be suboptimal since most calls are to functions with known argument types that can be implemented with less overhead than varadic functions. □

In particular, even if B is a public base of D we have

```
D* f();
B* (*p1)() = &f;          // error

void g(D*);
void (*p2)(B*) = &g;      // error
```

■ Had these examples been allowed, we could – without using explicit type conversion – call *g()* with an argument that wasn't a *D*.

```
void h1()
{
    B b;
    p2(&b);       // p2 requires only a B*
}
```

Simply modifying the return type would cause a more subtle problem if allowed. The function *f()* returns a pointer to a *D*, that is, a pointer to the beginning of a *D*. The base *B* may not be allocated at the beginning of the *D*. For example,

```
class D : public A, public B {
    // The B might be 1000 bytes
    // from the beginning of the D
};

D* f() { return new D; }

void h2()
{
    B* (*p1)() = &f;          // error
    B* p = p1();
}
```

There is no way for the compiler to know that it has to adjust the value of the pointer returned from a call through *p1* to refer to the *B* sub-object of a *D*.

This problem could be circumvented by generating pointer adjusting code at the point of the initialization of *p1* and letting *p1* point to that (see §10.3c, §10.6c). Such cleverness, however, seems excessive. □

13.4 Overloaded Operators

Most operators can be overloaded.

        operator-function-name:
                operator *operator*

operator: one of

```
new   delete
+     -      *      /      %      ^      &      |      ~
!     =      <      >      +=     -=     *=     /=     %=
^=    &=     |=     <<     >>     >>=    <<=    ==     !=
<=    >=     &&     ||     ++     --     ,      ->*    ->
()    []
```

The last two operators are function call (§5.2.2) and subscripting (§5.2.1). Both the unary and binary forms of

```
+      -      *      &
```

can be overloaded.

▪ A scheme for encoding overloaded operator names is presented in §7.2.1c. □

The following operators cannot be overloaded:

```
.      .*     ::     ?:     sizeof
```

nor can the preprocessing symbols # and ## (§16).

▪ The reason for disallowing the overloading of `.`, `.*`, and `::` is that they already have a predefined meaning for objects of any class as their first operand. Overloading of `?:` simply didn't seem worthwhile. □

Operator functions are usually not called directly; instead they are invoked to implement operators (§13.4.1, §13.4.2). They can be explicitly called, though. For example,

```
complex z = a.operator+(b);   // complex z = a+b;
void* p = operator new(sizeof(int)*n);
```

The operators `new` and `delete` are described in §5.3.3 and §5.3.4 and the rules described below in this section do not apply to them.

An operator function must either be a member function or take at least one argument of a class or a reference to a class. It is not possible to change the precedence, grouping, or number of operands of operators.

▪ This implies, for example, that if `operator^` is defined it must be defined as a member function taking one argument or as a global function taking two arguments. There is no unary or ternary form of `^` and no way of defining such. □

The predefined meaning of the operators `=`, (unary) `&`, and `,` (comma) applied to class objects may be changed. Except for `operator=()`, operator functions are inherited; see §12.8 for the rules for `operator=()`.

▪ This implies that the meaning of operators applied to nonclass types cannot be redefined. The intent is to make C++ extensible, but not mutable. This protects the C++ programmer from the most obvious abuses of operator overloading, such as redefining + on integers to mean subtraction.

Note that – except for *operator new()*, *operator delete()*, and *operator->()* – there are no restrictions on the return types of overloaded operators.

It would be an obvious extension to allow users to define their own operators in addition to the built-in ones.

```
**          // exponentiation
max
min
//          // division with remainder stored in '__rem'
*.          // my multiplication
+.          // my addition
```

This extension, however, would imply a significant extension of complexity of syntax analysis and an uncertain gain in readability. It would be necessary either to allow the user to specify both the binding strength and the associativity of new operators or to fix those attributes for all user-defined operators. In either case, the binding of expressions such as

```
a = b**c**d;      // (a**b)**c or a**(b**c) ?
```

would be surprising or annoying to many users. It would also be necessary to resolve clashes with the syntax of the usual operators. Consider this, assuming `**` and `//` to be defined as binary operators:

```
a = a**p;       // a**p OR a*(*p)
a = a//p;
*p = 7;         // a = a*p = 7; maybe?
```

□

Identities among operators applied to basic types (for example, ++a ≡ a+=1) need not hold for operators applied to class types. Some operators, for example, +=, require an operand to be an lvalue when applied to basic types; this is not required when the operators are declared for class types.

■ It is, however, usually a good idea to use operator overloading to mimic conventional usage. It follows that operators, such as *+=*, that require lvalues for built-in types should be defined as member functions, thus in effect requiring the overloaded versions to accept only lvalues as their first operand just as their built-in counterparts do. Similarly, operators such as *+*, that do not require lvalues for built-in types should be defined as global functions (often as *friends*) to allow standard and user-defined operators to be applied uniformly to both operands.

Similarly, it is typically a good idea to maintain the usual equivalences between operators. For example if more than one of the operators *->*, ***, and *[]* are defined for a class *V*, one would expect *v->m*, *(*v).m*, and *v[0].m* to have identical values for all objects *v* of class *V*. □

An overloaded operator cannot have default arguments (§8.2.6).

Operators not mentioned explicitly below in §13.4.3 to §13.4.7 act as ordinary unary and binary operators obeying the rules of section §13.4.1 or §13.4.2.

■ In particular, overloaded operators `,` and `->*` obey exactly the same rules as other overloaded binary operators, such as `^` and `%`. □

13.4.1 Unary Operators

A prefix unary operator may be declared by a nonstatic member function (§9.3) taking no arguments or a nonmember function taking one argument. Thus, for any prefix unary operator `@`, `@x` can be interpreted as either `x.operator@()` or `operator@(x)`. If both forms of the operator function have been declared, argument matching (§13.2) determines which, if any, interpretation is used.

■ For example,

```
struct B {
    int operator!();
    g1();
};

struct D: B { g2(); };

int operator!(D&);

int f(D& d)
{
    return !d;
}
```

calls `::operator!(D&)` because calling `B::operator!()` would require a standard conversion of a `D*` to a `B*`, and

```
int operator!(B&);

int ff(B& b)
{
    return !b;   // error: ambiguous
}
```

is obviously ambiguous given the definition of class *B* above.

Note that the transformation of an operator application to an overloaded function is not context sensitive, so applying the operator within a class member function has the same resolution as the application outside.

```
int D::g2()
{
    return !*this;      // calls ::operator!(D&)
}

int B::g1()
{
    return !*this;      // error: ambiguous
}
```

□

See §13.4.7 for an explanation of postfix unary operators, that is, ++ and −−.

■ Note that when the *x.operator@ ()* interpretation is used no user-defined conversions will be applied to *x* (§12.3). □

13.4.2 Binary Operators

A binary operator may be declared either by a nonstatic member function (§9.3) taking one argument or by a nonmember function taking two arguments. Thus, for any binary operator @, x@y can be interpreted as either x.operator@ (y) or operator@ (x,y). If both forms of the operator function have been declared, argument matching (§13.2) determines which, if any, interpretation is used.

■ Note that when the *x.operator@ (y)* interpretation is used no user-defined conversions will be applied to *x* (§12.3). □

■ When both forms of the operator function have been declared, ambiguity control is necessary. For example,

```
class X {
public:
    X operator+(int);
};

X operator+(X,double);

void g(X b)
{
    X a;
    a = b+1;     // call X::operator+(int)
    a = b+1.0;   // call ::operator+(X,double)
    a = b+1L;    // error: ambiguous
}
```

□

■ Allowing only individual operators to be overloaded leaves the user with the minimal amount of specification and the compiler with a major optimization problem. In particular, handling the problems of possible aliasing and minimization of the use of temporaries is usually not possible for compilers since they don't know the semantics of the functions called to interpret the expressions containing overloaded operators. □

■ It might be possible to let the user help the compiler generate better code by specifying what is to be done for common combinations of operations. For example, the two multiplications in

```
Matrix a, b, c, d;
// ...
a = b * c * d;
```

might be implemented by a specially defined "double multiplication" operator defined like this:

```
Matrix operator * * (Matrix&, Matrix&, Matrix&);
```

that would cause the statement above to be interpreted like this:

```
a = operator * * (b,c,d);
```

In other words, having seen the declaration

```
Matrix operator * * (Matrix&, Matrix&, Matrix&);
```

the compiler looks for patterns of repeated *Matrix* multiplications and calls the
function to interpret them. Patterns that are different or too complicated are handled
using the usual (unary and binary) operators.

   This extension has been independently invented several times as an efficient way
of coping with common patterns of use in scientific computing using user-defined
types. For example,

```
Matrix operator = * + (
    Matrix&,
    const Matrix&,
    double,
    const Matrix&
);
```

for handling statements like this:

```
a=b*1.7+d;
```

This scheme would also allow the overloading of the ternary operator *?:*. For
example,

```
operator?:(int,const X&,const Y&);

void f(int i, X a, Y b)
{
        int j = i?a:b;
}
```

   □

13.4.3 Assignment

The assignment function `operator=()` must be a nonstatic member function; it
is not inherited (§12.8). Instead, unless the user defines `operator=` for a class X,
`operator=` is defined, by default, as memberwise assignment of the members of
class X.

```
X& X::operator=(const X& from)
{
    // copy members of X
}
```

■ The assignment operator is the only operator function that is not inherited. Assignment has a useful and necessary generalization across all classes (memberwise copy; see §12.8). No other operator has that. Assignment resembles constructors and destructors more than it resembles operators such as *+* and *+=*.

Assignment must be a member function to avoid absurdities caused by defining an assignment operator after assignments of objects of a class have taken place. For example,

```
class X {
    // ...
};

void f()
{
    X a,b;
    // ...
    a = b;          // default meaning of assignment
}


X& operator=(X&,const X&);        // fortunately an error

void g()
{
    X a,b;
    // ...
    a = b;          // nonstandard meaning of assignment
}
```

Further problems could be created by providing different definitions of assignment in different files or even in different scopes within the same file.

Assignment operators, such as *+=*, however, have no predefined meaning for class objects and can be defined as global functions. □

13.4.4 Function Call

Function call

primary-expression (*expression-list*$_{opt}$)

is considered a binary operator with the *primary-expression* as the first operand and the possibly empty *expression-list* as the second. The name of the defining function is operator(). Thus, a call x(arg1,arg2,arg3) is interpreted as x.operator()(arg1,arg2,arg3) for a class object x. operator() must be a nonstatic member function.

■ Consider a class *string*, for manipulating strings of characters.

```
class Substring;
class String {
    // ...
```

```
public:
    String(const char*);
    String& operator=(const String&);
    String& operator=(const Substring&);
    Substring operator()(int position, int length);
    // ...
};

class Substring {
    // ...
public:
    operator String();
    String& operator=(const String&);
    String& operator=(const Substring&);
};
```

With suitable definitions strings and substrings can be used like this:

```
String month = "June";
month(2,2) = "ly";        // month becomes "July"
```

Here the function call operator returns a *Substring* describing *month(2,2)*; that is, the last two characters of the value of *String* variable *month*. The assignment is then resolved to a call of *Substring*'s assignment operator with the operand *String("ly")* to place *ly* in the part of *month* described by the substring *month(2,2)* so *month* finally gets the value *"July"*.

Other common uses of overloaded function call operators are defining a call operator for objects that act as functions (usually containing a pointer to a member function and a pointer to an object) and defining a subscript operator for genuinely multidimensional arrays. □

13.4.5 Subscripting

Subscripting

> *primary-expression* [*expression*]

is considered a binary operator. A subscripting expression x[y] is interpreted as x.operator[](y) for a class object x. operator[] must be a nonstatic member function.

■ An *operator[]* function can be used to define subscripting for class objects. For example,

```
class String {
    // ...
public:
    String(const char*);
    char& operator[](int);
    // ...
};
```

Because the value returned by *String::operator[]()* here is a *char&*, that function can be used on either side of an assignment operator. For example,

```
String ss = "asdf";
ss[1] = ss[3];
```

The assignment is interpreted as

```
ss.operator[](1) = ss.operator[](3);
```

Thus, the new value of *ss* is *"afdf"*.

The second argument (the subscript) of an *operator[]* function may be of any type. This allows popular types, such as associative arrays, to be defined with conventional notation. □

13.4.6 Class Member Access

Class member access using ->

primary-expression -> *primary-expression*

is considered a unary operator. An expression x->m is interpreted as (x.operator->())->m for a class object x. It follows that operator->() must return either a pointer to a class or an object of or a reference to a class for which operator->() is defined. operator-> must be a nonstatic member function.

■ Consider creating classes of objects intended to behave like what one might call "smart pointers" – pointers that do some additional work, like updating a use counter on each access through them.

```
struct Y { int m; };

class Yptr {
    Y* p;
    // information
public:
    Yptr(const char* arg);
    Y* operator->();
};

Yptr::Yptr(const char* arg)
{
    p = 0;
    // store away information
    // based on 'arg'
}
```

```
Y* Yptr::operator->()
{
    if (p) {
        // check p
        // update information
    }
    else {
        // initialize p using information
    }
    return p;
}
```

Class *Yptr*'s -> operator could be used as follows:

```
void f(Yptr y, Yptr& yr, Yptr* yp)
{
    int i = y->m;     // y.operator->()->m
    i = yr->m;        // yr.operator->()->m
    i = yp->m;        // error: Yptr does not have
                      // a member m
}
```

Class member access is a unary operator. An *operator->()* must return something that can be used as a pointer.

Note that there is nothing special about the binary operator ->*. The rules in this section apply only to ->. □

13.4.7 Increment and Decrement

A function called `operator++` taking one argument defines the prefix increment operator ++ for objects of some class. A function called `operator++` taking two arguments defines the postfix increment operator ++ for objects of some class. For postfix `operator++`, the second argument must be of type `int` and the `operator++()` will be called with the second argument 0 when invoked by a postfix increment expression. For example,

```
class X {
public:
    X operator++();      // prefix ++a
    X operator++(int);   // postfix a++
};

void f(X a)
{
    ++a;            // a.operator++();
    a++;            // a.operator++(0);

    a.operator++();   // explicit call: like ++a;
    a.operator++(0);  // explicit call: like a++;
}
```

The prefix and postfix decrement operators `--` are handled similarly.

■ Originally, C++ did not provide a way of specifying separate functions for prefix and postfix application of `++`. A single `operator++` was used to overload both, and no way was provided to distinguish which notation was used to trigger an invocation of an `operator++()`. The ability to distinguish prefix and postfix application of the unary increment operators has been vigorously requested by users for years. It was particularly desired by users who defined "smart pointer" types (§13.4.6). □

■ The choice of the one-argument version of `operator++` for specifying prefix application and the two-argument version of `operator++` for specifying postfix application is not random. All other unary operators are prefix and are overloaded by a function taking one argument. Since a member function must have the implicit `this` pointer as its first or only argument, `operator++(int)` must define the postfix version.

```
class X {
    X operator++();      // ++a, syntactically like !a
    X operator++(int);   // a++0, syntactically like a+0
};
```

Similarly for global functions,

```
class Y {
    friend Y operator++(Y&);       // ++a, like !a
    friend Y operator++(Y&,int);   // a++0, like a+0
};

void g(Y a)
{
    ++a;         // operator++(a);
    a++;         // operator++(a,0);

    operator++(a);      // ++a;
    operator++(a,0);    // a++;
}
```

The notation `a++3` is illegal (as is `3++a`), but `a.operator++(3)` is legal and the argument (in this case `3`) will be passed. □

14

Templates

A class *template* defines the layout and operations for an unbounded set of related types. For example, a single class template `List` might provide a common definition for list of `int`, list of `float`, and list of pointers to `Shapes`. A function *template* defines an unbounded set of related functions. For example, a single function template `sort()` might provide a common definition for sorting all the types defined by the `List` class template.

14   Templates

■ The template design was first presented in Bjarne Stroustrup: *Parameterized Types for C++*, Proc. USENIX C++ Conference, Denver, October 1988. It was accepted as part of the language by the ANSI C++ standards committee (X3J16) in July 1990. □

14.1 Templates

A *template* defines a family of types or functions.

> *template-declaration:*
>   template < *template-argument-list* > *declaration*

> *template-argument-list:*
>   *template-argument*
>   *template-argument-list* , *template argument*

> *template-argument:*
>   *type-argument*
>   *argument-declaration*

> *type-argument:*
>   class *identifier*

The *declaration* in a *template-declaration* must declare or define a function or a class.

A *type-argument* defines its *identifier* to be a *type-name* in the scope of the template declaration.

Template names obey the usual scope and access control rules.

> ■ The template argument list cannot be empty. A template with an empty argument list would simply define a single class or function and is therefore redundant. □

A *template-declaration* is a *declaration*. A *template-declaration* may appear only as a global declaration.

> ■ The template mechanism provides a way of providing general container types such as *list*, *vector*, and *associative array* where the specific type of the elements is left as a parameter. It does so in a way that does not compromise the static type system and allows close to optimal run-time performance through macro expansion of definitions and inlining of function calls (§16.3, §7.1.2, §16.1c). Inheritance can be used to achieve flexibility in a dimension that the template concept does not serve, and vice versa. □

> ■ The restriction to global templates is stronger than necessary; some templates could be handled in some local and nested contexts. Some, however − such as a template for a function definition defined within a function − cannot, and a general and simple restriction seems more sensible than a detailed and possibly subtle list. □

14.2 Class Templates

A class template specifies how individual classes can be constructed much as a class declaration specifies how individual objects can be constructed. A vector class template might be declared like this:

```
template<class T> class vector {
    T* v;
    int sz;
public:
    vector(int);
    T& operator[](int);
    T& elem(int i) { return v[i]; }
    // ...
};
```

The prefix `template <class T>` specifies that a template is being declared and that a *type-name* `T` will be used in the declaration. In other words, `vector` is a parameterized type with `T` as its parameter.

A class can be specified by a *template-class-name*:

> *template-class-name:*
> > *template-name* < *template-arg-list* >

> *template-arg-list:*
> > *template-arg*
> > *template-arg-list* , *template-arg*

> *template-arg:*
> > *expression*
> > *type-name*

A *template-class-name* is a *class-name* (§9).

A class generated from a class template is called a template class, as is a class specifically defined with a *template-class-name* as its name; see §14.5.

A *template-class-name* where the *template-name* is not defined names an undefined class.

A class template name must be unique in a program and may not be declared to refer to any other template, class, function, object, value, or type in the same scope.

The types of the *template-args* specified in a *template-class-name* must match the types specified for the template in its *template-argument-list*.

> ■ Specifying no restrictions on what types can match a type argument gives the programmer the maximum flexibility. The cost is that errors − such as attempting to sort objects of a type that does not have comparison operators − will not in general be detected until link time (§7.2c). Only then are both the template that defines the sort operation and the type of the elements to be sorted available. □

Other *template-args* must be *constant-expression*s, addresses of objects or functions with external linkage, or of static class members. An exact match (§13.2) is required for nontype arguments.

> ■ Nontype template arguments are restricted to values that can be compared at compile time. This allows static type checking involving the resulting types. □

For example, `vectors` can be used like this:

```
vector<int> v1(20);
vector<complex> v2(30);

typedef vector<complex> cvec;    // make cvec a synonym
                                 // for vector<complex>
cvec v3(40);   // v2 and v3 are of the same type

v1[3] = 7;
v2[3] = v3.elem(4) = complex(7,8);
```

Here, `vector<int>` and `vector<complex>` are template classes, and their definitions will by default be generated from the `vector` template.

Since a *template-class-name* is a *class-name*, it can be used wherever a *class-name* can be used. For example,

```
class vector<Shape*>;

vector<Window>* current_window;

class svector : public vector<Shape*> { /* ... */ };
```

Definition of class template member functions is described in §14.6.

■ The syntax relying on the `template` keyword and the placement of the template arguments before the definition was chosen to make it as clear as possible when a template was defined and to ensure that type parameters were introduced lexically before their first use.

This alternative notation was considered:

```
class vector<class T> {
    T* v;
    // ...
};

void sort<class V>(vector<V>& v);
```

It is terser and in some ways more consistent, in that template arguments always appear just after the template name.

This notation, however, has no keyword to attract the attention of human readers and tools; it would compound the problems caused by C and C++ function declarations not starting with a specific keyword. Consider

```
T& index<class T>(vector<T>&,int) { /* ... */ };
```

Parsing this example requires unnecessary cleverness because the first use of the type parameter *T* occurs lexically before the declaration that makes it a *type-name*.

The chosen syntax has no such problem.

```
template<class T> T& index(vector<T>&,int) { /* ... */ };
```

□

14.3 Type Equivalence

Two *template-class-name*s refer to the same class if their *template* names are identical and their arguments have identical values. For example,

```
template<class E, int size> class buffer;

buffer<char,2*512> x;
buffer<char,1024> y;
buffer<char,512> z;
```

declares x and y to be of the same type and z of a different type, and

```
template<class T, void(*err_fct)()>
    class list { /* ... */ };

list<int,&error_handler1> x1;
list<int,&error_handler2> x2;
list<int,&error_handler2> x3;
list<char,&error_handler2> x4;
```

declares x2 and x3 to be of the same type. Their type differs from the types of x1 and x4.

14.4 Function Templates

A function template specifies how individual functions can be constructed. A family of sort functions, for example, might be declared like this:

```
template<class T> void sort(vector<T>);
```

A function template specifies an unbounded set of (overloaded) functions. A function generated from a function template is called a template function, as is a function defined with a type that matches a function template; see §14.5.

Template arguments are not explicitly specified when calling a function template; instead, overloading resolution is used. For example,

```
vector<complex> cv(100);
vector<int> ci(200);

void f(vector<complex>& cv, vector<int>& ci)
{
    sort(cv);    // invoke sort(vector<complex>)
    sort(ci);    // invoke sort(vector<int>)
}
```

A template function may be overloaded either by (other) functions of its name or by (other) template functions of that same name. Overloading resolution for template functions and other functions of the same name is done in three steps:

[1] Look for an exact match (§13.2) on functions; if found, call it.

[2] Look for a function template from which a function that can be called with

an exact match can be generated; if found, call it.

[3] Try ordinary overloading resolution (§13.2) for the functions; if a function is found, call it.

If no match is found the call is an error. In each case, if there is more than one alternative in the first step that finds a match, the call is ambiguous and is an error.

A match on a template (step [2]) implies that a specific template function with arguments that exactly matches the types of the arguments will be generated (§14.5). Not even trivial conversions (§13.2) will be applied in this case.

■ This can cause the generation of unnecessarily many function definitions. A good implementation might take advantage of the similarity of such functions to suppress spurious replication. Alternatively, a user can use a few well-chosen template function declarations to avoid such generation – after an explicit declaration, trivial conversions can be used to find a match (step [1]). □

The same process is used for type matching for pointers to functions (§13.3). Here is an example:

```
template<class T> T max(T a, T b) { return a>b?a:b; };

void f(int a, int b, char c, char d)
{
    int m1 = max(a,b);   // max(int a, int b)
    char m2 = max(c,d);  // max(char a, char b)
    int m3 = max(a,c);   // error: cannot generate
                         // max(int,char)

}
```

For example, adding

```
int max(int,int);
```

to the example above would resolve the third call, by providing a function that could be called for max(a,c) after using the standard conversion of char to int for c.

A function template definition is needed to generate specific versions of the template; only a function template declaration is needed to generate calls to specific versions.

Every *template-argument* specified in the *template-argument-list* must be used in the argument types of a function template.

```
template<class T> T* create();   // error

template<class T>
    void f() {   // error
        T a;
        // ...
    }
```

■ Should this restriction be a problem it is often possible to achieve a similar effect by using a static member function.

```
template<class T> class creator {
    static T* create();
};

int* creator<int>::create();
```

□

All *template-argument*s for a function template must be *type-argument*s.

■ The reason for this is that they must be deduced from actual arguments in calls of the template function. □

14.5 Declarations and Definitions

There must be exactly one definition for each template of a given name in a program. There can be many declarations. The definition is used to generate specific template classes and template functions to match the uses of the template.

Using a *template-class-name* constitutes a declaration of a template class.

Calling a function template or taking its address constitutes a declaration of a template function. There is no special syntax for calling or taking the address of a template function; the name of a function template is used exactly as is a function name. Declaring a function with the same name as a function template with a matching type constitutes a declaration of a specific template function.

If the definition of a specific template function or specific template class is needed to perform some operation and if no explicit definition of that specific template function or class is found in the program, a definition is generated.

■ These rules imply that the decision of what functions to generate from function template definitions cannot be made until a program is complete, that is, not until it is known what function definitions are available.

As stated, error detection has been postponed to the last possible moment: the point after initial linking where definitions are generated for template functions. This is too late for many people's tastes.

As stated, the rules also place the maximum reliance on the programming environment. It will be up to the system to find the definitions of the class templates, function templates, and classes needed for generating those template function definitions. This will be unacceptably complicated for some environments.

Both problems can be alleviated by the introduction of mechanisms allowing a programmer to say ''generate these template functions here for these template arguments.'' This can be made simple enough for any environment and will ensure that errors relating to a specific template function definition are detected on request.

It is not clear, however, whether such mechanisms should be considered part of the language or part of the programming environment. It was felt that more experience was needed and, for that reason, such mechanisms belonged in the environment − at least temporarily.

The simplest mechanism for ensuring proper generation of template function definitions is to leave the problem to the programmer. The linker will tell which definitions are needed, and a file containing noninline template function definitions can be compiled together with an indication of which template arguments are to be used. More sophisticated systems can be built based on this fully manual base. □

The definition of a (nontemplate) function with a type that exactly matches the type of a function template declaration is a definition of that specific template function. For example,

```
template<class T> void sort(vector<T>& v) { /* ... */ }

void sort(vector<char*>& v)  { /* ... */ }
```

Here, the function definition will be used as the sort function for arguments of type vector<char*>. For other vector types the appropriate function definition is generated from the template.

A class can be defined as the definition of a template class. For example,

```
template<class T> class stream { /* ... */ };

class stream<char> { /* ... */ };
```

Here, the class declaration will be used as the definition of streams of characters (stream<char>). Other streams will be handled by template functions generated from the function template.

No operation that requires a defined class can be performed on a template class until the class template has been seen. After that, a specific template class is considered defined immediately before the first global declaration that names it.

■ In particular, a template class, such as *stream<char>*, cannot be defined unless its class template has been defined. □

■ Note that the generation of template functions and template classes from templates can be done by a well behaved macro expansion process. This ensures that optimal run-time behavior can be achieved.

If done naively, such a code replication technique can also lead to excessive amounts of generated code. Often, inheritance can be used to achieve code sharing. This would involve deriving a template from an ordinary class. For example,

```
template<class T> class vector {  // general vector type
        T* v;
        int sz;
public:
        vector(int);
        T& elem(int i) { return v[i]; }
        T& operator[](int i);
        // ...
};
```

```
template<class T>
class pvector : vector<void*> {   // build all vector
                                  // of pointer classes
                                  // based on vector<void*>
public:
    pvector(int i) : (i) {}
    T*& elem(int i)
        { return (T*&) vector<void*>::elem(i); }
    T*& operator[](int i)
        { return (T*&) vector<void*>::operator[](i); }
    // ...
};


pvector<int*> pivec(100);
pvector<complex*> icmpvec(200);
pvector<char*> pcvec(300);
```

The implementations of the three vector of pointer classes will be completely shared. They are all implemented exclusively through derivation and inline expansion relying on the implementation of *vector<void*>*. The *vector<void*>* implementation is a good candidate for a standard library.

Another way of using inheritance to achieve code sharing is to derive one template from another. For example,

```
template<class T> class B { /* ... */ };

template<class T> class D : public B<T> { /* ... */ };
```

□

14.6 Member Function Templates

A member function of a template class is implicitly a template function with the template arguments of its class as its template arguments. For example,

```
template<class T> class vector {
    T* v;
    int sz;
public:
    vector(int);
    T& operator[](int);
    T& elem(int i) { return v[i]; }
    // ...
};
```

declares three function templates. The subscript function might be defined like this:

```
template<class T> T& vector<T>::operator[](int i)
{
    if (i<0 || sz<=i) error("vector: range error");
    return v[i];
}
```

■ Note that since the template argument is implicit, applying it to the constructor name in a declaration or definition of the constructor is wrong.

```
template<class T> class vector {
        // ...
        vector<T>(int);    // error
        vector(int);       // ok
};

template<class T>
    vector<T>::vector<T>(int) { /* ... */ }    // error

template<class T>
    vector<T>::vector(int) { /* ... */ }       // ok
```

□

The template argument for `vector<T>::operator[]()` will be determined by the vector to which the subscripting operation is applied.

```
vector<int> v1(20);
vector<complex> v2(30);

v1[3] = 7;                   // vector<int>::operator[]()
v2[3] = complex(7,8);        // vector<complex>::operator[]()
```

■ It follows that explicit calls of constructors and destructors looks like this:

```
void f(vector<int>* p)
{
        // ...
        p->vector<int>::~vector();
        // ...
        vector<int>& v = vector<int>(10);
        // ...
}
```

□

14.7 Friends

A friend function of a template is not implicitly a template function. For example,

```
template<class T> class task {
    // ...
    friend void next_time();
    friend task<T>* preempt(task<T>*);
    friend task* prmt(task*);          // error
    // ...
};
```

Here, next_time() becomes the friend of all task classes, and each task has an appropriately typed function called preempt() as a friend. The preempt functions might be defined as a template.

```
template<class T>
    task<T>* preempt(task<T>* t) { /* ... */ }
```

The declaration of prmt() is an error because there is no type task, only specific template types, task<int>, task<record>, and so on.

14.8 Static Members and Variables

Each template class or function generated from a template has its own copies of any static variables or members. For example,

```
template<class T> class X {
    static T s;
    // ...
};


X<int> aa;
X<char*> bb;
```

Here X<int> has a static member s of type int and X<char*> has a static member s of type char*.
    Similarly,

```
template<class T> f(T* p)
{
    static T s;
    // ...
};


void g(int a, char* b)
{
    f(&a);
    f(&b);
}
```

Here f(int*) has a static member s of type int and f(char**) has a static member s of type char**.

15

Exception Handling

Exception handling provides a way of transferring control and information to an unspecified caller that has expressed willingness to handle exceptions of a given type. Exceptions of arbitrary types can be thrown and caught and the set of exceptions a function may throw can be specified. The termination model of exception handling is provided. Exception handling can be used to support notions of error handling and fault-tolerant computing.

15 Exception Handling

■ The exception handling design is a variant of the scheme presented in Andrew Koenig and Bjarne Stroustrup: *Exception Handling for C++ (revised)*, Proc. USENIX C++ Conference, San Francisco, April 1990. It was accepted as part of the language by the ANSI C++ standards committee (X3J16) in November 1990. □

15.1 Exception Handling

Exception handling provides a way of transferring control and information from a point in the execution of a program to an *exception handler* associated with a point previously passed by the execution. A handler will be invoked only by a *throw-expression* invoked in code executed in the handler's *try-block* or in functions called from the handler's *try-block*.

> *try-block:*
> > try *compound-statement handler-list*

> *handler-list:*
> > *handler handler-list*_{opt}

> *handler:*
> > catch (*exception-declaration*) *compound-statement*

> *exception-declaration:*
> > *type-specifier-list declarator*
> > *type-specifier-list abstract-declarator*
> > *type-specifier-list*
> > . . .

> *throw-expression:*
> > throw *expression*_{opt}

A *try-block* is a *statement* (§6). A *throw-expression* is a *unary-expression* (§5) of type void. A *throw-expression* is sometimes referred to as a "*throw-point*." Code that executes a *throw-expression* is said to "throw an exception"; code that subsequently gets control is called a "*handler*."

> ■ Exception handling is intended to allow code that has encountered a condition it cannot cope with to return to some other code that directly or indirectly invoked it. There is no way for an exception handler to request the thread of control to resume from the throw-point. In other words, throw implements the termination model of exception handling. □

> ■ Ideally, we would like an exception handling mechanism for C++ to do all the following:
> > [1] provide type-safe transmission of arbitrary amounts of information from a throw-point to a handler,
> > [2] impose no added cost (in time or space) to code that does not throw an exception,
> > [3] provide a guarantee that every exception thrown is caught by an appropriate handler,
> > [4] provide a way of grouping exceptions so that exception handlers can be written to catch groups of exceptions as well as individual ones,
> > [5] work correctly by default in a multithreaded program,
> > [6] allow cooperation with other languages, especially with C,

[7] be easy to understand and use, and

[8] be easy to implement.

The mechanism described here provides [1], [4], [5], and [7]. It can be implemented so that it provides [2] and can, if necessary, be extended to provide [3]. Such implementations are *relatively* simple, thus providing [8]. In addition, it is possible to provide a portable implementation by generating C code from the C++ source. The commentary below (§15.5) will discuss how [3] clashes with other important aspects of programming, making it hard to provide a guarantee against uncaught exceptions without punting on "every" or "appropriate" or creating other problems for the programmer. ☐

■ The design here and the criteria for it evolved slowly. An earlier version of the design was presented at the "C++ at Work" conference in November 1989 by Andrew Koenig and Bjarne Stroustrup. The design presented here owes much to the discussion generated by that paper and in particular to comments by Toby Bloom, Peter Deutch, Ken Friedenbach, Keith Gorlen, Martin O'Riorden, Mike Powell, Jim Mitchell, Rob Seliger, Jonathan Shopiro, and Mike Tiemann. The design is clearly influenced by the exception handling mechanism in ML.

Another important source of inspiration was the work on fault-tolerant systems done in the University of Newcastle in England under the direction of Brian Randell. ☐

■ This design assumes that exceptions are to be used primarily for error handling. Alternative uses, such as loop termination and alternate "normal" return paths from functions, are clearly possible, but are considered secondary.

Exception handlers are assumed to be rare compared to function definitions, and exceptions are assumed to be thrown infrequently compared to function calls. The aim is to allow programs to be constructed out of fault-tolerant subsystems without requiring attention to exception handling in every function. In other words, for most programs it is not reasonable to make every function fault-tolerant. Rather, some functions will be given responsibility for handling all errors occurring both in themselves and in functions called by them.

Exception handling, as described here, is a language-level concept and not just the description of a single implementation; many alternative implementation strategies are possible. Nor do the exception handling mechanisms described here dictate a particular policy for error handling; many alternative strategies for fault tolerancy are possible. ☐

■ The word *throw* was chosen in preference to the more commonly used *signal* and *raise* because both *signal* and *raise* are functions in the ANSI C standard library. Similarly, the word *catch* was chosen in preference to *handle* because *handle* is a common identifier in C programs for PC and Mac computers. ☐

15.2 Throwing an Exception

Throwing an exception transfers control to a handler. An object is passed and the type of that object determines which handlers can catch it. For example,

```
throw "Help!";
```

can be caught by a *handler* of some char* type:

```
try {
    // ...
}
catch(const char* p) {
    // handle character string exceptions here
}
```

and

```
class Overflow {
    // ...
public:
    Overflow(char,double,double);
};

void f(double x)
{
    // ...
    throw Overflow('+',x,3.45e107);
}
```

can be caught by a handler

```
try {
    // ...
    f(1.2);
    // ...
}
catch(Overflow& oo) {
    // handle exceptions of type Overflow here
}
```

When an exception is thrown, control is transferred to the nearest handler with an appropriate type; "nearest" means the handler whose *try-block* was most recently entered by the thread of control and not yet exited; "appropriate type" is defined in §15.4.

A *throw-expression* initializes a temporary object of the static type of the operand of throw and uses that temporary to initialize the appropriately-typed variable named in the handler.

■ For example,

```
void g()
{
    // ...
    Overflow dummy('?',1,2);
    // ...
    throw dummy;
    // ...
}

void f()
{
    try {
        g();
    }
    catch (Overflow& oo) {
        // ...
    }
}
```

Here the reference *oo* will refer to a copy of *dummy*. It cannot refer to the automatic storage of function *g()* from which control is returned by *throw*. The copy of the object created by *throw*, however, will persist until exit from the exception handler. □

Except for the restrictions on type matching mentioned in §15.4 and the use of a temporary variable, the operand of throw is treated exactly as a function argument in a call (§5.2.2) or the operand of a return statement.

■ Note that the exception parameter does not have to be named. Often a name is not needed because the information that an exception of a certain type has been thrown is sufficient to handle it. □

If the use of the temporary object can be eliminated without changing the meaning of the program except for the execution of constructors and destructors associated with the use of the temporary object (§12.1c), then the exception in the handler may be initialized directly with the argument of the throw expression.

■ Note that defining the transfer of information from a throw-point to a handler as initialization makes the transfer type-safe, potentially maximally efficient, and safe against race conditions in concurrent systems; it is simply a copy − possibly using a copy constructor − of a value of a known type from one location on the stack to another. □

■ For exceptions caused by free store storage management, it is not feasible for the exception handling mechanism to allocate the temporary object using the ordinary free store allocation mechanisms. Further, using the general free store mechanisms would be inefficient and would render exception handling vulnerable to errors caused by the corruption of free store. Thus, an implementation may decide to keep a pool of memory preallocated for the exclusive use of the exception handling mechanism and to impose a limit on the amount of memory used for exception handling where exceptions related to free store management are involved. □

A *throw-expression* with no operand rethrows the exception being handled. A *throw-expression* with no operand may appear only in a handler or in a function directly or indirectly called from a handler. For example, code that must be executed because of an exception yet cannot completely handle the exception can be written like this:

```
try {
    // ...
}
catch (...) {   // catch all exceptions

    // respond (partially) to exception

    throw;      // pass the exception to some
                // other handler
}
```

■ An alternative and typically more elegant way of ensuring that code is executed under all manageable circumstances is to rely on the execution of destructors as described in §15.3. □

■ This definition of `throw;` implies that the exception handling implementation needs a concept of a "*current exception*." It also implies that although an exception is considered handled on entry to a handler, the current exception cannot be deallocated until exit from its handler. □

15.3 Constructors and Destructors

As control passes from a throw-point to a handler, destructors are invoked for all automatic objects constructed since the *try-block* was entered.

An object that is partially constructed will have destructors executed only for its fully constructed sub-objects. Also, should a constructor for an element of an automatic array throw an exception, only the constructed elements of that array will be destroyed.

The process of calling destructors for automatic objects constructed on the path from a *try-block* to a *throw-expression* is called "*stack unwinding*".

■ If a debugger is active for a running program and that program throws an exception that is not caught, it would be unfortunate if the stack were unwound before entry into the debugger. Users are not likely to be pleased with a debugger that does such unwinding. □

■ Destructors can be used to automate management of resources in the presence of exceptions. The fundamental idea is to represent the acquisition of a resource as the initialization of a local variable and then rely on the execution of the destructor to release the resource. Consider, for example, a lock in some system.

```
class lock {
    // ...
public:
    grab();
    release();
};

lock very_important;
```

To manage acquisition and release we define an auxiliary *grab_lock* class.

```
class grab_lock {          // store and reset class
    lock& l;
public:
    grab_lock(lock& ll) :l(ll) { l.grab(); }

    ~grab_lock() { l.release(); }
};
```

Then, by allocating a *grab_lock* we ensure the release of the lock by *grab_lock*'s destructor even in the presence of exceptions.

```
void my_function()
{
    grab_lock mine(very_important);

    // ...
}
```

□

15.4 Handling an Exception

A *handler* with type T, const T, T&, or const T& is a match for a *throw-expression* with an object of type E if

[1] T and E are the same type, or

[2] T is an accessible (§4.6) base class of E at the throw point, or

[3] T is a pointer type and E is a pointer type that can be converted to T by a standard pointer conversion (§4.6) at the throw point.

For example,

```
class Matherr { /* ... */ virtual vf(); };
class Overflow: public Matherr { /* ... */ };
class Underflow: public Matherr { /* ... */ };
class Zerodivide: public Matherr { /* ... */ };

void f()
{
    try {
        g();
    }
```

```
catch (Overflow oo) {
    // ...
}
catch (Matherr mm) {
    // ...
}
```

}

Here, the `Overflow` handler will catch exceptions of type `Overflow` and the `Matherr` handler will catch exceptions of type `Matherr` and all types publicly derived from `Matherr` including `Underflow` and `Zerodivide`.

■ An alternative style of error handling would be to catch only the base class and rely on a virtual function to distinguish between the derived classes.

```
void g();

void ff()
{
    try {
        g();
    }
    catch (Matherr& mm) {
        mm.vf();            // call appropriate vf()
    }
}
```

The exception parameter must be a reference; otherwise only the `Matherr` part of the thrown object would be passed (§12.8). □

The handlers for a *try-block* are tried in order of appearance. It is an error to place a handler for a base class ahead of a handler for its derived class since that would ensure that the handler for the derived class would never be invoked.

■ Examples for which order matters can be constructed with multiple inheritance. For example,

```
class network_error { /* ... */ };
class file_system_error { /* ... */ };
class NFerror :
    public network_error,
    public file_system_error { /* ... */ };

void f()
{
    try {
        // ...
    }
```

```
catch (network_error& ne) {
    // ...
}
catch (file_system_error& fse) {
    // ...
}
}
```

Here, the order of handlers is significant when catching an *NFerror*. □

A ... in a handler's *exception-declaration* functions similarly to ... in a function argument declaration; it specifies a match for any exception. If present, a ... handler must be the last handler for its *try-block*.

If no match is found among the handlers for a *try-block*, the search for a matching handler continues in a dynamically surrounding *try-block*.

   ■ Thus, not specifying a ... handler for a try block is equivalent to specifying

```
catch (...) { throw; }
```

   □

If no matching handler is found in a program, the function `terminate()` (§15.7) is called.

An exception is considered handled upon entry to a handler. The stack will have been unwound at that point.

   ■ For example,

```
struct Foo {
    char* p;
    Foo(char* p1): p(p1) { }
};

void toss()
{
    char buffer[10];
    strcpy(buffer, "Foo!");
    throw Foo(buffer);    // bad idea!
                          // pointer to local in exception
}
```

Here the *buffer* in *toss()* will most likely be corrupted by the stack unwinding before a handler gets a chance to look at it. □

15.5 Exception Specifications

Raising or catching an exception affects the way a function relates to other functions. It is possible to list the set of exceptions that a function may directly or indirectly throw as part of a function declaration. An *exception-specification* can be used as a suffix of a function declarator.

exception-specification:
> throw (*type-list*_{opt})

type-list:
> *type-name*
> *type-list* , *type-name*

For example,

```
void f() throw (X,Y)
{
    // ...
}
```

■ Murphy's Law for exception handling reads "Any exception that can be thrown will be thrown," so this function declaration should be read as "*f()* will throw *X* and *Y*". □

An attempt by a function to throw an exception not in its exception list will cause a call of the function unexpected(); see §15.8.

■ A simple way to enforce this rule would be to generate code like this for *f()*:

```
void f()
{
    try {
        // ...
    }
    catch (X) { throw; }
    catch (Y) { throw; }
    catch (...) { unexpected(); }
}
```

□

■ The default effect of *unexpected()* is to call *terminate()*; the default effect of *terminate()* is *abort()* (§15.7). That is, a violation of the guarantee expressed by an *exception-specification* is by default considered a serious design error. The programmer defining *f()* can ensure that this never happens by brute force. For example,

```
void f() throw(X,Y)
{
    try {
        // ...
    }
    catch (X) { throw; }
    catch (Y) { throw; }
    catch (...) { throw X(); }
}
```

More subtle approaches, however, such as a proof that only *X* and *Y* (or classes derived from *X* and *Y*) can be thrown by *f()* and code called from *f()*, are sometimes possible. □

An implementation may not reject an expression simply because it *may* throw an exception not specified in an *exception-specification* of the function containing the expression; the handling of violations of an *exception-specification* is done at run-time.

■ For example,

```
extern "C" f();      // we have no way of guessing
                     // which exceptions f() might throw

void g() throw(X);   // g() will throw X

void h() throw()     // h() may not throw any exceptions
{
    f();    // legal, but suspect
    g();    // legal, but highly suspect
}
```

This program must be accepted by a compiler and any errors caused by `f()` throwing an exception must be caught at run-time. Static analyzers can be provided to help programmers avoid such run-time errors, however. Compilers can also help by warning about suspect constructs such as the call of `g()` above. □

A function with no *exception-specification* may throw any exception.

A function with an empty *exception-specification*, `throw()`, may not throw any exception.

A function that may throw an exception of a class X may throw an exception of any class publicly derived from X.

An *exception-specification* is not considered part of a function's type.

■ Ideally, only exceptions mentioned in an *exception-specification* will be thrown. Why don't we make *exception-specification*s part of a function's type and perform a complete static type check? Why don't we enforce the ideal by requiring every function to have an *exception-specification* and reject every program where an unexpected exception occurs?

Preventing such errors at compile-time would be a great bother to the programmer and the checking would consequently be subverted. Such subversion could take many forms. For example, calls through C functions could be used to render the static checking meaningless, programmers could declare functions to throw all exceptions by default, or tools could be written to create *exception-specification*s automatically, listing all possible exceptions. The effect would be to eliminate the bother as well as the safety checks that were designed into the mechanism.

Further, if a function were changed to throw a new exception, all functions that directly or indirectly call it would have to be changed and recompiled. This would be a nuisance and could lead to significant delays since libraries would have to agree on a set of exceptions used to work together as part of a single program. For example, if subsystem X handles exceptions from subsystem Y and the supplier of Y introduces a new kind of exception, then X's code will have to be modified to cope. A user of X and Y will not be able to upgrade to a new version of Y until X has been modified. Where many subsystems are used this could cause cascading delays.

In other words, it is infeasible to recompile all code in a system simply because a subsystem has been modified to possibly throw a new exception. This implies that it should be possible to replace a function with another that differs only in its *exception-specification* without requiring recompilation of its callers.

Naturally, in a restricted environment one might impose stricter rules based on separate static analysis or compiler warnings, but for general use the flexibility seems essential. □

15.6 Special Functions

The exception handling mechanism relies on two functions, `terminate()` and `unexpected()`, for coping with errors related to the exception handling mechanism itself.

■ Note that these functions must be specific to individual threads in a multi-threaded program. However, exactly how that is achieved is not supposed to be visible to a user. A programmer need not know if a program is multithreaded to use exceptions correctly. □

15.6.1 The `terminate()` Function

Occasionally, exception handling must be abandoned for less subtle error handling techniques. For example,
- when the exception handling mechanism cannot find a handler for a thrown exception,
- when the exception handling mechanism finds the stack corrupted, or
- when a destructor called during stack unwinding caused by an exception tries to exit using an exception.

In such cases,

```
void terminate();
```

is called; `terminate()` calls the last function given as an argument to `set_terminate()`:

```
typedef void(*PFV)();
PFV set_terminate(PFV);
```

The previous function given to `set_terminate()` will be the return value; this enables users to implement a stack strategy for using `terminate()`. The default function called by `terminate()` is `abort()`.

Selecting a terminate function that does not in fact terminate but tries to return to its caller is an error.

■ Note that *terminate()* may enforce this rule by calling *abort()* should a user-supplied function return. The use of *terminate()* is reserved for problems beyond the scope of ordinary exception handling. An example of a reasonable *terminate ()* that does not *abort ()* is a function that discards all data within its address space as probably corrupted and re-initializes the process. □

15.6.2 The `unexpected()` Function

If a function with an *exception-specification* throws an exception that is not listed in the *exception-specification*, the function

```
void unexpected();
```

is called; unexpected() calls the last function given as an argument to set_unexpected():

```
typedef void(*PFV)();
PFV set_unexpected(PFV);
```

The previous function given to set_unexpected() will be the return value; this enables users to implement a stack strategy for using unexpected(). The default function called by unexpected() is terminate(). Since the default function called by terminate() is abort(), this leads to immediate and precise detection of the error.

■ The idea is that a violation of a promise to throw only a specified set of exceptions is a serious design error that must be fixed before any further progress can be made.

There are, however, cases where having a subsystem unconditionally terminate is unacceptable. Some such cases can be handled by having *terminate ()* re-initialize the offending process, but in other cases this approach is too Draconian or infeasible because of lack of hardware support. The caller of a function with an *exception-specification* can use *set_unexpected ()* to reset the penalty for throwing an unexpected exception by the called function to something more suitable for the caller. For example,

```
extern void f() throw(X,Y);

void pass_through() { throw; }

void g()
{
    PFV old = set_unexpected(&pass_through);
    try {
        f();
    }
```

```
        catch (X) {
            // ...
        }
        catch (Y) {
            // ...
        }
        catch (...) {
            // something strange happened in f()
            // recover!
        }
        set_unexpected(old);
    }
```

Here, if `f()` throws an exception that is not *X* or *Y*, unexpected() will call
pass_through(), which in turn will rethrow the exception for *g()* to catch.

The example above was deliberately naively written. Clearly much care will
have to be taken to reset *unexpected()* on *all* returns from *g()*. A better style
can be achieved using the "resource acquisition is initialization" approach described
in §15.2:

```
    extern void f() throw(X,Y);

    void pass_through() { throw; }

    class SUE {       // store and reset class
        PFV old;
    public:
        SUE(PFV f) { old = set_unexpected(f); }
        ~SUE() { set_unexpected(old); }
    };

    void g()
    {
        SUE mine(&pass_through); // set_unexpected to
                                 // pass_through and
                                 // guarantee reset
        try {
            f();
        }
        catch (X) {
            // ...
        }
        catch (Y) {
            // ...
        }
        catch (...) {
            // something strange happened in f()
            // recover!
        }
    }
```

□

■ It has been suggested that the proper response to an attempt to throw an unexpected exception through an interface would be to throw a special exception *UNEXPECTED*. This can be easily handled using *set_unexpected()*:

```
class UNEXPECTED { /* ... */ } ;

void throw_UNEXPECTED() { throw UNEXPECTED; }

// ...

set_unexpected(&throw_UNEXPECTED);
```

However, many users with experience with exception handling mechanisms where the default style is to raise a distinguished exception prefer termination. □

15.7 Exceptions and Access

The formal argument of a catch clause obeys the same access rules as an argument of the function in which the catch clause occurs.

An object may be thrown if it can be copied and destroyed in the context of the function in which the throw occurs.

■ Note that since a base class of a thrown object must be accessible, an object with two uses of a class as a base cannot be thrown unless both are virtual bases; otherwise the throw would be ambiguous.

Note also that an object cannot be caught by a handler for a class that is a private base class of the object's class; a private class is considered an implementation detail. □

16

Preprocessing

This chapter describes preprocessing in C++. C++ preprocessing, which is based on ANSI C preprocessing, provides macro substitution, conditional compilation, and source file inclusion. In addition, directives are provided to control line numbering in diagnostics and for symbolic debugging, to generate a diagnostic message with a given token sequence, and to perform implementation-dependent actions (the #pragma directive). Certain predefined names are available. These facilities are conceptually handled by a preprocessor, which may or may not actually be implemented as a separate process.

16   Preprocessing

A C++ implementation contains a preprocessor capable of macro substitution, conditional compilation, and inclusion of named files.

Lines beginning with #, optionally preceded by space and horizontal tab characters, (also called "*directives*") communicate with this preprocessor. These lines have syntax independent of the rest of the language; they may appear anywhere and have effects that last (independent of the scoping rules of C++) until the end of the translation unit (§2).

A preprocessing directive (or any other line) may be continued on the next line in a source file by placing a backslash character, \, immediately before the new-line at the end of the line to be continued. The preprocessor effects the continuation by deleting the backslash and the new-line before the input sequence is divided into tokens. A backslash character may not be the last character in a source file.

A preprocessing token is a language token (§2.1), a file name as in a #include directive, or any single character, other than white space, that does not match another preprocessing token.

■ Except for the treatment of C++ // comments and C++ tokens that are not also C
tokens (. *, ->*, and : :), C++ preprocessing is ANSI C preprocessing.

Because an ANSI C style preprocessor may not be available for all C++ implementations, the commentary (§16.3) describes Classic C preprocessing. □

16.1 Phases of Preprocessing

Preprocessing is defined to occur in several phases. An implementation may col-
lapse these phases, but the effect must be as though they had been executed.

If needed, new-line characters are introduced to replace system-dependent end-
of-line indicators and any other necessary system-dependent character set trans-
lations are done. Trigraph sequences are replaced by their single character
equivalents (§16.2).

Each pair of a backslash character \ immediately followed by a new-line is
deleted, with the effect that the next source line is appended to the line that
contained the sequence.

The source text is decomposed into preprocessing tokens and sequences of
white space. A single white space replaces each comment. A source file may
not end with a partial token or comment.

■ Unless a C preprocessor has been adapted for use with C++, it will not recognize
// comments. Thus, macro replacement will inappropriately be done for macro
names appearing within // comments, and // comments within macro definitions
will not be correctly translated to white space.

Similarly, an unmodified C preprocessor will not recognize . *, ->*, and : : as
single tokens. □

Preprocessing directives are executed and macros are expanded (§16.3, §16.4,
§16.5, §16.6, §16.7, and §16.8).

Escape sequences in character constants and string literals are replaced by their
equivalents (§2.5.2).

■ The value of a character constant within a preprocessing directive may or may not
have the same numeric value as it has within any other expression. □

Adjacent string literals are concatenated.

The result of preprocessing is syntactically and semantically analyzed and
translated, then linked together as necessary with other programs and libraries.

16.2 Trigraph Sequences

Before any other processing takes place, each occurrence of one of the following sequences of three characters (*"trigraph sequences"*) is replaced by the single character indicated in the table below.

```
??=   #        ??(   [
??/   \        ??)   ]
??'   ^        ??!   |
```

For example,

```
??=define arraycheck(a,b) a??(b??) ??!??! b??(a??)
```

becomes

```
#define arraycheck(a,b) a[b] || b[a]
```

■ ANSI C introduced the notion of trigraphs to allow implementation of C on systems that do not support the full ASCII character set. In particular, the trigraph definitions allow a mapping from the ISO 646-1983 Invariant Code Set character set to ASCII.

Unfortunately, this doesn't address the problem of writing C and C++ programs on terminals where the all the character positions reserved for alphabetic characters are assigned to letters. The reason is that the ASCII (ANSI3.4-1968) special characters [,], {, }, /, and \ occupy character positions that in most European national ISO 646 character sets are occupied by letters not found in the English alphabet. For example, the Danish representations of these character values are Æ, Å, æ, å, ø, and Ø. No significant amount of text can be written in Danish without them. This leaves Danish programmers with the unpleasant choice of acquiring computers systems that handle full 8 bit character sets, such as ISO 8859/1/2, not using three vowels of their native language, or not using C++. Speakers of French, German, Spanish, Italian, and so on, face the same dilemma. We speculate that this has been a notable barrier to the use of C in Europe, especially in commercial settings where the use of 7 bit national character sets is pervasive in many countries.

For example, consider this innocent-looking ANSI C and C++ program:

```
int main(int argc, char* argv[])
{
        if (argc<1 || *argv[1]=='\0') return 0;
        printf("Hello, %s\n",argv[1]);
}
```

On a standard Danish terminal or printer this program will appear like this:

```
int main(int argc, char* argvÆ Å)
æ
        if (argc<1 øø *argvÆ 1Å=='Ø0') return 0;
        printf("Hello, %sØn",argvÆ 1Å);
å
```

It is amazing to realize that some people can actually read and write this with ease.

The trigraph version is little better.

```
int main(int argc, char* arg??(??))
??<
        if (argc<1 ??!??! *argv??(1??)=='??/0') return 0;
        printf("Hello, %s??/n",argv??(1??));
??>
```

For a further discussion of these issues, see Keld Simonsen and Bjarne Stroustrup: *A European Representation for ISO C* in the Vol. 9 No. 2 Summer 1989 issue of the European UNIX® Systems Users Group Newsletter. A partial solution would be to augment the trigraphs, which are necessary to allow character constants and string values, with keywords and new character combinations, as is often done for national dialects of languages such as Pascal. A comprehensive solution is possible only through a pervasive upgrading of complete computer systems to allow national characters to coexist with special characters such as \ and { in all software. □

16.3 Macro Definition and Expansion

A preprocessing directive of the form

> #define *identifier token-string*

causes the preprocessor to replace subsequent instances of the identifier with the given sequence of tokens. White space surrounding the replacement token sequence is discarded. Given, for example,

> #define SIDE 8

the declaration

> char chessboard[SIDE][SIDE];

after macro expansion becomes

> char chessboard[8][8];

An identifier defined in this form may be redefined only by another #define directive of this form provided the replacement list of the second definition is identical to that of the first. All white space separations are considered identical.

A line of the form

> #define *identifier* (*identifier* , ... , *identifier*) *token-string*

where there is no space between the first identifier and the (is a macro definition with parameters, or a "*function-like*" macro definition. An identifier defined as a function-like macro may be redefined by another function-like macro definition provided the second definition has the same number and spelling of parameters and the two replacement lists are identical. White space separations are considered identical.

Subsequent appearances of an identifier defined as a function-like macro followed by a (, a sequence of tokens delimited by commas, and a) are replaced by the token string in the definition. White space surrounding the replacement token sequence is discarded. Each occurrence of an identifier mentioned in the parameter list of the definition is replaced by the tokens representing the corresponding actual argument in the call. The actual arguments are token strings separated by commas; commas in quoted strings, in character constants, or within nested parentheses do not separate arguments. The number of arguments in a macro invocation must be the same as the number of parameters in the macro definition.

Once the arguments to a function-like macro have been identified, argument substitution occurs. Unless it is preceded by a # token (§16.3.1) or is adjacent to a ## token (§16.3.2), a parameter in the replacement list is replaced by the corresponding argument after any macros in the argument have been expanded (§16.3.3).

For example, given the macro definitions

```
#define index_mask      0XFF00
#define extract(word,mask)      word & mask
```

the call

```
index = extract(packed_data,index_mask);
```

expands to

```
index = packed_data & 0XFF00;
```

■ Semicolons in, or at the end of, a *token-string* are part of that sequence. Thus

```
#define MAX     256;
int upperbound=MAX-1;
```

expands to the two statements

```
int upperbound=256;-1;
```

which is probably not what the user intended. □

In both forms the replacement string is rescanned for more defined identifiers (§16.3.3).

16.3.1 The # Operator

If an occurrence of a parameter in a replacement token sequence is immediately preceded by a # token, the parameter and the # operator will be replaced in the expansion by a string literal containing the spelling of the corresponding argument. A \ character is inserted in the string literal before each occurrence of a \ or a " within or delimiting a character constant or string literal in the argument.

For example, given

```
#define path(logid,cmd)  "/usr/" #logid "/bin/" #cmd
#define joe              joseph
```

the call

```
char* mytool=path(joe,readmail);
```

yields

```
char* mytool="/usr/" "joe" "/bin/" "readmail";
```

which is later concatenated (§16.1) to become

```
char* mytool="/usr/joe/bin/readmail";
```

■ Note that the argument to the # operator is not available for further macro replace-ment so the result is *not*

char mytool="/usr/joseph/bin/readmail";*

□

16.3.2 The ## Operator

If a ## operator appears in a replacement token sequence between two tokens, first if either of the adjacent tokens is a parameter it is replaced, then the ## operator and any white space surrounding it are deleted. The effect of the ## operator, therefore, is concatenation.

Given

```
#define inherit(basenum)  public Pubbase ## basenum, \
                          private Privbase ## basenum
```

the call

```
class D : inherit(1) { };
```

yields

```
class D : public Pubbase1, private Privbase1 { };
```

Any macros in the replaced tokens adjacent to the ## are not available for further expansion, but the result of the concatenation is. Given

```
#define concat(a)      a ## ball
#define base           B
#define baseball       sport
```

the call

```
concat(base)
```

yields

```
sport
```

and *not*

```
Bball
```

16.3.3 Rescanning and Further Replacement

After all parameters in the replacement list have been replaced, the resulting list is rescanned for more macros to replace. If the name of the macro being replaced is found during this scan or during subsequent rescanning, it is not replaced.

A completely replaced macro expansion is not interpreted as a preprocessing directive, even if it appears to be one.

16.3.4 Scope of Macro Names and #undef

Once defined, a preprocessor identifier remains defined and in scope (independent of the scoping rules of C++) until the end of the translation unit or until it is undefined in a #undef directive.

A #undef directive has the form

    #undef *identifier*

and causes the identifier's preprocessor definition to be forgotten. If the specified identifier is not currently defined as a macro name, the #undef is ignored.

16.4 File Inclusion

A control line of the form

    #include <*filename*>

causes the replacement of that line by the entire contents of the file *filename*. The named file is searched for in an implementation-dependent sequence of places.

Similarly, a control line of the form

    #include "*filename*"

causes the replacement of that line by the contents of the file *filename*, which is searched for first in an implementation-dependent manner. If this search fails, the file is searched for as if the directive had been of the form

    #include <*filename*>

■ The intention of defining the two syntaxes for *#include* lines as above is that an implementation provide as closely as possible the functionality of Classic C, in which

    #include <*filename*>

meant that the file was to be searched for in a defined sequence of standard places, and

    #include "*filename*"

meant that the file was to be searched for first in the directory of the original source file and then in the sequence of standard places. It cannot be assumed, however, that the notion of ''directory'' will make sense for all implementations of C++. The semantics of `#include`, therefore, are highly implementation dependent. An implementation should specify the places that will be searched for a file to be included. □

Neither the new-line character nor > may appear in *filename* delimited by < and >. If any of the characters ', \, or ", or either of the sequences /* or // appear in such a *filename* the behavior is undefined.

Neither the new-line character nor " may appear in a *filename* delimited by a " pair, although > may appear. If either of the characters ' or \ or either of the sequences /* or // appear in such a *filename* the behavior is undefined.

■ How a sequence of preprocessing tokens between a < and > preprocessing token pair or a pair of "'s will be combined into a single file name preprocessing token will depend on the implementation. Treatment of white space within the delimiters will vary. Typically, a sequence of white space that is the result of a macro expansion will be treated as a single space character, while other sequences of white space will be preserved.

Some implementations will ignore case distinctions in file names. Further, the number of significant characters in a file name may be limited by an implementation. To provide functionality consistent with ANSI C, however, an implementation must provide at least six significant characters. □

If a directive appears of the form

    #include *token-string*

not matching either of the forms given above, the preprocessing tokens within *token-string* will be processed as normal text. The resulting directive must match one of the forms defined above and will be treated as such.

A `#include` directive may appear within a file that is being processed as a result of another `#include` directive.

An implementation may impose a limit on the depth of nesting of `#include` directives within source files that have been read while processing a `#include` directive in another source file.

■ Usually such a limit will be attributable to the host operating system's limit on the number of open files. □

16.5 Conditional Compilation

The preprocessor allows conditional compilation of source code. The syntax for conditional compilation follows:

> *conditional:*
>> *if-part elif-parts$_{opt}$ else-part$_{opt}$ endif-line*

> *if-part:*
>> *if-line text*

if-line:
> \# if *constant-expression*
> \# ifdef *identifier*
> \# ifndef *identifier*

elif-parts:
> *elif-line text*
> *elif-parts elif-line text*

elif-line:
> \# elif *constant-expression*

else-part:
> *else-line text*

else-line:
> \# else

endif-line:
> \# endif

The constant expression in the `#if` and `#elif`'s (if any) are evaluated in the order in which they appear until one of the expressions evaluates to a nonzero value. C++ statements following a line with a zero value are not compiled, nor do preprocessor directives following such a line have any effect. When a directive with a nonzero value is found, the succeeding `#elif`'s, and `#else`'s, together with their associated text (C++ statements and preprocessor directives) are ignored. The text associated with the successful directive (the first whose constant expression is nonzero) is preprocessed and compiled normally. If the expressions associated with the `#if` and all `#elif`'s evaluate to zero, then the text associated with the `#else` (if any) is treated normally.

Within the *constant-expression* in a `#if` or `#elif`, a unary operator `defined` can be used in either of the forms

> `defined` *identifier*

or

> `defined` (*identifier*)

When applied to an identifier, its value is 1 if that identifier has been defined with a `#define` directive and not later undefined using `#undef`; otherwise its value is 0. The identifier `defined` itself may not be undefined or redefined.

After any `defined` operators are evaluated, any remaining preprocessor macros appearing in the constant expression will be replaced as described in §16.3. The resulting expression must be an integral constant expression as defined in §5.19, except that types `int` and `unsigned int` are treated as `long` and `unsigned long` respectively, and it may not contain a cast, a `sizeof` operator, or an enumeration constant.

A control line of the form

>   #ifdef *identifier*

is equivalent to

>   #if defined *identifier*

A line of the form

>   #ifndef *identifier*

is equivalent to

>   #if !defined *identifier*

Conditional compilation constructs may be nested. An implementation may impose a limit on the depth of nesting of conditional compilation constructs.

16.6 Line Control

For the benefit of programs that generate C++ code, a line of the form

>   #line *constant* *"filename"*~opt~

sets the predefined macro   __LINE__ (§16.10), for purposes of error diagnostics or symbolic debugging, such that the line number of the next source line is considered to be the given constant, which must be a decimal integer. If *"filename"* appears, __FILE__ (§16.10), is set to the file named. If *"filename"* is absent the remembered file name does not change.

Macros appearing on the line are replaced before the line is processed.

16.7 Error Directive

A line of the form

>   #error *token-string*

causes the implementation to generate a diagnostic message that includes the given token sequence.

16.8 Pragmas

A line of the form

>   #pragma *token-string*

causes an implementation-dependent behavior when the token sequence is of a form recognized by the implementation. An unrecognized pragma will be ignored.

16.9 Null Directive

The null preprocessor directive, which has the form

> \#

has no effect.

16.10 Predefined Names

Certain information is available during compilation through predefined macros.

__LINE__ A decimal constant containing the current line number in the C++ source file.

__FILE__ A string literal containing the name of the source file being compiled.

__DATE__ A string literal containing the date of the translation, in the form "Mmm dd yyyy", or "Mmm d yyyy" if the value of the date is less than 10.

__TIME__ A string literal containing the time of the translation, in the form "hh:mm:ss".

In addition, the name __cplusplus is defined when compiling a C++ program.

These names may not be undefined or redefined.

__LINE__ and __FILE__ can be set by the #line directive (§16.6).

Whether __STDC__ is defined and, if so, what its value is are implementation dependent.

> ■ Some C++ implementations share a preprocessor, modified to handle // comments and C++ operators, with C. A C compiler that conforms to the ANSI C standard will define __STDC__ with the value 1 and will disallow applying a #define or #undef operator to __STDC__.
>
> C++ implementations that share header files with C may need to define __STDC__. □

> ■ Implementations are free to predefine additional macro names, which may be redefined through the #define directive or undefined through the #undef directive or a command line option. □

Commentary

16.1c C++ Constructs versus #define

The functionality of the C++ constructs *const* and *inline* can often be used where a C program would use a *#define*. The traditional C construct

    #define MAXCHARS 80

can be replaced by the C++ declaration

    const int MAXCHARS=80;

and the identifier *MAXCHARS* can be used within the program in the same way. The C++ construct has the advantage, however, that the symbol *MAXCHARS* can be made available to a symbolic debugger, while preprocessing symbols are generally not.
    A macro such as

    #define max(x,y)   ((x) > (y) ? (x) : (y))

can be replaced for integers by the C++ inline function

    inline int max(int x, int y)
    {
        return (x > y ? x : y);
    }

with no loss of efficiency. Templates (§14) can be used when a similar function will be needed for multiple types. The name of an inline or template function can be passed to a symbolic debugger. Further, the potential for error when a macro is invoked with an expression that has side effects, as in the following, for example,

    max(f(x),z++);

is eliminated when an inline or template function is used.

16.2c Compatibility

Differences between the ANSI C style preprocessing described above and older preprocessors are discussed in the following sections.

16.2.1c Tokenization Versus Characterization

The phases of translation specified by the ANSI C Standard, on which the definition of preprocessing for C++ is based, are "token-based;" the "Reiser" model, on which many existing preprocessors are built, is "character-based." Although it would be difficult to list all cases where the meaning of a program is affected by this change, two examples follow.

Given

```
#define MINUS -
i=MINUS-j;
```

a Reiser preprocessor will produce $i=--j;$, with the effect that i is assigned the result of applying the prefix decrement operator to the value of j. The output of an ANSI C conforming preprocessor will be in effect

```
i = - - j ;
```

Thus i will be assigned the result applying the minus operator to the result of applying the minus operator to the value of j.

Given

```
#define replace() NEW
#define NEWSTR getstr(Str)

replace()STR
```

a Reiser preprocessor yields $getstr(Str)$, while an ANSI C conforming preprocessor will produce in effect $NEW\ STR$.

Providing both token-based and character-based preprocessing may be unduly expensive, both in the complexity of implementation and in performance penalties. Furthermore, the affected code would have been inherently ambiguous, having relied on undefined and undocumented behavior. One would hope that little such code exists. An implementation may elect to provide a Reiser preprocessor for users who have existing programs that depend on "Reiser" behavior. Nevertheless, such users would be well advised to convert their programs to rely on well-defined constructs.

16.2.2c Tokenless Arguments

The ANSI C Standard says the behavior is undefined given an argument that contains no tokens, but many C and C++ implementations have treated a tokenless argument as a null token. That is,

```
#define SUB(x,y) (x-y)
SUB(,2)
```

would be translated to (-2). For compatibility, some implementations will continue to treat a tokenless argument as though a null argument were provided.

16.2.3c Rescanning and Further Replacement

The ANSI C Standard specifies that if the name of a macro being replaced is found during the scanning of the replacement list (or any subsequent rescanning), this occurrence of the macro name is not to be replaced. This may be interpreted to differ from Classic C, which says that a replacement string is to be rescanned for more defined identifiers. The following code fragment, for example,

```
#define m(a) a(w)
#define w 0,1
m(m)
```

will yield *0,1(0,1)* when compiled by some older preprocessors, but must yield *m(0,1)* in an ANSI C conforming implementation.

16.2.4c Stringizing

Although not defined in Classic C, many existing preprocessors provide the functionality of the ANSI C # operator, sometimes called "*stringizing*." If, in the replacement list of a function-like macro definition, there is a string literal token, the string contents are examined for the spelling of the formal arguments. If any formal arguments are found, their characters are replaced with the spelling of the actual arguments. For example, given

```
#define stringize(a)   "a"
stringize(hello world)
```

such a preprocessor yields *"hello world"*. An ANSI C conforming preprocessor, however, must yield *"a"*.

16.2.5c Charizing

Some old preprocessors also provide a functionality, called "*charizing*," that is not equivalent to any ANSI C operator, nor is it defined in Classic C. If, in the replacement list of a function-like macro definition, there is a character constant token, the character constant contents are examined for the spelling of the formal arguments. If any formal arguments are found, their characters are replaced with the spelling of the actual arguments. Given, for example,

```
#define charize(a) 'a'
charize(q)
```

such a preprocessor yields *'q'*, while an ANSI C conforming preprocessor must yield *'a'*.

16.2.6c Concatenation

Some old preprocessors provide the functionality of ANSI C's ## operator, not defined in Classic C, by concatenating a macro parameter and an identifier, an integral constant, or another macro parameter separated only by a comment in the replacement list. Given, for example,

```
#define paste(a,b)      a/* */b
paste(con,catenate)
```

such a preprocessor yields *concatenate*, while an ANSI C conforming preprocessor must yield *con catenate*.

16.2.7c   Trailing Tokens – #else and #endif

Although Classic C never defined the behavior when tokens follow an *#else* or *#endif* directive ("trailing tokens") and the ANSI C Standard disallows them, some implementations have accepted code that contains them. Many programmers use a programming style in which text following the *#else* and *#endif* identifies the matching *#if*, *#ifdef*, or *#ifndef* directive. For compatibility, some implementations may choose to ignore trailing tokens.

16.3c   Classic C Preprocessing

Because many C++ implementations will be used where an ANSI C style preprocessor is not available, this description of Classic C preprocessing is presented.

    Like the ANSI C-based preprocessor described above, a Classic C preprocessor is capable of macro substitution, conditional compilation, and inclusion of named files. Classic C did not define trigraph sequences, the *#*, *##* and *defined* operators, the *#elif* directive, error directives, pragmas, null directives, or the _ _*LINE*_ _, _ _*FILE*_ _, _ _*DATE*_ _, and _ _*TIME*_ _ macros. The name _ _*cplusplus*, however, is defined even when preprocessing a C++ program with a Classic C preprocessor.

    As with ANSI C style preprocessing, lines beginning with *#* are preprocessor directives. These lines have syntax independent of the rest of the language; they may appear anywhere and have effects that last (independent of scope) until the end of the translation unit.

    For the remainder of this section, "preprocessor" refers to a Classic C preprocessor.

16.3.1c   Classic C Token Replacement

A compiler control line of the form

                #define identifier token-string

causes the preprocessor to replace subsequent instances of the identifier with the given string of tokens. Semicolons in, or at the end of, the token string are part of that string.

    A line of the form

           #define identifier (identifier , ... , identifier) token-string

where there is no space between the first identifier and the *(,* is a macro definition with arguments. Subsequent instances of the first identifier followed by a *(,* a sequence of tokens delimited by commas, and a *)* are replaced by the token string in the definition. Each occurrence of an identifier mentioned in the formal argument list of the definition is replaced by the corresponding token string from the

call. The actual arguments in the call are token strings separated by commas; however commas in quoted strings or protected by parentheses do not separate arguments. The number of formal and actual arguments must be the same. Strings and
character constants in the token string are scanned for formal arguments, but strings
and character constants in the rest of the program are not scanned for defined identifiers.

> ■ Unless a Classic C preprocessor has been adapted for use with C++, it will not
> recognize // comments. Thus, macro replacement will inappropriately be done for
> macro names appearing within // comments, and // comments within macro defin-
> itions will not be correctly translated to white space. □

In both forms the replacement string is rescanned for more defined identifiers.
In both forms a long control line may be continued on another line by writing \ at
the end of the line to be continued.
    A control line of the form

$$\#undef\ identifier$$

causes the identifier's preprocessor definition to be forgotten.

16.3.2c Classic C File Inclusion

A compiler control line of the form

$$\#include\ "filename"$$

causes the replacement of that line by the entire contents of the file *filename*. The
named file is searched for first in the directory of the original source file, and then
in a sequence of specified or standard places. Alternatively, a control line of the
form

$$\#include\ <filename>$$

searches only the specified or standard places, and not the directory of the source
file. (How the places are specified is not part of the language.)

> ■ Because file systems vary on different operating systems and different machines,
> there are several implementation dependencies that affect source file inclusion. An
> implementation should specify the places that will be searched for a file, as well as
> how the file is to be identified.
>   Some implementations will ignore case distinctions in file names. Further, the
> number of significant characters in a file name may be limited by an implementation.
>   How a sequence of preprocessing tokens between a < and > preprocessing token
> pair or a pair of "'s will be combined into a single header name preprocessing
> token will also depend on the implementation. Implementations may differ in their
> treatment of white space within the delimiters. Typically, a sequence of white space
> that is the result of a macro expansion will be treated as a single space character,
> while other sequences of white space will be preserved. □

#include's may be nested.

Some implementations will impose a limit on the depth of nesting of `#include` directives within source files that have been read while processing a `#include` directive in another source file.

■ Usually such a limit will be attributable to a limit in the host operating system on the number of files that may be open. □

16.3.3c Classic C Conditional Compilation

A compiler control line of the form

> `#if` *expression*

checks whether the expression evaluates to nonzero. The expression must be a constant expression (§5.19). A control line of the form

> `#ifdef` *identifier*

checks whether the identifier is currently defined in the preprocessor; that is, whether it has been the subject of a `#define` control line. A control line of the form

> `#ifndef` *identifier*

checks whether the identifier is currently undefined in the preprocessor.

All three forms are followed by an arbitrary number of lines, possibly containing a control line

> `#else`

and then by a control line

> `#endif`

If the checked condition is true then any lines between `#else` and `#endif` are ignored. If the checked condition is false then any lines between the test and a `#else` or, lacking a `#else`, the `#endif`, are ignored.

These constructions may be nested. An implementation may impose a limit on the depth of nesting of conditional compilation constructs.

16.3.4c Classic C Line Control

For the benefit of other preprocessors that generate C++ programs, a line of the form

> `#line` *constant* *"filename "*$_{opt}$

causes the compiler to believe, for purposes of error diagnostics or symbolic debugging, that the line number of the next source line is given by the constant and the current input file is named by the identifier. If the optional file name is absent the remembered file name does not change.

Grammar Summary

This chapter provides a summary of the C++ grammar.

17 Appendix A: Grammar Summary

This appendix is not part of the C++ reference manual proper and does not define C++ language features.

This summary of C++ syntax is intended to be an aid to comprehension. It is not an exact statement of the language. In particular, the grammar described here accepts a superset of valid C++ constructs. Disambiguation rules (§6.8, §7.1, §10.1.1) must be applied to distinguish expressions from declarations. Further, access control, ambiguity, and type rules must be used to weed out syntactically valid but meaningless constructs.

17.1 Keywords

New context-dependent keywords are introduced into a program by `typedef` (§7.1.3), class (§9), enumeration (§7.2), and `template` (§14) declarations.

> *class-name:*
> > *identifier*

> *enum-name:*
> > *identifier*

> *typedef-name:*
> > *identifier*

Note that a *typedef-name* naming a class is also a *class-name* (§9.1).

#### Chapter 17

17.2 Expressions

expression:
        assignment-expression
        expression , *assignment-expression*

assignment-expression:
        conditional-expression
        unary-expression assignment-operator assignment-expression

assignment-operator: one of
        = *= /= %= += -= >>= <<= &= ^= |=

conditional-expression:
        logical-or-expression
        logical-or-expression ? *expression* : *conditional-expression*

logical-or-expression:
        logical-and-expression
        logical-or-expression || *logical-and-expression*

logical-and-expression:
        inclusive-or-expression
        logical-and-expression && *inclusive-or-expression*

inclusive-or-expression:
        exclusive-or-expression
        inclusive-or-expression | *exclusive-or-expression*

exclusive-or-expression:
        and-expression
        exclusive-or-expression ^ *and-expression*

and-expression:
        equality-expression
        and-expression & *equality-expression*

equality-expression:
        relational-expression
        equality-expression == *relational-expression*
        equality-expression != *relational-expression*

relational-expression:
  shift-expression
  relational-expression < *shift-expression*
  relational-expression > *shift-expression*
  relational-expression <= *shift-expression*
  relational-expression >= *shift-expression*

shift-expression:
  additive-expression
  shift-expression << *additive-expression*
  shift-expression >> *additive-expression*

additive-expression:
  multiplicative-expression
  additive-expression + *multiplicative-expression*
  additive-expression – *multiplicative-expression*

multiplicative-expression:
  pm-expression
  multiplicative-expression * *pm-expression*
  multiplicative-expression / *pm-expression*
  multiplicative-expression % *pm-expression*

pm-expression:
  cast-expression
  pm-expression .* *cast-expression*
  pm-expression –>* *cast-expression*

cast-expression:
  unary-expression
  (*type-name*) *cast-expression*

unary-expression:
  postfix-expression
  ++ *unary-expression*
  –– *unary-expression*
  unary-operator cast-expression
  `sizeof` *unary-expression*
  `sizeof` (*type-name*)
  allocation-expression
  deallocation-expression

unary-operator: one of
  * & + – ! ~

allocation-expression:
> $::_{opt}$ new *placement*$_{opt}$ *new-type-name new-initializer*$_{opt}$
> $::_{opt}$ new *placement*$_{opt}$ (*type-name*) *new-initializer*$_{opt}$

placement:
> (*expression-list*)

new-type-name:
> *type-specifier-list new-declarator*$_{opt}$

new-declarator:
> * *cv-qualifier-list*$_{opt}$ *new-declarator*$_{opt}$
> *complete-class-name* :: * *cv-qualifier-list*$_{opt}$ *new-declarator*$_{opt}$
> *new-declarator*$_{opt}$ [*expression*]

new-initializer:
> (*initializer-list*$_{opt}$)

deallocation-expression:
> $::_{opt}$ delete *cast-expression*
> $::_{opt}$ delete [ ] *cast-expression*

postfix-expression:
> *primary-expression*
> *postfix-expression* [*expression*]
> *postfix-expression* (*expression-list*$_{opt}$)
> *simple-type-name* (*expression-list*$_{opt}$)
> *postfix-expression* . *name*
> *postfix-expression* -> *name*
> *postfix-expression* ++
> *postfix-expression* --

expression-list:
> *assignment-expression*
> *expression-list* , *assignment-expression*

primary-expression:
> *literal*
> this
> :: *identifier*
> :: *operator-function-name*
> :: *qualified-name*
> (*expression*)
> *name*

name:
>> *identifier*
>> *operator-function-name*
>> *conversion-function-name*
>> ~ *class-name*
>> *qualified-name*

qualified-name:
>> *qualified-class-name* :: *name*

literal:
>> *integer-constant*
>> *character-constant*
>> *floating-constant*
>> *string-literal*

17.3 Declarations

declaration:
>> *decl-specifiers$_{opt}$ declarator-list$_{opt}$* ;
>> *asm-declaration*
>> *function-definition*
>> *template-declaration*
>> *linkage-specification*

decl-specifier:
>> *storage-class-specifier*
>> *type-specifier*
>> *fct-specifier*
>> friend
>> typedef

decl-specifiers:
>> *decl-specifiers$_{opt}$ decl-specifier*

storage-class-specifier:
>> auto
>> register
>> static
>> extern

fct-specifier:
>> inline
>> virtual

type-specifier:
    simple-type-name
    class-specifier
    enum-specifier
    elaborated-type-specifier
    `const`
    `volatile`

simple-type-name:
    complete-class-name
    qualified-type-name
    `char`
    `short`
    `int`
    `long`
    `signed`
    `unsigned`
    `float`
    `double`
    `void`

elaborated-type-specifier:
    class-key identifier
    class-key class-name
    `enum` *enum-name*

class-key:
    `class`
    `struct`
    `union`

qualified-type-name:
    typedef-name
    class-name `::` *qualified-type-name*

complete-class-name:
    qualified-class-name
     `::` *qualified-class-name*

qualified-class-name:
    class-name
    class-name `::` *qualified-class-name*

enum-specifier:
    `enum` *identifier$_{opt}$* `{` *enum-list$_{opt}$* `}`

enum-list:
> *enumerator*
> *enum-list* , *enumerator*

enumerator:
> *identifier*
> *identifier* = *constant-expression*

constant-expression:
> *conditional-expression*

linkage-specification:
> `extern` *string-literal* { *declaration-list$_{opt}$* }
> `extern` *string-literal* *declaration*

declaration-list:
> *declaration*
> *declaration-list* *declaration*

asm-declaration:
> `asm` (*string-literal*) ;

17.4 Declarators

declarator-list:
> *init-declarator*
> *declarator-list* , *init-declarator*

init-declarator:
> *declarator* *initializer$_{opt}$*

declarator:
> *dname*
> *ptr-operator declarator*
> *declarator* (*argument-declaration-list*) *cv-qualifier-list$_{opt}$*
> *declarator* [*constant-expression$_{opt}$*]
> (*declarator*)

ptr-operator:
> * *cv-qualifier-list$_{opt}$*
> & *cv-qualifier-list$_{opt}$*
> *complete-class-name* :: * *cv-qualifier-list$_{opt}$*

cv-qualifier-list:
> *cv-qualifier* *cv-qualifier-list$_{opt}$*

cv-qualifier:
>   const
>   volatile

dname:
>   *name*
>   *class-name*
>   ~ *class-name*
>   *typedef-name*
>   *qualified-type-name*

type-name:
>   *type-specifier-list abstract-declarator$_{opt}$*

type-specifier-list:
>   *type-specifier type-specifier-list$_{opt}$*

abstract-declarator:
>   *ptr-operator abstract-declarator$_{opt}$*
>   *abstract-declarator$_{opt}$ (argument-declaration-list) cv-qualifier-list$_{opt}$*
>   *abstract-declarator$_{opt}$ [constant-expression$_{opt}$]*
>   *(abstract-declarator)*

argument-declaration-list:
>   *arg-declaration-list$_{opt}$ ... $_{opt}$*
>   *arg-declaration-list , ...*

arg-declaration-list:
>   *argument-declaration*
>   *arg-declaration-list , argument-declaration*

argument-declaration:
>   *decl-specifiers declarator*
>   *decl-specifiers declarator = expression*
>   *decl-specifiers abstract-declarator$_{opt}$*
>   *decl-specifiers abstract-declarator$_{opt}$ = expression*

function-definition:
>   *decl-specifiers$_{opt}$ declarator ctor-initializer$_{opt}$ fct-body*

fct-body:
>   *compound-statement*

initializer:
>   *= assignment-expression*
>   *= { initializer-list $_{, opt}$ }*
>   *(expression-list)*

initializer-list:
> *assignment-expression*
> *initializer-list , assignment-expression*
> { *initializer-list* $,_{opt}$ }

17.5 Class Declarations

class-specifier:
> *class-head* { *member-list*$_{opt}$ }

class-head:
> *class-key identifier*$_{opt}$ *base-spec*$_{opt}$
> *class-key class-name base-spec*$_{opt}$

member-list:
> *member-declaration member-list*$_{opt}$
> *access-specifier* : *member-list*$_{opt}$

member-declaration:
> *decl-specifiers*$_{opt}$ *member-declarator-list*$_{opt}$;
> *function-definition* ;$_{opt}$
> *qualified-name* ;

member-declarator-list:
> *member-declarator*
> *member-declarator-list* , *member-declarator*

member-declarator:
> *declarator pure-specifier*$_{opt}$
> *identifier*$_{opt}$: *constant-expression*

pure-specifier:
> = 0

base-spec:
> : *base-list*

base-list:
> *base-specifier*
> *base-list* , *base-specifier*

base-specifier:
> *complete-class-name*
> `virtual` *access-specifier*$_{opt}$ *complete-class-name*
> *access-specifier* `virtual`$_{opt}$ *complete-class-name*

access-specifier:
       ```private```
       ```protected```
       ```public```

conversion-function-name:
       ```operator``` *conversion-type-name*

conversion-type-name:
       type-specifier-list ptr-operator$_{opt}$

ctor-initializer:
       : *mem-initializer-list*

mem-initializer-list:
       mem-initializer
       mem-initializer , mem-initializer-list

mem-initializer:
       complete-class-name (*expression-list$_{opt}$*)
       identifier (*expression-list$_{opt}$*)

operator-function-name:
       ```operator``` *operator*

operator: one of
```
        new   delete
        +     -     *     /     %     ^     &     |     ~
        !     =     <     >     +=    -=    *=    /=    %=
        ^=    &=    |=    <<    >>    >>=   <<=   ==    !=
        <=    >=    &&    ||    ++    --    ,     ->*   ->
        ()    []
```

17.6 Statements

statement:
       labeled-statement
       expression-statement
       compound-statement
       selection-statement
       iteration-statement
       jump-statement
       declaration-statement
```

labeled-statement:
>   *identifier* : *statement*
>   case *constant-expression* : *statement*
>   default : *statement*

expression-statement:
>   *expression$_{opt}$* ;

compound-statement:
>   { *statement-list$_{opt}$* }

statement-list:
>   *statement*
>   *statement-list statement*

selection-statement:
>   if (*expression*) *statement*
>   if (*expression*) *statement* else *statement*
>   switch (*expression*) *statement*

iteration-statement:
>   while (*expression*) *statement*
>   do *statement* while (*expression*) ;
>   for (*for-init-statement expression$_{opt}$* ; *expression$_{opt}$*) *statement*

for-init-statement:
>   *expression-statement*
>   *declaration-statement*

jump-statement:
>   break ;
>   continue ;
>   return *expression$_{opt}$* ;
>   goto *identifier* ;

declaration-statement:
>   *declaration*

17.7 Preprocessor

#define *identifier token-string*
#define *identifier* (*identifier* , ... , *identifier*) *token-string*

#include "*filename*"
#include <*filename*>

```
#line constant "filename"opt
#undef identifier
```

conditional:
> *if-part elif-parts*_{opt} *else-part*_{opt} *endif-line*

if-part:
> *if-line text*

if-line:
```
# if constant-expression
# ifdef identifier
# ifndef identifier
```

elif-parts:
> *elif-line text*
> *elif-parts elif-line text*

elif-line:
```
# elif constant-expression
```

else-part:
> *else-line text*

else-line:
```
# else
```

endif-line:
```
# endif
```

17.8 Templates

template-declaration:
```
template < template-argument-list > declaration
```

template-argument-list:
> *template-argument*
> *template-argument-list , template argument*

template-argument:
> *type-argument*
> *argument-declaration*

type-argument:
```
class identifier
```

template-class-name:
> *template-name* < *template-arg-list* >

template-arg-list:
> *template-arg*
> *template-arg-list* , *template-arg*

template-arg:
> *expression*
> *type-name*

17.9 Exception Handling

try-block:
> `try` *compound-statement handler-list*

handler-list:
> *handler handler-list$_{opt}$*

handler:
> `catch` (*exception-declaration*) *compound-statement*

exception-declaration:
> *type-specifier-list declarator*
> *type-specifier-list abstract-declarator*
> *type-specifier-list*
> . . .

throw-expression:
> `throw` *expression$_{opt}$*

exception-specification:
> `throw` (*type-list$_{opt}$*)

type-list:
> *type-name*
> *type-list* , *type-name*

18

Compatibility

This chapter summarizes the evolution of C++ since the first edition of *The C++ Programming Language* and explains in detail the differences between C++ and C. Because the C language as described by the ANSI C Standard differs from the dialects of Classic C used up till now, we discuss the differences between C++ and ANSI C as well as the differences between C++ and Classic C.

18   Appendix B: Compatibility

This appendix is not part of the C++ reference manual proper and does not define C++ language features.

C++ is based on C (K&R78) and adopts most of the changes specified by the ANSI C standard. Converting programs among C++, K&R C, and ANSI C may be subject to vicissitudes of expression evaluation. All differences between C++ and ANSI C can be diagnosed by a compiler. With the following three exceptions, programs that are both C++ and ANSI C have the same meaning in both languages:

In C, `sizeof('a')` equals `sizeof(int)`; in C++, it equals `sizeof(char)`.

In C, given

```
enum e { A };
```

`sizeof(A)` equals `sizeof(int)`; in C++, it equals `sizeof(e)`, which need not equal `sizeof(int)`.

A structure name declared in an inner scope can hide the name of an object, function, enumerator, or type in an outer scope. For example,

```
int x[99];
void f()
{
    struct x { int a; };
    sizeof(x);  /* size of the array in C */
                /* size of the struct in C++ */
}
```

■ The aim of C++ was and is to be as close to C as possible. Historically, that has been complicated by there being no single obvious definition or implementation of C with which to be compatible. C++ compilers will still show anachronisms reflecting the various Classic C dialects. More important, though, C++ relies on static type checking much more than C does, which necessitates some differences. These differences relate to the degree of type checking provided and to the central role of the class − the user-defined type − in C++. The remaining differences are deemed essential for the integrity of the C++ type system. □

18.1 Extensions

This section summarizes the major extensions to C provided by C++.

18.1.1 C++ Features Available in 1985

This subsection summarizes the extensions to C provided by C++ in the 1985 version of this manual:

The types of function arguments can be specified (§8.2.5) and will be checked (§5.2.2). Type conversions will be performed (§5.2.2). This is also in ANSI C.

Single-precision floating point arithmetic may be used for float expressions; §3.6.1 and §4.3. This is also in ANSI C.

Function names can be overloaded; §13.

Operators can be overloaded; §13.4.

Functions can be inline substituted; §7.1.2.

Data objects can be const; §7.1.6. This is also in ANSI C.

Objects of reference type can be declared; §8.2.2 and §8.4.3.

A free store is provided by the new and delete operators; §5.3.3, §5.3.4.

Classes can provide data hiding (§11), guaranteed initialization (§12.1), user-defined conversions (§12.3), and dynamic typing through use of virtual functions (§10.2).

The name of a class or enumeration is a type name; §9.

A pointer to any non-const and non-volatile object type can be assigned to a void*; §4.6. This is also in ANSI C.

A pointer to function can be assigned to a void*; §4.6.

A declaration within a block is a statement; §6.7.

Anonymous unions can be declared; §9.5.

18.1.2   C++ Features Added Since 1985

This subsection summarizes the major extensions of C++ since the 1985 version of this manual:

A class can have more than one direct base class (multiple inheritance); §10.1.

Class members can be `protected`; §11 .

Pointers to class members can be declared and used; §8.2.3, §5.5.

Operators `new` and `delete` can be overloaded and declared for a class; §5.3.3, §5.3.4, §12.5. This allows the "assignment to `this`" technique for class specific storage management to be removed to the anachronism section; §18.3.3.

Objects can be explicitly destroyed; §12.4.

Assignment and initialization are defined as memberwise assignment and initialization; §12.8.

The `overload` keyword was made redundant and moved to the anachronism section; §18.3.

General expressions are allowed as initializers for static objects; §8.4.

Data objects can be `volatile`; §7.1.6. Also in ANSI C.

Initializers are allowed for `static` class members; §9.4.

Member functions can be `static`; §9.4.

Member functions can be `const` and `volatile`; §9.3.1.

Linkage to non-C++ program fragments can be explicitly declared; §7.4.

Operators `->`, `->*`, and `,` can be overloaded; §13.4.

Classes can be abstract; §10.3.

Prefix and postfix application of `++` and `--` on a user-defined type can be distinguished.

Templates; §14.

Exception handling; §15.

> ■ The primary driving force in the evolution of C++ between 1985 and 1990 has been the desire to produce elegant and efficient libraries and to allow easy and safe composition of programs out of separately developed and separately compiled parts.
> □

18.2   C++ and ANSI C

In general, C++ provides more language features and fewer restrictions than ANSI C so most constructs in ANSI C are legal in C++ with their meanings unchanged. The exceptions are:

ANSI C programs using any of the C++ keywords

```
asm       catch      class      delete     friend
inline    new        operator   private    protected
public    template   try        this       virtual
throw
```

as identifiers are not C++ programs; §2.4.

Though deemed obsolescent in ANSI C, a C implementation may impose

Draconian limits on the length of identifiers; a C++ implementation is not permitted to; §2.3.

In C++, a function must be declared before it can be called; §5.2.2.

The function declaration `f();` means that `f` takes no arguments (§8.2.5); in C it means that `f` can take any number of arguments of any type at all. Such use is deemed obsolescent in ANSI C.

In ANSI C a global data object may be declared several times without using the `extern` specifier; in C++ it must be defined exactly once; §3.3.

In C++, a class may not have the same name as a typedef declared to refer to a different type in the same scope; §9.1.

In ANSI C a `void*` may be used as the right-hand operand of an assignment to or initialization of a variable of any pointer type; in C++ it may not; §7.1.6.

C allows jumps to bypass an initialization; C++ does not.

In ANSI C, a global `const` by default has external linkage; in C++ it does not; §3.3.

"Old style" C function definitions and calls of undeclared functions are considered anachronisms in C++ and may not be supported by all implementations; §18.3.1. This is deemed obsolescent in ANSI C.

A `struct` is a scope in C++ (§3.2); in ANSI C a `struct`, an enumeration, or an enumerator declared in a `struct` is exported to scope enclosing the `struct`.

Assignment to an object of enumeration type with a value that is not of that enumeration type is considered an anachronism in C++ and may not be supported by all implementations; §7.2. ANSI C recommends a warning for such assignments.

Surplus characters are not allowed in strings used to initialize character arrays; §8.4.2.

The type of a character constant is `char` in C++ (§2.5.2) and `int` in C.

The type of an enumerator is the type of its enumeration in C++ (§7.2) and `int` in C.

In addition, the ANSI C standard allows conforming implementations to differ considerably; this may lead to further incompatibilities between C and C++ implementations. In particular, some C implementations may consider certain incompatible declarations legal. C++ requires consistency even across compilation boundaries; §3.3.

18.2.1 How to Cope

In general, a C++ program uses many features not provided by ANSI C. For such a program, the minor differences of §18.2 don't matter since they are dwarfed by the C++ extensions. Where ANSI C and C++ need to share header files, care must be taken so that such headers are written in the common subset of the two languages.

No advantage must be taken of C++ specific features such as classes, overloading, and so on.

A name should not be used both as a structure tag and as the name of a different type.

A function `f` taking no arguments should be declared `f(void)` and not simply `f()`.

Global `const`s must be declared explicitly `static` or `extern`.

Conditional compilation using the C++ predefined name `__cplusplus` may be used to distinguish information to be used by an ANSI C program from information to be used by a C++ program.

Functions that are to be callable from both languages must be explicitly declared to have C linkage.

18.3 Anachronisms

The extensions presented here may be provided by an implementation to ease the use of C programs as C++ programs or to provide continuity from earlier C++ implementations. Note that each of these features has undesirable aspects. An implementation providing them should also provide a way for the user to ensure that they do not occur in a source file. A C++ implementation is not obliged to provide these features.

> ■ It is easy to deem an undesirable feature an anachronism and remove it from the reference manual; it is an entirely different matter to modify a compiler to disallow a feature that a programmer relies on. The problem of how to manage transitions from old code (often C code) to a more up-to-date implementation is often handled like this:
>
> [1] Release N contains the old feature (only).
>
> [2] Release N+1 issues a warning for uses of the old feature and provides the alternative new feature.
>
> [3] Release N+2 provides the alternative new feature (only).
>
> Sometimes it takes more than two releases to fade out a feature, so this process may be extended. □

The word `overload` may be used as a *decl-specifier* (§7) in a function declaration or a function definition. When used as a *decl-specifier*, `overload` is a reserved word and cannot also be used as an identifier.

The definition of a static data member of a class for which initialization by default to all zeros applies (§8.4, §9.4) may be omitted.

An old style (that is, pre-ANSI C) C preprocessor may be used.

An `int` may be assigned to an object of enumeration type.

The number of elements in an array may be specified when deleting an array of a type for which there is no destructor; §5.3.4.

A single function `operator++()` may be used to overload both prefix and postfix `++` and a single function `operator--()` may be used to overload both prefix and postfix `--`; §13.4.6.

18.3.1 Old Style Function Definitions

The C function definition syntax

> *old-function-definition:*
>   *decl-specifiers$_{opt}$ old-function-declarator declaration-list$_{opt}$ fct-body*

> *old-function-declarator:*
>   *declarator (parameter-list$_{opt}$)*

> *parameter-list:*
>   *identifier*
>   *parameter-list , identifier*

For example,

```
max(a,b) int b; { return (a<b) ? b : a; }
```

may be used. If a function defined like this has not been previously declared its argument type will be taken to be (...), that is, unchecked. If it has been declared its type must agree with that of the declaration.

Class member functions may not be defined with this syntax.

18.3.2 Old Style Base Class Initializer

In a *mem-initializer*(§12.6.2), the *class-name* naming a base class may be left out provided there is exactly one immediate base class. For example,

```
class B {
    // ...
public:
    B (int);
};

class D : public B {
    // ...
    D(int i) : (i) { /* ... */ }
};
```

causes the B constructor to be called with the argument i.

18.3.3 Assignment to `this`

Memory management for objects of a specific class can be controlled by the user by suitable assignments to the `this` pointer. By assigning to the `this` pointer before any use of a member, a constructor can implement its own storage allocation. By assigning a zero value to `this`, a destructor can avoid the standard deallocation operation for objects of its class. Assigning a zero value to `this` in a destructor also suppressed the implicit calls of destructors for bases and members. For example,

```
class Z {
    int z[10];
    Z()   { this = my_allocator( sizeof(Z) ); }
    ~Z() { my_deallocator( this ); this = 0; }
};
```

On entry into a constructor, this is nonzero if allocation has already taken place (as it will have for auto, static, and member objects) and zero otherwise.

Calls to constructors for a base class and for member objects will take place (only) after an assignment to this. If a base class's constructor assigns to this, the new value will also be used by the derived class's constructor (if any).

Note that if this anachronism exists either the type of the this pointer cannot be a *const or the enforcement of the rules for assignment to a constant pointer must be subverted for the this pointer.

18.3.4 Cast of Bound Pointer

A pointer to member function for a particular object may be cast into a pointer to function, for example, (int (*)())p->f. The result is a pointer to the function that would have been called using that member function for that particular object. Any use of the resulting pointer is − as ever − undefined.

18.3.5 Nonnested Classes

Where a class is declared within another class and no other class of that name is declared in the program that class can be used as if it was declared outside its enclosing class (exactly as a C struct). For example,

```
struct S {
    struct T {
        int a;
    };
    int b;
};

struct T x;      // meaning 'S::T x;'
```

Index

B

O

U